Reading the Wife/Sister Narratives in Genesis

Reading the Wife/Sister Narratives in Genesis

A Textlinguistic and Type-Scene Analysis

Hwagu Kang

FOREWORD BY
Richard E. Averbeck

☙PICKWICK *Publications* · Eugene, Oregon

READING THE WIFE/SISTER NARRATIVES IN GENESIS
A Textlinguistic and Type-Scene Analysis

Copyright © 2018 Hwagu Kang. All rights reserved. Except for brief quotations in critical publications or reviews, no part of this book may be reproduced in any manner without prior written permission from the publisher. Write: Permissions, Wipf and Stock Publishers, 199 W. 8th Ave., Suite 3, Eugene, OR 97401.

Pickwick Publications
An Imprint of Wipf and Stock Publishers
199 W. 8th Ave., Suite 3
Eugene, OR 97401

www.wipfandstock.com

PAPERBACK ISBN: 978-1-5326-3517-5
HARDCOVER ISBN: 978-1-5326-3519-9
EBOOK ISBN: 978-1-5326-3518-2

Cataloguing-in-Publication data:

Names: Kang, Hwagu, author. | Averbeck, Richard E., foreword.

Title: Reading the wife/sister narratives in Genesis : a textlinguistic and type-scene analysis / Hwagu Kang.

Description: Eugene, OR: Pickwick Publications, 2018 | Includes bibliographical references.

Identifiers: ISBN 978-1-5326-3517-5 (paperback) | ISBN 978-1-5326-3519-9 (hardcover) | ISBN 978-1-5326-3518-2 (ebook)

Subjects: LCSH: Bible–Genesis–Criticism, interpretation, etc. | Abraham-(Biblical patriarch) | Old Testament

Classification: BS1235.52 H81 2018 (print) | BS1235.52 (ebook)

Manufactured in the U.S.A.   10/02/18

To
Young Nam, my beloved wife
Gayoung and Minseok, my precious gifts

Contents

List of Illustrations | viii
List of Tables | ix
Foreword by Richard E. Averbeck | xi
Preface | xv
List of Abbreviations | xvii

Introduction | 1
1 Wife/Sister Stories within the Context | 39
2 The First Wife/Sister Story (Genesis 12:10—13:1) | 62
3 The Second Wife/Sister Story (Genesis 20:1–18) | 101
4 The Third Wife/Sister Story (Genesis 26:1–11) | 140
5 Conclusion | 170

Bibliography | 177

Illustrations

1. Types of Generation | 53
2. The Plotline of Story A | 100
3. The Plotline of Story B | 138
4. The Plotline of Story C | 168

Tables

1. Three Wife/Sister Stories in Form | 9
2. Comparison of The Three Wife/Sister Stories | 10
3. Niccacci's The Mainline of Communication | 28
4. Occurence of The Characters in Story A | 92
5. The Change of Speaker and Addressee in Gen 20:3–7 | 112
6. Pharaoh's Questions in Stories A and B | 121
7. Delimitation of Story C | 141
8. Comparison between Genesis 26 and Genesis 12:10—14:20 | 146
9. Comparison between Genesis 26 and Genesis 20:1—21:31 | 146
10. Comparison of God's Promise | 151
11. Isaac's Defense | 156

Foreword

THE PRIMEVAL NARRATIVES IN Genesis 1–11 level the ground of our human experience in this world. They provide the foundation for a sound biblical understanding of who we are, how we got here, what we are supposed to be doing here, and why we experience so many struggles physically, personally, and relationally as we make our way in this world from life to death. This is the start of the biblical metanarrative—the story that explains all other stories.

The patriarchal narratives in Genesis 12–50 form the basis of God's historical plan of redemption for the world. The primeval narratives already anticipated this redemptive plan, but Genesis 12–50 recounts God's historical work in and through the patriarchs as the ancestors of the nation of Israel. It was through Israel that he would work his covenant plan to redeem the world. If it were not for God's promises to the patriarchs there would be no redemption of Israel out of Egypt: "God heard their groaning and he remembered his covenant with Abraham, with Isaac and with Jacob" (Exod 2:24; cf. Lev 26:42; Deut 7:7–8; and many other passages). The history of Israel led to the birth of Jesus the Christ, the ultimate descendant of Abraham (Matt 1:2, 17–25). And it is through Abrahamic faith that we enter into the redemptive plan of God (Rom 4:1–3, 16–25; Gal 3:7–9).

When we read the patriarchal narratives it is readily apparent that they contain realistic accounts of real people who became heroes of redemptive covenantal faith in spite of the fact that they were so often fearful, frail, weak, and downright selfish. The three so-called "wife-sister" stories stand out, partly because there are, in fact, three of them (Gen 12:10—13:1; 20:1–18; and 26:1–11), and partly because they are so transparently illustrative of how much the patriarchs struggled to entrust themselves to the Lord. The first wife-sister story gives us Abram's rationale for his wife-sister ruse as he put it to Sarai, "I know what a beautiful woman you are. 12 When the Egyptians see you, they will say, 'This is his wife.' Then they will kill me but will let you live. 13 Say you are my sister, so that I will be treated well for your sake and my life will be spared because of you" (Gen 12:11–13). If Sarai was Abram's wife, Abram would be seen as an obstacle to gaining her as a wife. If she was his sister, he would be seen as an avenue through which to approach and gain her (see, e.g., Gen 24:28–60 for the role of Laban, Rebekah's brother, in giving her to Isaac as a wife). It was all about Abram protecting himself, not protecting Sarai, and the same with Isaac later with regard to his wife Rebekah (Gen 26:7).

Although there were precursors in earlier centuries, the historical critical approach to the Bible began in earnest with the so-called "Enlightenment," especially the biblical work of the Dutch philosopher Baruch Spinoza (1632–77) and the French priest Richard Simon (1638–1712). This set the stage for the following two centuries, leading up to the source critical approach of Julius Wellhausen (1844–1918) in his well-known *Prolegomena to the History of Israel* (1885), first written and published as his *History of Israel* (1878). Without going into all the details, this led to separating what we have in Genesis into three documentary strands of tradition: the J or "Yahwist" account, the E or "Elohist" account, and the P or "priestly" account. As applied to the wife-sister stories, it was determined that the three wife-sister stories were originally only one story in two different traditions: J in Genesis 12 and 26, and E in Genesis 20. The Genesis 12 and 26 accounts are both from J, but assigned to two different patriarchs, Abraham and Isaac, respectively. The E account in Genesis 20 is a variant of the same story recorded by J in Genesis 12. According form critical analysis of Hermann Gunkel (1862–1932), many of the variants between these stories arose in the process of oral composition and transmission that preceded the written accounts of J and E, but again, there was only one original story that gave rise to the others.

As one reads the stories they do indeed seem quite similar at first glance even though there are variations in the details. So given their compositional assumptions and methods, one can understand why source and form critics might conclude that they are variants of only one original. It is interesting to observe, however, that as Abraham put it in his response to Abimelek of Gerar in the second wife-sister story, "she really is my sister, the daughter of my father though not of my mother; and she became my wife. 13 And when God had me wander from my father's household, I said to her, 'This is how you can show your love to me: *Everywhere we go*, say of me, He is my brother'" (Gen 20:12–13; emphasis added). There is good reason to believe that Abraham's confession to Abimelek is true, and that this was his regular practice. If so, we could potentially have had many more such stories included in the Abraham narratives. The ones included were selected for a purpose.

This brings us to the work in Dr. Hwagu Kang's dissertation. Although he carefully reviews the historical critical issues and approaches, and other points noted above, he focuses his attention on how the wife-sister stories as a series contribute to the synchronic substance and shaping of the patriarchal narratives. He combines a text-linguistic approach with type-scene analysis. The text-linguistic approach shows how the wife-sister stories fits into their respective contexts. He argues that each of them relates to the special development of one the three main points in God's promises to the patriarchs: the Genesis 12 wife-story story emphasizes the promise of the land, the Genesis 20 account develops the seed promise, and the Genesis 26 wife-sister story is focused on God's promise of blessing.

Kang's type-scene analysis enables him to carefully take account of both the similarities and the differences between the wife-sister stories. Historical critical scholars have long noticed the obvious similarities between the three accounts and have discounted the differences between them as variant traditions about the same incident. The problem with this approach is that it is not verifiable, and moreover, the writer of the narratives are quite aware of the relationships between the stories. For example, Gen 26:1 tells the reader that "there was a famine in the land—besides the previous famine in Abraham's time," referring back to wife-sister incident in Genesis 12. In the next verse the Lord told Isaac specifically not to go down to Egypt as Abraham did.

We are in Dr. Kang's debt for his detailed analysis of the texts and contexts of the wife-sister stories. He has shown that they are part of the glue that holds the patriarchal narratives together on a literary level. They were included specifically for this purpose, not manufactured out of imaginative reuse of one original story in oral or written stages of composition.

Richard E. Averbeck
January 9, 2018

Preface

THIS BOOK GOT ITS start as my doctoral dissertation at Trinity Evangelical Divinity School. Working on my dissertation was a long journey. I struggled for several years to find a way to the proper understanding of the passage. I often felt that I was passing alone through the darkness. Without the assistance, guidance, and encouragement of various people, whom I would like to thank, my dissertation would not have been completed.

First of all, I cannot say how much I appreciate Dr. Richard E. Averbeck, my supervisor and mentor. He always provided me with wise advice and invaluable inspiration, and suggested a right direction throughout my study for the dissertation. In fact, my dissertation topic came from his classes on Pentateuchal Criticism and on Genesis. After the defense was completed, he encouraged me to publish my dissertation. When I asked him to write a foreword for this book, he was happy to do that. I am also thankful to Dr. K. Lawson Younger for his encouragement and insightful criticism of my dissertation.

I would like to express deep appreciation to the members of Jesurun Presbyterian Church. Over the last eight years, my service to the church, particularly the Young Adult group, has helped me to finish this dissertation and to keep going on my spiritual journey. Their love and encouragement always inspire me. Also, many churches and friends supported me with prayers and financial help. I am especially thankful to Jamsil Jungang Presbyterian Church, Yeonji Presbyterian Church, and Ulsan Presbyterian Church. They have supported my studies in various ways.

My gratitude also goes to my family members in South Korea for their constant support and prayers. My parents, Sung Yoon Kang and Seok Soon Kim, and my mother-in-law, Sam Soon Lee, have supported me with prayers and financial support over the years. Above all, my deepest appreciation goes to my prudent, wise wife, Young Nam Park, and my beloved children, Gayoung and Minseok. They are the best gifts from God for my life. Without their patience, sacrificial support, invaluable encouragement, and constant presence at my side, I would not have been able to complete this dissertation.

I appreciate Wipf & Stock for the wonderful opportunity to publish this book. The staff there was very passionate and diligent. Their endeavors breathed a new life into my work.

Finally, my preface would be incomplete without mentioning how grateful I am for everything God has done throughout my journey. He has constantly showed His favor and faithfulness to me even when I walked through the valley of the shadow of death.

Serving Him and His churches is the purpose and the reason for this book. All the glory to the LORD, my ultimate Love.

SOLI DEO GLORIA

Hwagu Kang

Abbreviations

ABC	The Anchor Bible Commentary
ASV	American Standard Version
BHS	Biblia Hebraica Stuttgartensia
ESV	English Standard Version
GKC	*Gesenius' Hebrew Grammar*. Edited by E. Kautzsch. Translated by A. E. Cowley. 2nd ed. Oxford: Clarendon, 1910.
HALOT	The Hebrew and Aramaic Lexicon of the Old Testament
IBHS	*An Introduction to Biblical Hebrew Syntax*. Bruce K. Waltke and M. O'Connor. Winona Lake, IN: Eisenbrauns, 1990.
JPS	Jewish Publication Society OT
JSOTSup	Journal for the Study of the Old Testament: Supplement Series
KJV	King James Version
LXX	The Septuagint
MT	the Masoretic Text
NAC	The New American Commentary
NASB	New American Standard Bible
NEB	New English Bible
NET	New English Translation
NICOT	New International Commentary on the Old Testament
NIV	New International Version
NLT	New Living Translation
RSV	Revised Standard Version
TOTC	The Tyndale Old Testament Commentaries
WBC	Word Biblical Commentary

I

Introduction

THROUGHOUT CHRISTIAN HISTORY, ABRAHAM[1] has been considered the father of our faith. If one word could sum up Abraham's character, it would be "faith."[2] Not only did he leave his birthplace, kin, and father's house but he was even willing to sacrifice his own beloved son, Isaac. At a glance, Abraham has a faith so great that we cannot come anywhere close to following his example. If we read the Abraham narrative as a whole, however, we immediately recognize that he had weaknesses like us. We find good examples of Abraham's weakness in the wife/sister stories, in which Abraham passes off his wife as a sister before foreign rulers, thus putting his wife in danger (Gen 12:10—13:1 and 20:1–18). Isaac also did this (Gen 26:1–11). Surprisingly, the first wife/sister account occurs right after Abraham makes a great decision of faith (Gen 12:1–9). Similarly, the second account appears after he hears God's promise of offspring through Sarah (Gen 18:10–15). In truth, Abraham appears as a two-faced person throughout the narrative. This is also true of Isaac in Gerar: like his father, Isaac deceived a foreign ruler for his own benefit by claiming his wife was actually his sister.

Because many scholars have various views on the lives of the patriarchs, readers have concluded that different sources have been jumbled together in the Genesis narratives. For the past two centuries, many scholars have endeavored to discover the sources used in Genesis. Others have argued that if we are interested in the final form of the text, we can easily recognize how the texts have been carefully arranged to enhance the author's intention throughout the book of Genesis. This leads to some questions. Why does Genesis include three wife/sister stories in which the patriarchs' faith seems to fail? How do these three stories function within the whole narrative of Genesis? What are the literary intentions of the three stories? The present work seeks to answer these questions.

1. For the sake of consistency of discussion I will use the names "Abraham" and "Sarah" even when discussing texts before the change their names (Gen 17).

2. Williams, "Abraham," 11.

Research Problem

The book of Genesis contains three stories of a patriarch who deceives a foreign ruler by claiming that his wife is actually his sister (12:10—13:1; 20:1-18; and 26:1-11).[3] These stories have created long discussions among a variety of scholars. Scholars employing source criticism and form criticism tend to focus on issues of origin and historical development. For these scholars, the wife/sister stories provide formidable evidence of different sources. The many questions raised by these approaches still generate much controversy. Which story is the original? Why are three stories needed? What is the relationship among the stories? Do they have an oral tradition? Do they have an ur-story? Are they historical? What are the theological implications of the stories in their own context? Did three authors, or different sources, make three distinctly separate stories? Or are all three stories the work of a single author?

While a number of answers to these questions have been proposed, no consensus has emerged. It appears that discussions of historical, compositional, and theological considerations are largely based on misunderstandings of the texts themselves. In fact, scholars have brought their own perspectives to the text in order to arrive at preconceived conclusions. After thorough investigation, T. Desmond Alexander concludes that "it is now possible to view all three episodes as deriving from a single author, who composed each of the wife-sister pericopes with a clear knowledge of what

---

3. Henceforth, this paper will use the name "Story A" for Gen 12, "Story B" for Gen 20, and "Story C" for Gen 26. It is difficult to define the extent of each text. In Story A, וַיְהִי is usually a good sign of the new beginning of a pericope, but the end of this story is more difficult to define. In relation to v. 9, some scholars consider 13:1 as the proper end of Story A. Others, like Casutto, argue that Story A may end at 13:4. Yet it is worth noting that there is another initial disjunctive clause in 13:2, which indicates the beginning of a new section. Thus, from a grammatical perspective, Story A includes 12:10—13:1. Story B is easily defined except for the source critical interpolation issue in v. 1 and v. 18. Story C involves even more complicated issues than Story A. There is wide agreement in seeing 26:1 as the beginning of the story because of the expression וַיְהִי. However, scholars define the end of the story differently and may see the full extent of the story as vv. 1-11, vv. 1-13, vv. 7-11, vv. 1-14, or vv. 1-33. We will discuss the extent of each story in later chapters. Considering the similar forms of the wife/sister stories, as Van Seters points out, Story C may extend through the whole chapter of Gen 26 because it contains God's blessing in the same territory, Gerar, which is included in the main story of Stories B and C. But if we consider the wife/sister motif itself, it is necessary to define Story C as Gen 26:1-11. Cf. Maly, "Genesis 12:10-20; 20:1-18; 26:7-11 and the Pentateuchal Question," 255-62; Speiser, *Genesis*, 89-94; Koch, *The Growth of the Biblical Tradition*, 111-32; Cassuto, *A Commentary on the Book of Genesis, Part 2*, 334-65; Alexander, *Abraham in the Negev*, 33-35; Culley, *Studies in the Structure of Hebrew Narrative*, 33-41; von Rad, *Genesis*, 271; Schmitt, "Zu Gen 26:1-14," 143-56; Van Seters, *Abraham in History and Tradition*, 167-91.

he had already written earlier."[4] However, Alexander does not deny the possibility of oral tradition or earlier versions. R. N. Whybray maintains that the Pentateuch was not a simple collection of various sources, but rather an intentional product of a single author who lived in the post-exilic period and considered ancient sources ahistorical.[5] He, therefore, takes a similar position to that of Alexander. Whybray suggests that one author generated three different versions out of the same wife/sister story: "All three stories, despite the variation in the participants and in the location, are clearly different versions of the same story."[6]

In summary, throughout the history of the study of the wife/sister stories, arguments have moved from viewing the stories in terms of different sources to viewing them as the intentional product of a single author—or, put differently, from diachronic to synchronic readings. Although both Alexander and Whybray argue for the possibility of a single author, they still utilize earlier source critical methods. This study will summarize the scholarly approaches and their assumptions, evaluate their methodologies, and propose a synthesis of these methodologies. Furthermore, from a synchronic point of view, this study will consider these three stories as a typescene, in that these stories demonstrate intentional connections as well as literary and linguistic developments.

History of Research

Despite the fact that several explanations have been proposed for the three wife/sister stories and some would consider the matter settled, no true scholarly agreement has been reached. This section will explore what scholars have historically argued as well as the issues that remain unresolved.

Source Criticism

In general, source critics have paid attention to literary features of the Pentateuch such as repetitions, use of different divine names, contradictions, and stylistic differences. As a result, they conclude that the Pentateuchal stories can be divided and credited to different sources. Traditionally, they have assigned Stories A and C to the J source and Story B to the E source. S.

---

4. Alexander, *Abraham in the Negev*, 50; Alexander, "Are the Wife/Sister Incidents of Genesis Literary Compositional Variants?," 145–53.

5. Whybray, *The Making of the Pentateuch*, 221–25. He maintains that the Pentateuch is a religious fiction (240).

6. Ibid., 76.

R. Driver, for example, comes to this conclusion based on differing uses of divine names.[7] On the other hand, there are also different views regarding these designations.[8] Gunkel, for example, believes that Story A does not belong to the original J source, so he assigns it to J[b]. In Story C, Gunkel assigns verses 7–11 to J[a] and verses 1–6 to a redactor of J (J[r]).[9]

Source critics view the use of different divine names (YHWH and Elohim), the appearance of various themes such as dream and prayer, and several inconsistencies apparent in the repetitive narratives as good reasons for dividing the text into sources. However, not all source critics have arrived at the same conclusions regarding the sources. In regard to inconsistency, the wife/sister stories are often seen as providing important evidence for the presence of different sources. Joel S. Baden, however, argues against this approach because the three stories are not simply a triplet. The incidents take place in different regions and at different times, and they involve different people. For this reason, Baden concludes that the three wife/sister stories belong to a single author.[10]

Moreover, in terms of sources, the fact that Story B may be considered as an E source is problematic. Different divine names and some general terminologies belonging to the E source have led some scholars to assign Story B to the E source. It is probable, however, that the use of different divine names, YHWH and Elohim, should be understood in light of different literary intentions. For instance, the personal divine name (YHWH) is not commonly used by foreigners, and the Israelites generally use Elohim when speaking to foreigners.[11] This is why Abraham uses Elohim rather than YHWH in 20:11–13. Abimelech uses only Elohim in Story B. Therefore, the use of different divine names in the wife/sister stories is not necessarily evidence of different sources. Furthermore, as Frederick V. Winnett shows,[12] the E source cannot be understood as an independent source, but rather as a simple revision of the J source. If, as is usually understood, Gen 20 and the

---

7. Driver, *An Introduction to the Literature of the Old Testament*, 13–16; Skinner, *A Critical and Exegetical Commentary on Genesis*, 240–41, 315. According to Skinner, since Gen 20:18 uses YHWH instead of God, it should be considered a gloss.

8. Noth, *A History of Pentateuchal Traditions*, 28–37; von Rad, *Genesis*, 167, 226, 270; Speiser, *Genesis*, xxxi–xxxii. Noth regards Gen 20:1a as a secondary addition from the J source.

9. Gunkel and Biddle, *Genesis*, 168, 293–94.

10. Baden, *The Composition of the Pentateuch*, 17.

11. Sarna, *Genesis*, 273; Cassuto, *The Documentary Hypothesis*, 40. Cassuto provides basic rules for using the divine name, Elohim: (1) when the reference is to alien people, (2) when God reveals himself to a member of Gentile nations, (3) in conversations with Gentiles, etc.

12. Winnett, "Re-Examining the Foundations," 5–7.

majority of 21 can be assigned to E and Gen 26:15–18 can be assigned to J,[13] it is strange to see the earlier J source referring to the later E source, since 26:15–18 assumes Gen 21:22–34.[14] Gen 26:16 and 18 clearly refer to the time of Abraham and the author's use of these references shows his intention to connect the incident of Abraham and that of Isaac at Beersheva. For this reason, the traditional source criticism should be reexamined.

Alexander goes one step further. He concludes that "a re-examination of the arguments in favour of assigning chap. 20 to E. reveals that, apart from the presence of the divine name Elohim, there is no reason why the entire narrative should not be assigned to J." The words and expressions typically attributed to the E source should be reexamined because they cannot be assigned exclusively to E. For example, the prophetic character of Abraham also appears in Gen 15:1, which is generally viewed as J source. Furthermore, Biddle argues that there are some significant features of J in Story B. The curse/blessing theme, which is introduced in Gen 12:1–3 (i.e., in the J source) is very important in Story B. Additionally, the role of Abraham praying for the foreign king may be the best example of the thematic connection to Gen 18, which is from the J source.[15] Due to these questions raised by several scholars, the traditional source critical approach has achieved no consensus even among source critics. Their arguments thus hardly offer support for source criticism.

Nevertheless, the distinctiveness of Genesis itself makes it necessary to refer to the possibility of the existence and use of sources in the book. First, the author—that is, Moses—lived long after the patriarchs. He was not an eyewitness. Second, Genesis contains clear signs of sources—Gen 5:1, for example, indicates that the *Toledot* of Adam was a book. We can therefore assume that Moses used some sources from the past.[16] Based on this conclusion, further study on the sources of the book of Genesis is necessary, but will differ from the traditional source critical approach.

---

13. Most critics assign vv. 1a, 2a, and 33 to J and vv. 1b and 2b–5 to P.

14. For further study, see Baden, *J, E, and the Redaction of the Pentateuch*, 214–18. We will come back to the issue of similarities between Genesis 21 and 26 in chapter 4.

15. For a more detailed discussion of Biddle's four conclusions, see Biddle, "The 'Endangered Ancestress' and Blessing for the Nations," 609–11.

16. Garrett, *Rethinking Genesis*, 91–106.

Form Criticism

Form Criticism attempts to determine the possible oral stage, genre, structure, and *Sitz im Leben* of a text.[17] It is worthwhile to question whether or not the three similar wife/sister stories in Genesis originated from actual events comparable to those found in history.

Scholars have attempted to identify the origin of the wife/sister stories, as they show remarkable similarities in form and pattern. The basic concept of the form critical approach accepts the premise that the original story existed in an oral form, which was transmitted to diverse places over a long period of time. As far as possible, the form critic attempts to recover the original story. Herman Gunkel, for example, is interested in the oral stages that he assumes lie behind the written text. He concludes that the patriarchal narratives are a collection of legends and that the task of scholars is to deduce the previous stages of the narratives.[18] It is appropriate here to quote Koch's reconstruction of the original wife/sister story:

> Because of famine Isaac travelled from the desert in southern Palestine to the nearby Canaanite city of Gerar, to live there as "sojourner," i.e. to keep within the pasturage rights on the ground belonging to the city. He told everyone that his wife was his sister so that his life would not be endangered by those who desired her. However, Rebekah's beauty could not pass unnoticed. The king of the city, Abimelech, took Rebekah into his harem, amply compensating Isaac. As a material sin was about to be committed, God struck the people of the palace with a mysterious illness. Through the medium of his gods, or a soothsayer, Abimelech recognized what had happened. Abimelech called Isaac to account: "What is this that you have done to me?" He then restored him his wife and sent him away, loaded with gifts.[19]

For Koch, this original oral story has been changed by deletion, addition, and editing. Some scholars, however, recognize that the stories should be viewed as literary compositions rather than oral ones.

Van Seters argues that Story A, originally an oral variant, can be assigned to an early J source—that is, a primitive folktale form. For Van Seters, Story B, a literary variant, assumes Story A, while Story C assumes both Stories A and B. Van Seters only acknowledges only Story C as belonging

---

17. For the basic ideas, see Tucker, *Form Criticism of the Old Testament*; Sweeney, "Form Criticism: The Question of the Endangered Matriarchs in Genesis," 17–38.

18. Gunkel, *The Folktale in the Old Testament*, 21–27; Gunkel and Biddle, *Genesis*.

19. Koch, *The Growth of the Biblical Tradition*, 126.

INTRODUCTION 7

to the J source, assigning Stories A and B to different pre-J stages.[20] He argues that Story A has the form of an oral folktale in terms of simplicity and self-containment, while Stories B and C have clear literary features that are dependent on the previous stories. Therefore, Story A is the oldest one: Story B knew of and depended on Story A; and Story C knew of and depended on Stories A and B.[21] Van Seters identifies four guidelines for determining literary dependence:

1. The account with the simplest form and structure will most likely be the earliest one.

2. The second version often shortens or summarizes the material that it borrows from the first one, although by adding new materials of its own it may result in a longer story.

3. Occasionally, in a latter version there occurs a "blind motif;" that is, some unexplained action or detail that assumes consciously or unconsciously that the earlier account is known.

4. The strongest evidence for literary dependence is verbal similarity.[22]

Based on these criteria, Van Seters observes that Stories B and C intentionally avoid repetition of the same story lines and that the former story provides background information for the latter. Story A is focused on Abraham's intention to deceive (vv. 11–13), while Story B is mainly concerned with the dialogues between God and Abimelech, and Abimelech and Abraham. We can understand Gen 20:2 by considering Gen 12:11–15, and Gen 26:1 directly connects to Story A. Following Van Seters, Alexander concludes that if the three stories are oral variants, some considerable overlaps should be seen. Since the latter stories intentionally avoided duplications of the former ones, it is therefore proper to suggest that these are not oral variants but literary compositions.[23] However, it is necessary to explore here whether Story A is an oral or a literary composition. Van Seters argues that Story A is an oral composition because it is a self-contained unit barely related to the surrounding narratives, and because it shares similar

---

20. Van Seters, *Abraham in History and Tradition*, 167–92; Alexander, *Abraham in the Negev*, 48–49. Following Van Seters, Westermann rejects the idea that Story B can be considered the E source; instead, he would leave it as an open question and only consider Story A as the J source. Thus, Van Seters and Westermann do not agree on the J source. In fact, Westermann only acknowledges Story A as the J source.

21. Van Seters, *Abraham in History and Tradition*, 175–83, esp. 177.

22. Ibid., 162–63.

23. Alexander, *Abraham in the Negev*, 42.

structures with a folktale. The basic elements of the folktale, for Van Seters, are as follows:

a. A situation of need, problem, or crisis,
b. A plan to deal with the problem (wise or foolish),
c. The execution of the plan with some complications,
d. An unexpected outside intervention,
e. A fortunate or unfortunate consequence.[24]

Van Seters depends on Olrik's laws to confirm his argument,[25] observing that the features of Story A are similar to Olrik's laws and thus arguing for the oral composition of Story A. Other scholars, however, are quite unconvinced by this conclusion. In particular, Alexander raises serious questions about the general assumptions of oral transmission[26] pointing out that they should not always be applied to the stories in the same way. The fact that there are duplicate stories of the same event does not mean that they have a long oral history. In addition, as mentioned above, the fact that Stories B and C presuppose Story A indicates that the readers may have known Story A as a literary composition, allowing Stories B and C to intentionally avoid unnecessary repetition of detail.[27] The lack of further evidence thus leaves us hesitant to firmly identify Story A as an oral composition. Alexander concludes, "Unfortunately, in the past, many scholars have jumped too quickly to the assumption that the wife/sister episodes must all relate to one original incident, and that the differences between them are due to the process of oral transmission. But . . . one cannot assume that the present shape of the narratives represents accurately their form during oral transmission."[28] Therefore, even though Story A has some features of an oral composition, such as brevity, scholars should be more cautious before concluding that it was an oral composition.

In contrast, many other scholars take an almost opposite view, arguing that Story C is the original and oldest of the three wife/sister stories.[29] In

---

24. Van Seters, *Abraham in History and Tradition*, 168.
25. Ibid., 168–72; Olrik, "Epic Laws of Folk Narrative," 129–41.
26. Alexander, "The Wife/Sister Incidents of Genesis: Oral Variants?," 17–19.
27. Ibid., 18–19; Alter, *The Art of Biblical Narrative*, 48. Alter successfully uses the example of a dozen surviving Hollywood films to show that literary variants do not necessarily indicate literary dependence.
28. Alexander, "The Wife/Sister Incidents of Genesis," 19; also see Niditch, *A Prelude to Biblical Folklore*, 29–40; Biddle, "The 'Endangered Ancestress' and Blessing for the Nations," 600. Niditch concludes that three stories were composed in different styles: "economic" for Story A, "baroque" for Story B, and "anthological" for Story C.
29. Noth, *A History of Pentateuchal Traditions*, 103–6; Maly, "Genesis 12:10–20;

general, the story featuring the least-known character is considered to be the original. It follows that Isaac, seen in Story C, was the original name in the story, before being gradually replaced by Abraham.[30] In addition, Noth argues that Story C is the original because it is profane. He states,

> This story, as distinct from the two variants in the corresponding Abraham story (Gen. 12:10–20[J]; 20:1–18 [E]), appears here in a still completely 'profane' form . . . It may be here that we find ourselves relatively close to the original form of this frequently utilized narrative material, though we must notice that in Genesis 26 this form is apparently present in a condensed literary formulation, at least in the opening.[31]

We may doubt, however, whether a story's "profane" character can be seen as evidence for its originality, as there is no consensus on this among form critics.[32]

In terms of their overall structure, the three wife/sister stories obviously contain remarkable similarities in vocabulary, theme, form, and pattern. Therefore, in terms of form criticism, it is worthwhile to compare each story and describe their overall structures. Alexander places the three stories side by side as follows:[33]

Table 1: Three Wife/Sister Stories in Form

	Ch. 12	Ch. 20	Ch. 26
Reason for locale	v. 10	v. 1	v. 1–6a
The deception occurs	v. 11–13	v. 2a	vv. 6b–7
Abduction of wife	vv. 14–16	v. 2b	–
Discovery of ruse	v. 17	vv. 3–7	v. 8
Interview with foreigner	vv. 18–19	vv. 8–16	vv. 9–10
Final outcome	v. 20; 13:1	vv. 17–18	vv. 11–13

20:1–18; 26:7–11 and the Pentateuchal Question," 260–61; von Rad, *Genesis*, 271.

30. Koch, *The Growth of the Biblical Tradition*, 126. Also note the change from the king of Gerar to the king of Egypt.

31. Noth, *A History of Pentateuchal Traditions*, 105.

32. Koch, *The Growth of the Biblical Tradition*, 124; Pappas, "Deception as Patriarchal Self-Defense in a Foreign Land," 49–50.

33. Alexander, *Abraham in the Negev*, 42.

At a glance, the three stories are very similar. For this reason, many scholars have regarded them as variants of one story (A or C) or an Ur-story. A detailed examination of each story, however, reveals that the three stories could not have originated from a single original. The similarities and differences between each story are summarized in the following chart.[34]

Table 2: Comparison of The Wife/Sister Stories

	A	B	C
Location	Egypt	Gerar	Gerar
Characters	Abraham, Sarah, and Pharaoh	Abraham, Sarah, and Abimelech	Isaac, Rebekah, and Abimelech
Reason	Famine	No explanation	Famine (like the famine that occurred in the time of Abraham)
Divine Presence	Not mentioned	Not mentioned	vv. 2–5
Deception Plan	Before entering Egypt (Abraham's speech)	Not mentioned, but occurs after exposure	Narrator
Process	The Egyptian's praise of her beauty	No reference to her beauty	Reference to Rebekah's beauty, but no reference to people's praise
What Happened	Sarah was taken to Pharaoh's harem	Abimelech took Sarah	Nothing happened
Wealth	After taking of Sarah by Pharaoh	After exposure by Abimelech	After exposure, but wealth grows through Isaac's labor
Divine Intervention	The LORD sent serious disease	God's presence in Abimelech's dream	No intervention
Exposure	Not mentioned	God's prevention	By chance
Summon	Pharaoh summons and rebukes Abraham, who does not reply	Abimelech summons Abraham, who gives a long answer (motivation of deception)	Abimelech rebukes Isaac, who answers (motivation of deception)
Ruler's order			Abimelech orders the people not to harm Isaac

---

34. Ibid., 34–38. For Alexander, each story differs considerably from the others, even though they share "a common basic motif."

INTRODUCTION 11

	A	B	C
Result	Pharaoh expels Abraham	Abimelech provides wealth and allows them to live anywhere	Isaac plants crops and God blesses him (wealth)
		Abimelech's speech to Sarah	
		Abraham prays for Abimelech as a prophet, so God heals his people	

As we can see, one cannot simply conclude that the wife/sister stories have similar structures and storylines, for they also include many differences in their details.[35] It may be better to say that the three stories are independent accounts that simply use similar literary motifs.

Social-Historical Study

Many parallels between ancient Near Eastern contexts and biblical accounts are observed in the areas of social customs and laws, though scholars have not reached consensus regarding all such parallels. Notably, the discoveries of Mari and Nuzi make it possible to understand the patriarchal narratives in relation to the environment of the second millennium BCE.[36] On the other hand, materials from the first millennium BCE are relatively rare compared to those from the second millennium. As Van Seters constructively points out, however, the first millennium materials can usually be applied to both periods: "most of the first millennium materials have been available for a long period of time, much of it before the major part of the second millennium materials even came to light."[37] Because of the considerable continuity, one should be cautious in arguing that a certain material is

---

35. I do not agree with Thompson who argues that Story C has no parallels to Stories A and B. Thompson, *The Origin Tradition of Ancient Israel*, 56–59.

36. Selman, "Comparative Customs and the Patriarchal Age," 91–139. Selman suggests that the fourteen cases in Genesis can be supported by extrabiblical material from the Ancient Near East. For a more detailed history of scholarly discussions see Eichler, "Nuzi and the Bible," 107–19. Speiser, *Oriental and Biblical Studies*; Gordon, "Biblical Customs and the Nuzi Tablets," 1–12; Merrill, "Ebla and Biblical Historical Inerrancy," 302–21; Pettinato, "Ebla and the Bible," 203–16; Kitchen, *On the Reliability of the Old Testament*, 324–28.

37. Van Seters, *Abraham in History and Tradition*, 67.

available only for a specific time period. On this basis, Van Seters rejects the second millennium background of the patriarchs and places these social customs and laws within the first millennium background.[38]

The wife/sister motif has been the topic of heated discussions in relation to comparative studies of ancient Near Eastern culture. The work of E. A. Speiser offers a good starting point on this issue. Speiser's article on how the wife/sister motif may be understood from extrabiblical data suggests very valuable insights by drawing our attention to the Hurrians in the eighteenth century BCE.[39] Based on investigation of the cuneiform tablets at Nuzi, which were influenced by the Hurrians, Speiser suggests that a girl who was given as a wife in a Nuzi text HSS V 80 (*ana aššūti*) was also given as a sister in HSS V 69 (*ana aḫāti*). Based on this, he concludes that "a wife could have simultaneously the status of sister."[40] What is more, HSS V 25 informs us that a girl should give personal consent, which means that the girl had independence. Finally, Speiser concludes as follows:

> To sum up, the Hurrian family system contained various fratriarchal features one of which was the wife-sister concept. Under it, a woman given in marriage by her brother, either natural or adoptive, became legally her husband's sister: Such a wife-sister had the advantage of exceptional socioreligious solicitude and protection which was not enjoyed by ordinary wives. The practice was characteristic of, though not restricted to, the top levels of Hurrian society. It was evidently a mark of superior status.[41]

From this information, we can infer that Speiser thinks Abraham and Isaac, either directly or indirectly influenced by Hurrian culture, were married to women who were of very noble status in their society.[42] This argument is followed by Nahum M Sarna, who avers that according to Hurrian custom, a woman had dual status, "wife-sistership," in which she could hold superior privileges and protection.[43]

As Freedman points out, however, Speiser's conclusion is dependent on a small amount of data from Nuzi. In fact, only thirteen out of over sixty tablets mention that distinct relationship between a man and a woman,

---

38. Ibid., 70–71.

39. Speiser, "The Wife-Sister Motif in the Patriarchal Narratives," 62–82; Speiser, *Genesis*, 91–94.

40. Speiser, "The Wife-Sister Motif in the Patriarchal Narratives," 68–69.

41. Ibid., 75.

42. Ibid., 81.

43. Sarna, *Understanding Genesis*, 103.

and only one is related to the wife-sister relationship.[44] Like Freedman, Thompson also uncovers a methodological problem with Speiser's assumption. He contends that Speiser's argument is built not on the basis of biblical accounts, but on a historical hypothesis, drawing on historical records.[45] While we may concede and accept that Nuzi customs are related to the Genesis accounts, we cannot conclude that the patriarchs lived by Hurrian customs and laws, because it is apparent that wife-sistership contracts were rare even at Nuzi.[46]

Regarding vocabulary, Speiser considers the word *aḫātī*, used in HSS 5.69, to have the same meaning as the word *aḫātūti*, which means "sistership." According to Freedman, however, *aḫātī* is not the same as *aḫātūti*, nor is it used elsewhere.[47] Again, it is worth noting Thompson's strong rejection of Speiser's ideas: "Even so, the most important objection to Speiser's interpretation is that he does violence to the biblical stories. The story element found in each of our passages in which the patriarch calls his wife, his sister, is basically integrated into the stories as a motif of intended deception."[48] Consequently, at this point there is no reason to understand the patriarchs as simply following Hurrian law.

Van Seters also disagrees with Speiser's argument. In addition, he tries to push the wife/sister motif into the first millennium situation. Van Seters believes that the three stories in the book of Genesis are more aligned with Egyptian marriage contracts from the sixth century BCE.[49] However, as Egyptologist James K. Hoffmeier suggests, this argument is also problematic. If the patriarchs acted according to Egyptian custom, it is strange that the Pharaoh and the Egyptians misunderstood the patriarchs' intentions. What is more, the Egyptian word "sister" can be applied to both late and early periods of Egyptian history.[50]

In order to make an argument, it is necessary to gather more data regarding the wife/sister situation. We may therefore conclude at this point that it is doubtful that the wife/sister narratives in Genesis are related to the

---

44. Greengus, "Sisterhood Adoption at Nuzi," 5–31; Greengus, "The Patriarchs' Wives as Sisters," 22–26; also see Mullo Weir, "The Alleged Hurrian Wife-Sister Motif in Genesis," 16–18.

45. Thompson, *Historicity of the Patriarchal Narratives*, 235.

46. Ibid.

47. Freedman, "A New Approach to the Nuzi Sistership Contract," 80–81.

48. Thompson, *Historicity of the Patriarchal Narratives*, 245–46.

49. Van Seters, *Abraham in History and Tradition*, 74–76; Greengus, "Sisterhood Adoption at Nuzi"; Mullo Weir, "The Alleged Hurrian Wife-Sister Motif in Genesis," 14–25; Freedman, "A New Approach to the Nuzi Sistership Contract," 77–85.

50. Hoffmeier, "The Wives' Tales of Genesis 12, 20 and 26," 85–86.

extrabiblical data. Nowhere in the extrabiblical data does the term "wife-sister" or "sister-wife" appear and there is no evidence of a woman's status being changed in marriage. More significantly, there is no reason why a woman should have received honored status or privilege in marriage.[51]

James K. Hoffmeier points out that proposals emphasizing possible parallels with ancient Near Eastern cultures have failed to achieve consensus for more than thirty years. He therefore proposes a new approach. For him, the wife/sister stories reflect diplomatic marriage.[52] Wiseman observes that because Abraham was already well known to the Egyptians as a high-ranking prince, the foreign ruler would inevitably seek to make a covenantal relationship.[53] Since neither Abraham nor Isaac had a daughter, they each had to deceive the foreign rulers by saying their wife was a sister.[54] Hoffmeier thus concludes that the three wife/sister stories include possible socio-political factors, and therefore originally appeared as separate stories.[55] Hoffmeier's arguments and conclusion present a plausible interpretation of the background of the wife/sister stories. However, Hoffmeier does not discuss whether all three of the patriarchs' attempts failed; whether, if they were successful, they actively intended to send their wives to foreign rulers; or why the author wrote these three stories together in the patriarchal narrative. Furthermore, we need to note that the texts themselves clearly mention that Abraham and Isaac were afraid of death at the hands of the people of a foreign land (Gen 12:11–13; 20:11–13; and 26:7). It seems, then, that diplomatic marriage may provide a possible background to the wife/sister stories, but Hoffmeier's argument needs to focus more on the biblical texts than other ancient Near Eastern ones. Regardless of the success of his attempt, then, Hoffmeier's argument will not be considered in detail in this study. Instead, we will endeavor to address issues about which Hoffmeier is silent—that is, how the three stories function on a literary level and their connections with each other and the larger narrative.

---

51. Mullo Weir, "The Alleged Hurrian Wife-Sister Motif in Genesis," 21.

52. For more details on the Ancient Near Eastern background, see Hoffmeier, "The Wives' Tales of Genesis 12, 20, and 26," 87–95. He notes that diplomatic marriages between nations, city-states, and peoples are well known in the Near East.

53. Wiseman, "Abraham Reassessed," 147–50; Kidner, Genesis, 116–17. Kidner thinks that only the wife/sister story in Genesis 20 is related to diplomatic marriage because Sarah was ninety years old and there is no mention of her beauty in this passage.

54. The patriarchs, as shepherds, might obtain water, grass, and security, while the foreign rulers, as agriculturalists, might receive fields fertilized by the herd and other economic benefits through trade. See, Matthews, "Pastoralists and Patriarchs," 215–18.

55. Hoffmeier, "The Wives' Tales of Genesis 12, 20, and 26," 99.

Literary Criticism

Since diachronic approaches have not resolved all of the issues that have been raised, some scholars have examined the connections among the wife/sister stories through synchronic lenses. Robert Polzin, for example, points out lamentable aspects of diachronic approaches, including their failure to consider how each story fits into its own context or take into account the weight of particular texts within the context of the larger storylines of the patriarchal narrative.[56] Furthermore, scholars have observed that the repetitions in biblical narratives, which are often regarded as strong evidence of different sources, are used to emphasize necessary themes.[57] Robert Alter categorizes repetition in biblical narratives as cases of *Leitwort*, Motif, Theme, Sequence of actions, or Type-scene. He sees the wife/sister stories belonging to the type-scene category, which includes compositions with "a fixed sequence of motifs."[58]

As previously explained, the three wife/sister stories need to be read as parts of a whole, reflecting the author's intention for each story to be understood in relation to the others. If this is the case, the concern of scholars naturally moves to the relationship and thematic development of the stories. David L. Petersen asserts that the thematic flow in the wife/sister motif is "the divergence between YHWH's and men's plan."[59] Similarly, Polzin attempts to understand the theme of the wife/sister motif in terms of "wealth, progeny and blessing by God."[60] Niditch sees independent developments of a single folktale pattern. For her, Story A contains the underdog/trickster motif, Story B highlights a courtly interest in the status quo, and Story C emphasizes a homiletical/theological treatment.[61] David J. A. Clines sees that the danger in each story is different, while the theme is transformed through the three stories.[62]

---

56. Polzin, "'The Ancestress of Israel in Danger' in Danger," 82–83.

57. Gunn and Fewell, *Narrative in the Hebrew Bible*, 148; Alter, *The Art of Biblical Narrative*, 49–50, 88–113.

58. Alter, *The Art of Biblical Narrative*, 96. For a detailed discussion of type-scene, consult Alter's third chapter (pp. 47–62). Sailhamer presents a similar idea called "narrative typology," which he defines as a technique by which "the author develops central themes and continually draws them to the reader's attention," so that "the earlier events foreshadow and anticipate later events." Sailhamer, *The Pentateuch as Narrative*, 37–39.

59. Petersen, "A Thrice-Told Tale," 38.

60. Polzin, "'The Ancestress of Israel in Danger' in Danger," 89.

61. Niditch, *A Prelude to Biblical Folklore*, 44–52.

62. Clines, *What Does Eve Do to Help?*, 67–84.

On the other hand, some scholars attempt to connect the wife/sister stories to the Exodus motif and other narratives such as the David story. U. Cassuto observes that there are remarkable parallels between the wife/sister story and the Exodus story, even claiming that "there is hardly a verse or half a verse in this passage that does not remind us of a parallel in connection with the children of Israel."[63]

Many scholars attempt to explain the overall theme of the wife/sister stories and the relationship between the stories. One of the crucial questions they ask is why there are three wife/sister stories. Based on Abraham's words in Gen 20:13 ("This is how you can show your love to me: Everywhere we go, say of me, 'He is my brother'"), we may assume that it was possible to carry out this deception more than three times because wherever Abraham went, Sarah repeated the same thing. Also, 26:1 differentiates Story C from Story A by mentioning a famine that was different from the famine of Abraham's time. If we assume that the deception occurred more than three times, then we must question why the author specifically recorded three such occurrences. Duane A. Garrett identifies a "two-out-of-three pattern," in which, "most remarkably, the three stories are bound by a pattern in which a narrative element is consistently present in two out of the three accounts."[64] Based on this observation, he argues that there is a clear unity of the three stories as a whole. However, even though there are indeed some-two-out-of-three patterns in the texts, it is doubtful that this pattern is dominant. We can easily observe some important features that occur in all the three stories, such as the patriarch's journey, the deception motif, the foreign rulers' rebuke, and the patriarch's increase in wealth. Additional evidence would be needed

---

63. Cassuto, *The Documentary Hypothesis*, 78–83. In this book, Cassuto presents a number of detailed examples of parallels. Furthermore, Reis, ("Take My Wife," 315) extends Cassuto's approach to the historical books. According to Reis, Story B can be connected to the capture of the holy ark (1 Sam 4–6) and Story C parallels to the story of return of the ark by David (2 Sam 6:16–23). Also see Sailhamer, *The Pentateuch as Narrative*, 307–9; Sailhamer, *Introduction to Old Testament Theology*, 293–95. Sailhamer provides more extended parallels between Gen 12:10–20 and stories from Genesis 41 to Exodus 12. We should, however, be careful in applying this approach because it is hard to establish connections between two or more passages through the use of some of the same terminology and imagery. For example, Reis tries to connect Story C to 2 Sam 6:16–23 by observing a connection between Isaac's sporting (Gen 26:8) and David's joyful accompanying of the ark into Jerusalem, but the only support for this link is the use of the same Hebrew root for "sporting" and "making merry" (Reis, "Take My Wife," 314). Furthermore, it is very unlikely that Story A should be compared to the Exodus story. Doing so seems to ignore the other two wife/sister stories and thus results in breaking up the intention of the author, who wants to bind the wife/sister stories together as a whole.

64. Garrett, *Rethinking Genesis*, 131.

to establish the significance of the two-out-of-three pattern, so Garrett's approach thus requires further explanation.

The synchronic discussions presented above can be summarized as follows. First, the three wife/sister stories have similar storylines—namely, they share the same motif. Second, the three stories differ considerably from one another—that is, they are independent from each other, even though they share the same motif. Third, each story is best understood individually and in its own context. Finally, it is clear that the shared wife/sister motif may provide a crucial key for understanding these stories together as intended by the author. Furthermore, observing a pattern through the three stories allows us to understand the author's intention in presenting this motif three times within the book of Genesis.

Reading Strategies

By nature, biblical texts are products of language. It is therefore common sense that we should understand the common theories and praxes of linguistics and apply them to biblical texts.[65] During the last century, biblical scholars have shifted their perspective away from a focus on large units of text toward a concern for smaller units. Scholars have attempted to discover the smallest unit of a text.[66] This has resulted in the identification of many different sources in a single narrative unit. Following this approach, other scholars have tried to discover the *Sitz im Leben* of each unit.

Since the 1960s, scholars have achieved remarkable agreement concerning the locus of meaning. James Barr criticized what was then the widespread view on the meaning of words, arguing that proper meaning of a text should be detected not by examining words, but by applying a broader perspective focused on units such as sentences, paragraphs, discourses, and texts.[67] It is clear that holding a holistic perspective on texts is crucial for unfolding their proper meaning. We will therefore apply a holistic point of view—that is, a textlinguistic approach—that looks at a text as a whole by exploring it in three analytical aspects: syntactics, semantics, and pragmatics.

---

65. Lowery, "The Theoretical Foundations," 105; Porter, "Discourse Analysis and the New Testament Studies," 14–35. Porter mentions, "The study of the New Testament is essentially a language-based discipline . . . Whatever else may be involved in the study of the New Testament . . . it always remains textually based, since the only direct access that we have into the world of the New Testament is through the text of the Greek New Testament." This comment of Porter may be applied to the Old Testament as well.

66. Lowery, "The Theoretical Foundations," 104.

67. Barr, *Semantics of Biblical Language*; For a good summary, see Cotterell and Turner, *Linguistics & Biblical Interpretation*, 106–28.

In order to examine these three dimensions of the text, we first need to focus on where the meaning is to be found.

Locus of Meaning

In order to correlate these three dimensions of the text—that is, syntactics, semantics, and pragmatics—it will be helpful to first examine the nature of meaning. Thinkers throughout history have made innumerable attempts to locate the meaning of texts. Plato, in his pioneer study of the nature of meaning and language,[68] argued that reality is only an idea and earthly things are only imitations of the ideas.[69] Aristotle disagreed with Plato's argument—for him, reality must be understood to be a particular thing, which is in fact related to Cratylus's suggestion in Plato's dialogues.[70] Immanuel Kant has been seen as a figure who terminated the long debates between Platonic ideas and Aristotelian form and matter.[71] Vanhoozer summarizes Kant's view: "Words express thoughts. This 'turn to the subject' implied that language expresses an individual's experience of the world rather than the world itself. What words represent in the first instance is not the world itself, nor Plato's eternal ideas, but rather human ideas or subjectivity. Words are signs not of things but of thoughts."[72] Attempts to discovering the locus of meaning can be categorized by their focus on author, text, or reader.

First, according to the author-centered approach, the locus of meaning is in the author. E. D. Hirsch rejects the idea that textual meaning changes over time, arguing that the meaning of the text will never change. In order to explain this, he separates meaning and significance: "Meaning is that which is represented by a text; it is what the author meant by his use of a particular sign sequence; it is what the signs represent. Significance, on the other hand, names a relationship between that meaning and a person, or a conception, or a situation, or indeed anything imaginable."[73] Accordingly, for Hirsch, significance (a relationship between a meaning and a person)

---

68. Vanhoozer, "Language, Literature, Hermeneutics and Biblical Theology," 13–15. Vanhoozer provides a good summary of Plato's Cratylus, which is a less known dialogue than some of his other works. In this book, Plato argued that the reality is only in the idea, while appearance is a copy of the idea.

69. Ibid., 15–16.

70. Ibid., 14; Russell, *A History of Western Philosophy*, 162.

71. Vanhoozer, "Language, Literature, Hermeneutics and Biblical Theology," 17. He calls this, "Copernican Revolution."

72. Ibid.

73. Hirsch, Jr., *Validity in Interpretation*, 8.

changes, but meaning (what the author intends the text to mean) does not.[74] Hirsch asserts that a text without a fixed authorial meaning would lack any determinateness, with the result that no interpretation could fit into the meaning of the text. He explains, "To say that verbal meaning is determinate is not to exclude complexities of meaning but only to insist that a text's meaning is what it is and not a hundred other things."[75]

Second, Hans-Georg Gadamer and Paul Ricoeur emphasize the importance of the text itself rather than the author.[76] By clarifying the difference between speaking and writing, Ricoeur argues that authorial intention does not coincide with the meaning of the text.[77] Because the text no longer has its author or speaker, there is a disconnection between the author's mental intention and the textual meaning. So, he concludes, "the text's career escapes the finite horizon lived by its author."[78] From this perspective, then, the meaning of the text is more than the authorial meaning. Both Ricoeur and Gadamer acknowledge the importance of the reader. For them, a true understanding of the text can be discovered at the contact point between the horizon of the text and that of the reader.[79]

Finally, the reader-centered approach focuses on the role of the reader in determining the meaning of the text. Reader response theory can be divided into two groups: radical and conservative. The radical tends to focus on the reader in the process of deciding the textual meaning, while the conservative stresses both the reader and the text.[80] Stanley Fish, a radical reader response critic, held that meaning simply becomes known from the text through the practice of reading. However, his investigation of the questions "Is the meaning coming only from the activity of reading?" and "Do the texts play a certain role in producing the meaning, namely, limiting interpretation of the readers?" changed after he encountered Umberto Eco's relatively conservative reader response theory.[81]

74. Ibid., 6–10; Osborne, *The Hermeneutical Spiral*, 393.
75. Hirsch, *Validity in Interpretation*, 230.
76. Ricoeur, *Interpretation Theory*; Gadamer, *Truth and Method*.
77. Ricoeur, *Interpretation Theory*, 28–29.
78. Ibid., 30.
79. Vanhoozer, *Is There a Meaning in This Text?*, 106–9. However, Vanhoozer maintains that the meaning of the text cannot be separable from the authorial intention (109); Gadamer, *Truth and Method*, 317. Gadamer also mentions, "Rather, understanding is always the fusion of these horizons supposedly existing by themselves."
80. Vanhoozer, "The Reader in New Testament Interpretation," 306–7.
81. Eco, *The Role of the Reader*; Eco, *The Limits of Interpretation*, 55–56; Eco, *Interpretation and Overinterpretation*, 63. In reality, Eco also turned to conservative position in the reader response criticism. He differentiates the use of a text and the interpretation

According to reader response theory, which follows postmodernity,[82] meaning is subjective, such that there is no single correct meaning of a text. Instead, understandings of the text are produced in readers' minds. Adherents of this view do not ignore the role of author or text, but they argue that the meaning of the text must be completed by the interpretation and understanding of the reader.[83] This view represents a paradigm shift.[84] Since contemporary readers may know nothing about a text's original authors, original contexts, or even original readers, the meaning of the text should be produced through the interplay of text and reader. Simply put, "the reader is not a passive spectator but actively contributes something to the meaning. He or she is more than a passive observer."[85]

These three hermeneutical perspectives are not entirely mutually exclusive in biblical interpretation. In order to understand the text in synthesis, we need to acknowledge that each approach has significant flaws and advantages, and that the three approaches should therefore be considered together. Keck argues that the different approaches are complementary, and that a "plurality of methods" is therefore necessary.[86] If we are trying to discover the meaning of something that does not originate from ourselves, we must try to decipher the text, and that which lies beyond the text, in a way that was intended by the author. Vanhoozer's argument on this point is worth noting,

---

of a text. He argues that Stanley Fish simply uses a text in order to get something else, so there are no limits to the interpretation of the radical reader response critics like Fish. Eco himself sees that the meaning of a text is limited by the intention of the work.

82. Harvey, *The Condition of Postmodernity*, 8–9, 43; Thiselton, *Hermeneutics*, 328. Despite its ubiquity, it is very hard to define the word "postmodernism." Basically, postmodernism presumes the end of modernism. According to Harvey, postmodernism was a reaction to the modernism, which can be identified as "positivistic, technocentric, and rationalistic." Thiselton summarizes: "Modernism, he claims, is characterized by purpose and form; postmodernism by play and antiform or dysfunction. Modernism strives for coherence, hierarchy, presence, and semantics; against these, respectively, postmodernism represents chance, anarchy, absence, and rhetoric. Finally, modernism aims at metaphysics, determinacy, and transcendence; postmodernity replaces these with irony, indeterminacy, and immanence." He follows Harvey's *The Condition of Postmodernity*, 43.

83. Thiselton, *Hermeneutics*, 306.

84. Vanhoozer, "The Reader in New Testament Interpretation," 301. "Reading is not merely a matter of perception but also of production."

85. Thiselton, *Hermeneutics*, 306.

86. Keck, "Will the Historical-Critical Method Survive?," 123–24; also see Nahkola, *Double Narratives in the Old Testament*, 192–93. Nahkola argues that "a synthesis of the existing theories" will yield a more satisfactory solution.

My appeal to the Trinity arises rather from the perception that the literary crisis about textual meaning is related to the broader philosophical crisis concerning realism, rationality, and right, and that this crisis, summed up by the term "postmodern," is in turn explicitly theological. After all, it was Nietzsche's announcement of the "death of God" that eventually led to the "death of the author."[87]

It is clear that we cannot access the original authors' intentions because the authors are no longer available. By the same token, we cannot access the original text or the original readers' contexts. In fact, the only thing we can do is to deal with the text itself. The voice of the author should be discovered in the text. It is therefore important to make every effort to understand the text by examining the text itself as well as its various contexts (literary, historical, and cultural, etc.). However, as mentioned above, absolute objectivity may not be confirmed. Because meaning is always laden with "unconscious assumptions between sender and receiver" we also should consider the "subjective 'life-world' of the reader or the 'inter-subjective social world' of the text."[88] Naturally the author is bound to the text, and readers can recognize the authorial meaning by looking into the encoded texts.[89] In order to avoid two extremes of meaning, we must examine the discourse meaning of the text. By looking into authorial intention, we can avoid autonomy of the text; by looking into the readers' context, we can avoid a complete relativity of meaning.[90] In order to determine the proper meaning, then, we need to examine what the text means. From there, we can discover both the authorial meaning and its implication for the readers.

Textlinguistics

The meaning of a text is that which was intended by the author. Therefore, discovering textual meaning is a proper way to obtain the authorial meaning. In order to do this, we will now examine some important approaches to obtaining the proper meaning of the text. In particular, I will adopt the textlinguistic method for this study.[91] Two different terms are used

---

87. Vanhoozer, *Is There a Meaning in This Text?*, 456.
88. Osborne, *The Hermeneutical Spiral*, 386.
89. Vanhoozer, "Language, Literature, Hermeneutics and Biblical Theology," 30.
90. Cotterell, "Semantics, Interpretation, and Theology," 140–42.
91. For more general studies, consult followings: Halliday and Matthiessen, *An Introduction to Functional Grammar*; Longacre, *The Grammar of Discourse*; Beaugrande and Dressler, *Introduction to Text Linguistics*; Lyons, *Language and Linguistics*; Groom,

interchangeably in discussions of this method: discourse analysis and textlinguistics.[92]

The term "textlinguistics" describes not a simple theory for understanding a text but "any work in language science devoted to the text as the primary object of inquiry."[93] Even though there are slight differences between discourse analysis and textlinguistics, Jeffrey T. Reed's definition is worth noting. According to him, textlinguistics (discourse analysis) refers to "(1) the linguistic units surrounding a sentence (cotext), (2) the immediate situation (context of situation), and (3) the wider cultural background of the text (context of culture)."[94]

Due to the difficulty of defining textlinguistics, Lowery divides textlinguistic approaches into just two categories: the first is focused on human behavior, and the second focuses on language itself.[95] Based on their seven standards of textuality, Lowery's two categories also can be classified either text-centered or reader-centered.[96] At this point, we need to consider three dimensions of the text: syntactics, semantics, and pragmatics.[97]

Linguistic Analysis of Biblical Hebrew; Dawson, *Text-Linguistics and Biblical Hebrew*; and Wiklander, *Prophecy as Literature*.

92. Bodine, "Introduction," 2. He distinguishes these two terms. Generally speaking, discourse analysis has been called in United States, while textlinguistics is in Europe.

93. Beaugrande and Dressler, *Introduction to Text Linguistics*, 14.

94. Reed, "Discourse Analysis as New Testament Hermeneutic," 225; Stubbs, *Discourse Analysis*, 10. Stubbs applies it "both to the study of language above the sentence, and also to the study of naturally occurring language."

95. Lowery, "The Theoretical Foundations," 11.

96. Ibid., 111. For further study on the seven standards of textuality—cohesion, coherence, intentionality, acceptability, informativity, situationality, and intertextuality—see Beaugrande and Dressler, *Introduction to Text Linguistics*, 1–13. Bodine, "Introduction," 3. The most important assumption of textlinguistics is that the meaning of the text does not rest simply in words, sentence, or even discourse, but is larger than the sum of the whole unit of the text. Bodine avers, "In discourse there is a linguistic entity that is greater than any distilled, logical summary sentence and also greater than only the sequence of sentences that make up the discourse."

97. VanGemeren, "Preface," 7–9. VanGemeren states, "The discourse is held together at three levels: syntactics, semantics, and pragmatics. Grammar and syntax help in seeing 'grammatical and syntactical cohesion' of a text, but the study of the meaning of words enhances the study by two additional dimensions: semantic coherence and intentionality ... Pragmatics as the third dimension of linguistics helps the reader of the text to connect the author with his intended audience ..."

Syntactics, Semantics, and Pragmatics

In its essence, a text can be seen as a communicative act in which an author communicates with a reader through the text. In order to uncover the textual meaning intended by the author, we should focus on the linguistic aspects of the text. Syntactics is primarily the study of the relationship between the sequences of words in a sentence and beyond.[98] It has long been observed that the meaning of a text comes from words and their relationships. Simply put, a text should contain words and employ certain sequences of words. For de Beaugrande and Dressler, surface text is "mutually connected within a sequence."[99] This connection constitutes of cohesion in a text. Therefore, in order to investigate the text, we must first focus on the words and their relationships within the text. The major task here is to observe the grammatical relationships within the text, including phonology, morphology, and syntax.

Scholars generally agree that the locus of meaning is larger than word meaning.[100] In general, a word itself does not hold a specific meaning outside its context. As J. P. Louw rightly states, "More specifically this implies that a word does not have a meaning without a context, it only has possibilities of meaning. Context, situation and syntactic environment contribute to the choice between the several possibilities of meaning. The word has a specific meaning in that context."[101] As James Barr suggests, a better way to understand biblical language is to study "larger linguistic complexes such as the sentences," rather than words in isolation.[102] By creating grammatical dependencies between words, textual interrelationships establish grammatical and lexical cohesion within and beyond the sentence.[103] Since words have certain meanings defined by their contexts on the semantic level, it

---

98. Yule, *Pragmatics*, 4. He defines, "Syntax is the study of the relationships between linguistic forms, how they are arranged in sequence, and which sequences are well-formed."

99. Beaugrande and Dressler, *Introduction to Text Linguistics*, 3.

100. For more detailed explanation about the general fallacies of word study, see Carson, *Exegetical Fallacies*, 27–64; Osborne, *The Hermeneutical Spiral*, 65–75; Barr, *Semantics of Biblical Language*; Louw, *Semantics of New Testament Greek*, 23–31. But to seek word meaning is relatively valuable to the Old Testament study because the Hebrew Old Testament more frequently contains *hapax legomena* than the Greek New Testament. See Carson, *Exegetical Fallacies*, 33.

101. Louw, *Semantics of New Testament Greek*, 40.

102. Barr, *Semantics of Biblical Language*, 263.

103. Halliday and Hasan, *Cohesion in English*, 8–13; Beaugrande and Dressler, *Introduction to Text Linguistics*, 48–51.

is necessary to study beyond the surface text. This brings us to the second dimension of the text: semantics.

As mentioned, meaning is not just the sum of words and phrases, but goes beyond them. According to Yule, semantics can be defined as "the study of the relationships between linguistic forms and entities in the world; that is, how words literally connect to things."[104] Ferdinand de Saussure's work, which is grounded in a study of language as a structural system of linguistics, brings us to the realization that basic meaning should be determined by the structural relationships within and beyond the text. As Saussure contends, "A language is a system in which all the elements fit together, and in which the value of any one element depends on the simultaneous coexistence of all the others."[105] He continues, "Its value is therefore not determined merely by that concept or meaning for which it is a token. It must also be assessed against comparable values, by contrast with other words. The content of a word is determined in the final analysis not by what it contains but by what exists outside it."[106] Semantics thus allows us to take a holistic approach to a sentence and helps us synthesize all of its components.

At the same time, language is still a communicative act, and in order to get the full meaning we must shift our focus from the "what of meaning (texts as communicative acts)" to the "who of meaning (authors as communicative agents)."[107] It is necessary to expand our concern to the third dimension of linguistics: pragmatics.

According to Yule, pragmatics is "the study of the relationships between linguistic forms and the users of those forms."[108] In this step, pragmatics can add the author's intended meaning, purpose, or assumption to the previous two linguistic dimensions (syntactics and semantics). Uncovering the meaning of the text requires proper understanding of words, syntax, sentence, and discourse, as well as an extended concern for the historical, social, and literary contexts in which authorial intention is located. Pragmatics enhances semantic coherence and helps us discover the whole meaning of the text as the author originally intended. In terms of de Beaugrande and Dressler's categories, pragmatics is related to intentionality, informativity, and situationality. Because we cannot infer an author's intention from gesture and intonation, we should focus on grammatical forms, the features of the sentences, and contexts of the text (literary, historical, social, etc.).

---

104. Yule, *Pragmatics*, 4.
105. Saussure, *Course in General Linguistics*, 113.
106. Ibid., 114.
107. Vanhoozer, *Is There a Meaning in This Text?*, 218–59.
108. Yule, *Pragmatics*, 4.

One of the most helpful ways to uncover the context of the text is to study deixis. According to Stephen C. Levinson, "Essentially deixis concerns the ways in which languages encode or grammaticalize features of the *context of utterance* or *speech event*, and thus also concerns ways in which the interpretation of utterances depends on the analysis of that context of utterance."[109] Deixis thus explains the various ways in which a sentence can be structured. More specifically, we need to know the speaker, audience, and time and place of speaking in order to more fully and properly understand the text. It is therefore of first and foremost importance to examine the context of a text if we wish to understand it properly. Traditionally, there are three basic categories of deixis: person, place, and time.[110] Levinson adds two additional categories: discourse and social deixis. For him, discourse deixis is related to "[the] reference to portions of the unfolding discourse," while social deixis manifests the social distinctions related to both speaker and addressee.[111]

These three dimensions of the text allow us to arrive at the meaning of a discourse, not just a word or sentence. Textlinguistics, with its use of syntactics, semantics, and pragmatics, is thus an appropriate tool for studying the text. Additionally, it is important to balance micro and macro structure in the study of textlinguistics. We must synthesize word, sentence, discourse, and even book in order to gain an appropriate understanding of the text.

We now come to the next two steps of analyzing texts in order to enhance their relationship. First, at the foundation of linguistic theory, it is important to utilize the "functional sentence perspective," which provides us with a better understanding of sentences, including their morphology, syntax, and semantics. Second, we will consider innerbiblical interpretation as an appropriate tool with which to observe a macro structure of a text.

---

109. Levinson, *Pragmatics*, 54; emphasis in the original.

110. Ibid., 62. According to Levinson, person deixis manifests the role of participants, place deixis concerns the location of the participants, and time deixis encodes the temporal points and span.

111. Ibid., 62–63; Cotterell and Turner, *Linguistics & Biblical Interpretation*, 236–40; Longacre, *The Grammar of Discourse*, 84–86. Similarly Cotterell and Turner categorize deixis into five: personal (personal pronoun), social (social relationships), temporal (tense and aspect), locational (spatial aspect like here, there, this and that), and discourse deixis (indicators of discourse structure like therefore, subsequent, so, and following).

Functional Sentence Perspective

Since the meaning of text resides not only at the sentence level, but also at the discourse and text levels, it is essential to observe the connectivity of the sentences. As Hannes Rieser argues, sentence grammar fails to demonstrate linguistic phenomena. The sentences must incorporate into a larger unit of text.[112] In this regard, Functional Sentence Perspective (FSP) is a good method for connecting and recognizing textual progress of the phrase, sentence, paragraph, and discourse at the textlinguistic level.

FSP examines the thematic progression and connection of sentences. Because it relates to the sequence in the text and moves forward the communication acts, it enhances biblical interpretation by enabling recognition of textual cohesion and coherence. On a basic level, sentences are organized by a theme-rheme structure. This structure represents thematic systems, in which the speaker/author organizes clauses as a message.[113] The terms "theme" and "rheme" were originally used by the Prague School, and have been referred to as "topic" and "comment" by American linguists.[114] In general, theme is defined as "what we are talking about (the topic), while rheme is "what we are saying about it (the comment)."[115] By definition, theme is usually placed at the starting point and rheme is placed at the point of arrival. In terms of information, although theme-rheme and given-new structures are not exactly the same, there are significant semantic relationships between them. In most cases, theme is given information, while rheme is new information.[116] Through the relationship between theme/given and rheme/new in sentences, we can see connections and even progressions in texts. Through these connections, it is clear that sentences are closely related to one another.

Theme-rheme analysis enhances our understanding of textual connectivity and structural coherence by shedding light on the text's functional progression. Leonard F. M. Scinto states that "the necessity for such functional

---

112. Rieser, "On the Development of Text Grammar," 9–10; Van Dijk, "Episodes as Units of Discourse Analysis," 177. Van Dijk mentions, "Roughly speaking, paragraphs or episodes are characterized as coherent sequences of sentences of a discourse, linguistically marked for beginning and/or end, and further defined in terms of some kind of 'thematic unity.'"

113. Halliday, "Text as Semantic Choice in Social Contexts," 182; Halliday and Matthiessen, *An Introduction to Functional Grammar*.

114. Heimerdinger, *Topic, Focus and Foreground*, 102.

115. Palmer, *Semantics*, 158; Payne, "Functional Sentence Perspective," 62–82.

116. Payne, "Functional Sentence Perspective," 63–64; Halliday and Matthiessen, *An Introduction to Functional Grammar*, 119–21. Halliday argues that the theme-rheme is speaker-oriented, while given-new is listerner-oriented.

relations between successive sentences of text is a result of the thematic progression operative in a text ... This functional requirement leads to the establishment of what may be termed 'functional-communicative coherence.'"[117] Theme-rheme analysis can thus show thematic progressions, including thematic developments, through the connectivity of the sentences.[118]

Now we need to take this one step further. Continuity is presupposed by the nature of a text, but it may be expressed differently in Hebrew than in English. For example, the basic structure of the sentence in English is subject-verb-object, while in Hebrew it is verb-subject-object. It is therefore doubtful that the FSP theory for English can be applied to Hebrew in the exactly same way. Hebrew has its own way to express continuity and discontinuity in sentences, paragraphs, and discourses. Christo H. J. van der Merwe discusses two approaches to functional grammar in Hebrew: the bottom-up approach, which moves from sentence to text, and the top-down approach, which begins with the whole text and moves down to the sentence level.[119] In these approaches, there are two distinctive connections "between the mainline and the subsidiary line of communication."[120]

The mainline usually consists of the *Wayyiqtol* and the *WeQatal*. In particular, the *Wayyiqtol* constitutes the mainline and independent sentences of the narrative. Robert E. Longacre argues, "Here the waw-consecutive imperfect is seen to be mainline in that it is punctiliar and sequential in function."[121] So, an important feature of the *Wayyiqtol* form is that it advances the mainline of the story.[122] Of course, there are some exceptions.

---

117. Scinto, "Functional Connectivity and the Communicative Structure of Text," 81–82; Van Dijk, *Text and Context*, 132.

118. For more specific patterns of theme-rheme structure, see Scinto, "Functional Connectivity and the Communicative Structure of Text"; Daneš, "Functional Sentence Perspective and the Organization of the Text," 106–28. There are three basic patterns: a simple linear; a continuous theme, and theme derived from "hypertheme." First, simple linear is the most basic thing, in which rheme becomes the theme in the next. Second, a continuous theme denotes that one same theme continues to the following utterances but has different rhemes. And third is the combination of first and second. They also provide very useful diagrams for helping understand thematic progression of the sentences.

119. Merwe, "Discourse Linguistics and Biblical Hebrew Grammar," 18–21; For the bottom-up approach in detail, see Niccacci, "On the Hebrew Verbal System," 117–37; and for the top-down approach in detail, see Longacre, "Weqatal Forms in Biblical Hebrew Prose," 50–98; Longacre, "Discourse Perspective on the Hebrew Verb," 177–89.

120. Merwe, "Discourse Linguistics and Biblical Hebrew Grammar," 23.

121. Longacre, *Joseph*, 59.

122. Heimerdinger, *Topic, Focus, and Foreground*, 76–85. So, Heimerdinger reviews Longacre's approaches to the *Wayyiqtol* as foreground, action advancing events, and sequence.

Sometimes the *Wayyiqtol* form can be used in a flashback, which returns the storyline to an earlier point.[123] These cases represent a break in the mainline of time even though the *Wayyiqtol* form is used. On the same basis, an overlap can be understood as a non-chronological usage of the *Wayyiqtol* form.[124] An overlap appears when two events that are sequentially linked happen partially or completely at the same time. Finally, the *Wayyiqtol* form can also be used for a summarizing statement, evaluation, or recapitulation of a whole storyline.[125]

The *WeQatal* form functions in the same way as the *Wayyiqtol* in predictive, procedural, and instructional discourse.[126] According to Niccacci, the *Weqatal* constitutes the mainline for the future tense in direct speech. He describes the mainline of communication as follows:[127]

Table 3: Niccacci's The Mainline of Communication

Temporal Axis	Narrative	Direct Speech
Past	Wayyiqtol	Qatal
Present	—	Simple nominal clause
Future	—	WeQatal

The *WeQatal* thus shows sequence in time and logic, and as a temporal aspect denotes habitual actions, modality, and possibility.[128]

While the *Wayyiqtol* and the *WeQatal* forms express the sequential aspect as a mainline of the story—that is, they serve to advance the story—the *We-X-Qatal* and *We-X-Yiqtol* forms perform the secondary function of providing background information.[129] For example, Gen 3:1a uses the *We+X+Qatal* structure. Since it displays different word order, it introduces a new topic or the beginning of a paragraph. Its syntax also breaks up

---

123. Ibid., 86.
124. Ibid., 89.
125. Ibid., 90–93.
126. Longacre, "*Weqatal* Forms in Biblical Hebrew Prose," 50–55.
127. Niccacci, "Analysis of Biblical Narrative," 177.
128. Merwe, Kroeze, and Naudé, *A Biblical Hebrew Reference Grammar*, 169.
129. Heimerdinger, *Topic, Focus, and Foreground*, 58; Merwe, "Discourse Linguistics and Biblical Hebrew Grammar," 30; Longacre, *Joseph*, 74–82. Longacre states, "Clauses that begin with a non-preterite (perfect) verb portray secondary actions; for example, actions that are in some sense subsidiary to the main action, which is described by a following preterite (65)."

a sequence of mainline in the story. Verse 3:1a thus provides background information for the mainline of the story. Since the information about the serpent does not contribute to the stream of the story, it is not mainline but secondary.

In sum, FSP is closely related to a grammatical approach and to discourse analysis, in which it enhances understanding of the continuity and progression of discourses. By examining the functional grammar of text we can gain a good deal of insight that will help us denote textual meanings and properly respond to historical critical approaches that explore the smallest units of texts.

Inner-Biblical Interpretation

The problem with Robert Alter's type-scene model, which takes the synchronic approach, is that it does not take seriously the historical aspect of the text.[130] A historical approach can provide the setting and literary, social, geographical, cultural, and religious background necessary for a better understanding of the text. Anthony Thiselton, therefore, argues that a reading that ignores or underestimates historical aspects in order to emphasize the literary aspects "becomes docetic."[131] As Werner G. Jeanrond rightly observes,

> The individual meaning of linguistic expressions is not determined solely by the choice of words, or by the way in which the sentence is structured, but also by the context in which an expression is embedded. This embedding comes about through the linguistic context on the one hand, and, on the other, through the situation of communication which is also constitutive of meaning.[132]

---

130. Alter, *The Art of Biblical Narrative*, 49–50. Alter divides his new literary approach from form criticism by rejecting historical aspects of the texts, even though they share similar approach in terms of form and structure.

131. Thiselton, *Hermeneutics*, 28–29; For more extended discussion and example, see Thiselton, "On Models and Methods," 337–57.

132. Jeanrond, *Text and Interpretation*, 76; Williams, "The Beautiful and the Barren," 107–19; Edelman, "An Appraisal of Robert Alter's Approach," 19–25. Edelman mentions, "I feel that any analysis that fails to deal with the historical dimension of a biblical text, even if the focus is on compositional methods and intentions, has not evaluated the full available data, and therefore is incomplete and potentially misleading. Conclusions need to be based on the largest available data pool and must explain as many facts as possible (p.22–23)."

Clearly, meaning lies not only in the connection of words, sentences, and discourses, but also beyond the text. It is therefore necessary to maintain a balance between historical and literary analysis. Aulikki Nahkola, for example, has done a significant amount of research on double narratives in the Old Testament.[133] He suggests that "a synthesis of the existing theories" is necessary for a more satisfactory solution to the issues involved.[134] Nahkola's argument for a synthetic or holistic approach does not mean that we should accept historical-critical approaches. Although he argues that there is a need to maintain a balance by placing diachronic approaches alongside synchronic approaches, he generally fails to actually maintain a balance because he considers source criticism to be of pivotal significance in the study of the texts.[135] Within this study, however, the term "historical" it used simply to refer to the fact that the texts have historical backgrounds (cultural, contextual, social, etc.), and that these historical aspects can help the readers determine textual meaning.

Bearing all this in mind, an innerbiblical interpretation is a good tool with which to explore the text from both literary and historical perspectives. Michael Fishbane has developed the idea of innerbiblical interpretation of the Bible,[136] which involves studying the relationships between texts. Fishbane maintains that "in so far as the 'latter correspondents' occur in history and time, they will never be precisely identical with their prototype, but inevitably stand in a *hermeneutical* relationship with them."[137] Relationships between or among texts can be drawn explicitly through quotations or implicitly through allusions. Focusing on the exegetical developments of texts can help us notice the textual relationships.[138] Innerbiblical interpretation thus allows us to thoroughly examine the text itself as well as its own context, noting that later texts should be understood in light of earlier ones. To say that the later texts are related to earlier texts does not, however, necessarily imply the ideas of derived source, form, or redaction criticism. Monika Lindner suggests some important questions that we should raise in relation to innerbiblical interpretation, suggesting that we should examine how the author deals with the earlier story, how the ideas from the earlier text develop in the later text, and what the author intended to achieve by

---

133. Nahkola, *Double Narratives in the Old Testament*.
134. Ibid., 192–93.
135. Ibid., 195–96.
136. Fishbane, *Biblical Interpretation in Ancient Israel*.
137. Ibid., 351; emphasis in the original.
138. Schniedewind, "Innerbiblical Exegesis," 503.

including those texts.[139] Attention can be given to all of these questions while undertaking innerbiblical interpretation can be applied to the wife/sister motif in Genesis.[140]

As we have seen, looking at a text as a whole, both in its literary context—the most important and most basic process—and in its historical background, enables us to reach a better understanding of the text.[141] For our present purposes, we must examine the wife/sister stories using the tools of type-scene and innerbiblical interpretation. In addition, because the three stories appear in two different *Toledot* formulae, we must consider them seriously and try to discover the overall structure connecting the two different *Toledots* from the point of view of the wife/sister motif. This synthetic approach will lead us to a better understanding of: (1) the literary meaning of each story, (2) the function of each story in its own context, (3) the continuities and variations among the stories, and finally (4) the overall structure and function of the wife/sister stories as a whole within the Abraham and Isaac *Toledots*.

Type-Scene

In the previous section, we explored the textlinguistic approach, which is the most basic method for understanding the text itself. We now come to another important method for this study: type-scene.

Definition

Scholars consider Walter Arend, author of the 1933 book *Die typischen Scenen bei Homer*, as a pioneer of type-scene study. Arend observes sequences of elements such as "arrival, sacrifice, meal preparation, journeys by sea and by land, donning armor and clothing, retiring to sleep, deliberation, assembly, oath-taking, and bathing"[142] and argues that the repetition of such stories is a result not of interpolations but of literary purpose. Robert Alter

---

139. Lindner, "Integrationsformen Der Intertextualität," 116–35.

140. Zakovitch, "Juxtaposition in the Abraham Cycle," 509–24; Fishbane, *Biblical Interpretation in Ancient Israel*.

141. For three dimensions for biblical narrative study, see Averbeck, "Factors in Reading the Patriarchal Narratives," 115–37.

142. Arend, *Die Typischen Szenen bei Homer*. For full discussion on the history of the study on the type-scene, see Edwards, "Homer and Oral Tradition: The Type-Scene," 290. Here Edwards provided an earlier study on type-scene by Radlov, which has to do with Turkic oral poetry. Also see Foley, *The Theory of Oral Composition*, 10–13.

was the first scholar to apply Arend's type-scene model to biblical study. Although previous form critical scholars had recognized recurrent patterns as literary conventions, Alter considered "how the patterns actually work."[143] According to Alter, form criticism, focusing on *Gattung*, mainly addresses *Sitz im Leben* in the texts by investigating recurrent patterns. However, Alter maintains, "in contrast to a *Gattung*, a literary convention may in some instances reflect certain social or cultural realities but is bound to offer a highly mediated, stylized image of such realities: in the literary convention, culture has been transformed into text, which is rather different from form-criticism's tendency to insist on the function performed by text in culture."[144] This shift from a diachronic approach to *Gattung* to a synchronic approach that focuses on the literary function is Alter's major contribution.

Regarding type-scene, Alter proposes that "there is a series of recurrent narrative episodes attached to the careers of biblical heroes that are analogous to Homeric type-scenes in that they are dependent on the manipulation of a fixed constellation of predetermined motifs."[145] He includes the following motifs in his analysis: (1) the annunciation of the birth of the hero to his barren mother, (2) the encounter with the future betrothed at a well, (3) the epiphany in the "field," (4) the initiatory trial, (5) danger in the desert and the discovery of a well or other source of sustenance, and (6) the testament of the dying hero.[146] Though he considers the three wife/sister stories as a type-scene, he does not deal with them in detail.

It is important to note, then, that while Alter was the first scholar to apply specific type-scenes to biblical studies, he for the most part simply followed Arend's idea about type-scenes. Thus, following Arend, Alter maintains that a type-scene should have a fixed pattern. For example, the type-scene of the visit should include the following: "a guest approaches, someone spots him, gets up, hurries to greet him, the guest is taken by the hand, led into the room, invited to take the seat of honor, the guest is enjoined to feast, the ensuing meal."[147] While Alter argues that some fixed

---

143. Alter, "How Convention Helps Us Read," 119.

144. Ibid.

145. Alter, *The Art of Biblical Narrative*, 51.

146. Since Alter proposed these type-scene models, many other scholars have tried to identify them in other biblical narratives. See, Kim, *Incubation as a Type-Scene*; Bullard, "Genesis 18:1–15 through the Lens of a Covenant Meal Type-Scene"; Kee, "The Heavenly Council and Its Type-Scene," 259–73; Savran, "Theophany as Type Scene," 119–49; Britt, "Prophetic Concealment in a Biblical Type Scene," 37–58; Green, "A Type-Scene Approach to Jacob's Encounter at the Jabbok"; Fuchs, "Structure, Ideology and Politics," 273–81; Fleming, "The Divine Council as Type-Scene"; McMahan, "Meals as Type-Scenes"; Williams, "The Beautiful and the Barren."

147. Alter, *The Art of Biblical Narrative*, 50–51.

motifs—those required in type-scenes—are joined with other free motifs, his basic understanding of a type-scene is no different than Arend's.

Many biblical scholars have accepted Alter's approach. For example, Victor R. Salanga develops Alter's type-scene model and applies it to the wife/sister stories in his dissertation. He summarizes a possible basic type-scene in the wife/sister stories as follows:

First, the hero sojourns in a place where the couple is not recognized at all as married. Second, the husband perceives danger and peril to his own life. Third, he resorts to the wife-sister trick. Fourth, depending on how long the trick holds, the baseline requirement is the possibility of the wife being imperiled and endangered. Fifth, the trick finally must be unmasked.[148]
The understanding of type-scene as a recurrent fixed motif has not been challenged, however.

Some scholars have offered significant challenges to Arend's basic concept of type-scenes (that is, recurrent fixed motifs). Michael N. Nagler, for example, maintains that typical scenes are not fixed patterns of words or ideas, but "an inherited pre-verbal *Gestalt* for the spontaneous generation of a 'family' of meaningful details."[149] In a crucial 1967 article, Nagler wrote,

> With the conceptual framework in question, a group . . . would be considered not a closed "system" but an open-ended "family," and each phrase in the group would be considered an allomorph, *not of any other existing phrase*, but of some central Gestalt—for want of a better term—which is the real mental template underlying the production of all such phrases.[150]

Nagler, therefore, expands the basic concept of type-scene by including "referentiality."[151] Instead of defining a type-scene as a recurrent fixed pattern, he introduces the concept of "family" into the subject matter. For Nagler, then, a type-scene is not required to follow a fixed pattern but need only maintain a family resemblance in the poet's mind. He calls this a "pre-verbal" *Gestalt*.

Following Nagler, Koowon Kim impressively applies this new concept of type-scenes to biblical Hannah stories.[152] Kim's argument contributes

---

148. Salanga, *Three Stories of the Endangered Wife*, 54.

149. Nagler, *Spontaneity and Tradition*, 82. He argues, "in practice . . . not only are no two passages normally the same verbatim, they need not be a pattern (an identical sequence of elements) in order to be recognized as the same motif. One could even cite examples of the same motif which do not share a single element in common."

150. Nagler, "Toward a Generative View of the Oral Formula," 281.

151. Nagler, *Spontaneity and Tradition*, 83–85; Foley, *Traditional Oral Epic*, 243.

152. Kim, *Incubation as a Type-Scene*.

to the scholarly discussions. Like Kim, Jonathan Kruschwitz attempts to loosen the strict type-scene concept and seek connections between the story of Judah and Tamar in Gen 38 and the Joseph story by observing the type-scene concept of deception and counter-deception.[153] It is important to note that Kruschwitz applies the type-scene model to two stories that are not closely connected to each other. Even though these stories do not share many fixed patterns compared to other type-scene stories, they do have "a similar plot progression" and "knowledge structure."[154] Kruschwitz moves far from the traditional definition of type-scene as understood by Arend and Alter. This is pertinent to the wife/sister stories because scholars have spent decades attempting to find recurring scenes and their importance. If we accept Nagler's theory of family resemblance, we can avoid endless discussion concerning what type or kind of motif should be used in type-scenes.[155]

In order to define the nature of type-scene, it is worth quoting Robert Tannehill's definition, who highlights the essential features of the subject matter.

> A type-scene is a basic situation, which recurs several times within a narrative. Each occurrence has a recognizably similar set of characteristics, sometimes highlighted by the repetition of key phrases, but this similarity permits- even requires, if boredom is to be avoided- new variations in the development of the scene.[156]

This definition shows that a type-scene is: (1) a repetitive element within a narrative, (2) a similar set of characteristics, and (3) capable of supporting new variations in order to avoid boredom and provide development in a narrative. According to this definition, type-scenes enhance the unity of a narrative through their similarities as well as the development of a narrative through variations in characterization, theme, and plot.[157]

---

153. Kruschwitz, "The Type-Scene Connection," 391–92.

154. Ibid., 391.

155. Arend, *Die Typischen Szenen bei Homer*, 28–63. Arend argues that a certain theme (type-scene) should contain certain elements. For example, he argues that the sleep scenes should have three elements: night, sleep, and dawn. But it seems to me that different scholars identify different scenes from their different perspectives. For this, see Morris, "'Dream Scenes' in Homer," 40–42.

156. Tannehill, *The Narrative Unity of Luke-Acts*, 170.

157. Fleming, "The Divine Council as Type-Scene," 44; McMahan, "Meals as Type-Scenes," 50, 62.

Function of Type-Scene

The use of type-scenes as a literary device can demonstrate that an author wrote well-crafted stories. The most basic feature of the type-scene is the repetition of scenes. In order to demonstrate similarities and connections, biblical narratives certainly contain recurrent motifs, *leitwort*, themes, sequences of actions, repetitions, and type-scenes.[158] We may therefore conclude that the biblical authors used type-scenes to achieve a special purpose. Following Alter's investigation of the formal elements of recurring narratives in the Old Testament, James Williams analyzed and discussed the essential elements of the wife/sister stories. Williams identified seven essential similarities in the wife/sister stories but did not take note of variations.[159] Neither Alter nor Williams focused on the function of variations.

It is clear that the most basic and crucial characteristic of type-scenes are repetition and recurrence. According to Sternberg, repetitions appear at different levels of the narrative, from the level of sound to the levels of plot and theme.[160] Through the repetitions of types, the texts reinforce: (1) reliability of recognition, (2) accuracy of transmission, (3) a greater level of assent to the views of the narrator, and (4) a sense of formalistic coherence in the narrative.[161] By observing repetitions in type-scenes, one can easily follow the continuity of the narrative. As Alter points out, a type-scene is "an elaborately integrated system of repetitions."[162] So, by using a type-scene, the author enhances the continuity of the stories within a larger context. What is more, the repetition does not simply manifest continuity but also provides for the development of the narrative. In this regard, repetitions in a type-scene lead the narrative to a climactic moment in the story as a whole.[163] According to Tannehill,

> Reading is a constant process of forming and revising expectation, both focal expectations, relating to the immediate context, and global expectations, stretching over large sections of the

---

158. Alter, *The Art of Biblical Narrative*, 88–113.

159. Williams, "The Beautiful and the Barren," 108–9.

160. Sternberg, *The Poetics of Biblical Narrative*, 365–66. Sternberg identifies different levels of repetitions as follows: on the levels of sound and linguistic sense, on the level of plot, on the thematic level, and on the generic level.

161. Fleming, "The Divine Council as Type-Scene," 49.

162. Alter, *The Art of Biblical Narrative*, 95–96. He includes *leitwort*, motif, theme, sequence of actions, and type-scene in this system of repetitions.

163. Thimmes, *Studies in the Biblical Sea-Storm Type-Scene*, 207–9; Fleming, "The Divine Council as Type-Scene," 44; McMahan, "Meals as Type-Scenes in the Gospel of Luke," 62.

> work. The need to continually revise expectations involves the reader actively in the work and can be a major means of holding the reader's interest... Furthermore, the process of building and revising expectations in reading can be used effectively to guide readers toward a climax in the narrative. Confirmation of expectations through a growing repetitive pattern allows the reader to anticipate a climactic instance of the pattern, which will fulfill expectations in the highest degree.[164]

Through repetition, narratives can preserve unity while continually revising and developing the story. In order to maximize readers' expectations and involvement, the narrative uses variations, another crucial function of type-scenes.

Type-scenes contain a variety of differences. At a glance, certain stories seem to repeat the same story line in different contexts—if we scrutinize these stories, however, we can discover considerable variation. As Meir Sternberg points out, these variations appear even in verbatim repetition. Sternberg states that "verbatim repetition is not precise repetition. It is precise only in the sense that its members vary in contextual rather than physical (verbal, grammatical) features."[165] Variations are crucial because they create tension between the reader's expectation of uniformity and the reality of variation. Through repetitions, authors ensure the continuity of the texts; through variations, they provide new information to readers. This new information established by variation contributes to the development of the narrative as a whole. According to McMahan, one can find clear evidence of development in particular variations in type-scenes. He maintains that the following three areas are important for narrative development: plot, characterization, and theme.[166]

Like repetition, variations are formal manifestations of dissimilar information. Variations can take the form of expansion or addition, truncation or ellipsis, change of order, grammatical transformation, or substitution.[167] In fact, variations challenge readers to perceive another essential meaning that is not provided by repetitions. In this regard, both repetition and variation are crucial to a proper understanding of a narrative. Nonetheless, we need to recognize that these two crucial elements do not function in contradiction for both can provide functional unity. Sternberg argues, "Below the surface, however, all this formal variety combines into functional unity. All

---

164. Tannehill, "The Composition of Acts 3–5," 239.
165. Sternberg, *The Poetics of Biblical Narrative*, 390–91.
166. McMahan, "Meals as Type-Scenes in the Gospel of Luke," 62.
167. Sternberg, *The Poetics of Biblical Narrative*, 391–92.

the variations go to dramatize a single point."[168] We can therefore conclude that both repetition and variation in a type-scene function to enhance narrative coherence and unity.

It is important to analyze the wife/sister stories as a unity because this scene appears not once but three times in the book of Genesis. The type-scene approach to examining the similarities and dissimilarities between the stories is a good starting point from which to gain a better understanding of each story and its distinct meaning within its own context. Further, as we look at these narratives through the lens of type-scene, we may establish the connections among the three stories and their intended function within the larger context of the book of Genesis.

Application and Summary

This book will investigate the three wife/sister stories that appear in Gen 12:1—13:1; 20:1–20; and 26:1–11. Although many scholars have observed the three wife/sister stories, very few have investigated them adequately from the perspectives of textlinguistic and type-scene analysis.

The methodology to be used in this study consists of two major parts. A textlinguistic analysis will be the first consideration. Since we do not have access to the original author and readers of these stories, the only way to determine meaning is to investigate the text itself. Through study of the text, we can establish what the author originally intended to communicate. In this regard, a textlinguistic study is essential for determining the textual meaning. For the purposes of textlinguistic analysis, this study will focus on three dimensions of the text: syntactics, semantics, and pragmatics. Further, we will employ functional sentence perspective and innerbiblical interpretation methods to observe relationships between the texts. These tools will allow us to highlight how the three wife/sister stories are closely connected to each other and how thematic coherence is maintained throughout the stories.

The second major part of the methodology used in this study is the type-scene method. Following Robert Alter, most scholars view the wife/sister stories as a good example of type-scene. When exploring the three stories with the type-scene method, scholars tend to focus on how these stories share similar scenes, and therefore attempt to find the recurrent fixed motif or pattern in the stories. Recently, however, there have been important developments in the study of type-scenes, particularly a shift in focus from recurrent fixed motifs to family resemblances. We must therefore spend

---

168. Ibid., 138; McMahan, "Meals as Type-Scenes in the Gospel of Luke," 63–64.

more time examining not the type or motif, but similarities and variations.[169] In this study, I will use the type-scene model to examine three areas: characterization, theme, and plot. Through this process, I will attempt to shed light on the three wife/sister stories' close connections, their thematic development, and their emphasis on the major themes of the book of Genesis.

Before examining each wife/sister story in turn, we need to investigate the wife/sister stories within their larger context from a textlinguistic point of view. The next chapter will include discussions of the *Toledot* formula, the macrostructure of Genesis, and the major themes of the book of Genesis, which should be applied to the wife/sister stories.

---

169. Fleming, "The Divine Council as Type-Scene," 44. Tannehill, *The Narrative Unity of Luke-Acts*, 170.

CHAPTER ONE

The Wife/Sister Stories Within the Context

BEFORE INVESTIGATING EACH WIFE/SISTER story, we need to examine the structure of each story within its own context. Stories A and B belong to the *Toledot* of Terah, while Story C belongs to the *Toledot* of Isaac. In this chapter we will examine the places of the wife/sister stories in their individual contexts, in the Abraham narrative, and in the Jacob narrative.

Narrative Structure of the Toledot of Terah

This section will examine the literary structure of the Abraham narrative. The Abraham narrative is complicated—Jean-Louis Ska argues that, unlike the Jacob and Joseph cycles, it contains no single chain of conflict and resolution. Ska explains:

> La trame du cycle d'Abraham n'est pas unifiée. Au contraire du cycle de Jacob et surtout de l'histoire de Joseph, Gn 12–25 n'est pas centré sur un seul épisode, un conflit et sa résolution, ou un problème et sa solution. Comme l'ont noté plusieurs auteurs, le lien entre les diverses péripéties du cycle d'Abraham est souvent assez lâche et la sequence n'est pas toujours très logique.[1]

It is true to say that the Abraham narrative is complicated, but contrary to Ska's assertion, there is clear evidence to confirm that the Abraham narrative was intentionally composed to be a unified literary work. One of the most important signals for the narrative structure in Genesis is the *Toledot* formula. The Abraham narrative begins in Gen 11:27 with the new *Toledot* formula—"This is the account of Terah"—and ends with Abraham's death and burial story in Gen 25:1–11. We then see a new beginning marked by a new *Toledot* formula—"This is the account of Ishmael"—in Gen 25:12. Scholars have offered many different analyses of the structure of the Abraham narrative. George W. Coats argues that the Abraham narrative

---

1. Ska, "Essai sur la Nature et la Signification," 159.

truly begins at Gen 11:10 and ends with the generation of Ishmael and Isaac in Gen 25:26.² He sees ten steps of genealogy in the Abraham narrative, beginning with the Shem genealogy. David A. Dorsey recognizes the Abraham narrative as beginning with Gen 12:1 and extending to Gen 21:7, and locates its center in the covenant section (17:1–21).³ However, neither Coats nor Dorsey take the *Toledot* formulae seriously in the Book of Genesis. We can also look at the obvious repetitions of double narrative patterns within the same narrative. It is natural to understand the structure of the Abraham narrative according to these patterns, yet neither Coats nor Dorsey connect one story to another corresponding story. For example, while Gen 15 and 17 clearly illustrate stories of covenant, Dorsey attempts to parallel Gen 15 to Gen 18:1–15, where God promises a son to Sarah.⁴ Further, while Dorsey ends the Abraham narrative at the birth of Isaac (21:1–7), Wenham points out that we should not overlook the strong connection between 12:1–3 and 22:1–3.⁵

It is clear that the Abraham narrative contains patterns of repetition and organization that cannot be written off as accidental. Here it is worth considering the work of Gary A. Rendsburg, who assumes that the Abraham narrative contains a series of parallels in corresponding stories, and argues that intended theme-words and catchwords function to connect these units.

Since so much of redactional structuring is tied to theme-words and catchwords, a description of these items is appropriate. They can be of several types. The most obvious cases are those where the same word is used in matching or successive episodes. In other cases we see the use of different words—or, to use more precise grammatical terminology, different inflections—from the same root. Some theme-words and catchwords can be like-sounding words derived from separate roots, and still others may be merely similar in meaning or share a similar connotation. What all of these variations share is their ability, if the writer or compiler has achieved his goal, to connect the different units of the cycle.⁶ Rendsburg, then, suggests the following outline:⁷

2. Coats, *Genesis*, 97–106.
3. Dorsey, *The Literary Structure of the Old Testament*, 56.
4. Ibid.
5. Wenham, *Genesis 1–15*, 263.
6. Rendsburg, *The Redaction of Genesis*, 4–5.
7. Ibid., 27–52. Rendsburg is heavily influenced by Cassuto's ten trial understanding of the Abraham narrative but tries to expand in detail. Cassuto analyzes the Abraham narrative in a chiastic structure (ABCDD'C'B'A'), in which the stories of Ishmael and Isaac (D: Chapters 16–17 and D': 18:1–15) from the center of the narrative. Cassuto

A Genealogy of Terah (11:27–32)

  B Start of Abram's Spiritual Odyssey (12:1–9)

    C Sarai in foreign palace; ordeal ends in peace and success; Abram and Lot part (12:10—13:18)

      D Abram comes to the rescue of Sodom and Lot (14:1–24)

        E Covenant with Abram; Annunciation of Ishmael (15:1—16:16)

        E' Covenant with Abraham; Annunciation of Isaac (17:1—18:15)

      D' Abraham comes to the rescue of Sodom and Lot (18:16—19:38)

    C' Sarah in foreign palace; ordeal ends in peace and success; Abraham and Ishmael part (20:1—21:34)

  B' Climax of Abraham's Spiritual Odyssey (22:1–19)

A' Genealogy of Nahor (22:20–24)

Many scholars agree with Rendsburg's basic analysis, though they suggest some subtle differences.[8] We see here the intended narrative structure, and we can conclude that it is effective because it exhibits an inner unity. For example, Gen 12:1–3 clearly corresponds to Gen 22:1–3, as seen in the passages' grammatical and syntactical correspondences. On the same basis, we can see correspondences between Genesis 15 and 17, Gen 12:10—13:1 and Genesis 20, and the Sodom motifs in Genesis 13–14 and Genesis 18–19.[9]

At the same time, we must remember that the *Toledot* of Terah continues through Gen 25:11. Therefore, scholars who regard Gen 22:20–24 as the end of the Abraham narrative actually ignore the last three chapters

---

also observes the close relationships between Abraham's first trial and the last trial, noting their grammatical and syntactical correspondences. See Cassuto, *A Commentary on the Book of Genesis, Part 2*, 291–300.

8. Yudkowsky, "Chaos or Chiasm?," 109–14; Mathews, *Genesis 11:27—50:26*, 89–91; Walsh, *Style and Structure In Biblical Hebrew Narrative*, 89–92; Radday, "Chiasmus in Hebrew Biblical Narrative," 104–5; Alexander, *Abraham in the Negev*, 102–6. In his 1982 dissertation, Alexander observes the narrative cycle only from 12:10—20:18. He broadened the extent of the Abraham narrative to 25:11 in this book. Alexander, "A Literary Analysis of the Abraham Narrative in Genesis," 26–27; Wenham, *Genesis 1–15*, 263; Sutherland, "The Organization of the Abraham Promise Narratives," 337–43.

9. Yudkowsky, "Chaos or Chiasm?," 110–11; Wheaton, "Focus and Structure in the Abraham Narratives," 152–57; Williamson, *Abraham, Israel and the Nations*, 26–77; Rendsburg, *The Redaction of Genesis*, 27–52.

(Gen 23:1—25:11). In relation to this, Anthony Abela observes that Gen 22:20—25:11 is a well-structured whole.[10]

(a) Gen 22, 20-24		A twelve-name genealogy. Rebekah, Isaac's future wife, is introduced—far away from Canaan
(b) Gen 23		Sarah's death and burial in the "land of Canaan". Abraham, the sojourner, buys the burial ground
(c) Gen 24		Abraham, blessed in everything, procures wife for Isaac. Rebekah, *Yhwh*'s chosen wife for Isaac is introduced into Sarah's tent.
(b') Gen 25, 1–11		Abraham's death and burial in the 'land of Canaan' besides his wife. The 'land of Canaan' cleared of possible contenders with Isaac.
(a') Gen 25, 12–18		A twelve-name genealogy: Ishmael, Abraham's son from Hagar grown to a people: dies away from Canaan?

According to Abela, the end of the Abraham narrative is not Gen 22:20-24 but Gen 25:11. Based on this understanding, Abela observes that Gen 22:20—25:11 is closely connected to Gen 11:27—12:9. In both passages, each unit contains the genealogies of Terah (11:27–32) and Nahor (22:20–24). Nahum Sarna further points out that Gen 22:20-24 assumes the previous passage. For example, Gen 22:20 mentions Milcah's bearing children to Nahor (Gen 11:29). This is also a reason why Gen 11:29 does not mention Milcah's children, although it acknowledges Sarah's barrenness.[11]

Sarna makes the important observation that the genealogies in Genesis serve "anticipatory and integral" functions in the unfolding narratives. Three wives are mentioned in Gen 11:27–32, and it is necessary to note how the descriptions of this genealogy work together in the subsequent Abraham narrative. First, Sarah is apparently more important than others, but the text does not provide Sarah's parentage, while it does give that of the

---

10. Abela, *The Themes of the Abraham Narrative*, 1–9; For his conclusion and complete diagram, see Abela, "The Redactional Structuring within the Abraham Narrative," 80–82; Also see, Rosenberg, *King and Kin*, 81. Rosenberg avers, "The latter complex of narrative and genealogy (22:20—25:18) is a self-contained composition in its own right, and dependent for its meaning on narrative information established throughout the cycle."

11. Sarna, "The Anticipatory Use of Information," 80.

others. Second, though both Sarah and Milcah lack children, only Sarah is described as barren (Gen 11:30). Third, Haran's wife is of no concern, even though she is the only woman who bore a son. As a substitute, her son Lot is described in the genealogy.[12] These observations on genealogy are crucial to an understanding of the Abraham story and following narratives. Therefore, as we consider Sarna's observations, we can conclude that the genealogy anticipates the subsequent narratives.

Regarding this observation, we may expand Sarna's argument to Gen 22:20–24 in order to determine the narrative structure of the Abraham story. As Sarna points out, the genealogy in Gen 22:20–24 provides important information regarding the subsequent narratives. By referring to Milcah and her bearing of children, we are reminded of the previous genealogy in Gen 11:27–32. In addition, the introduction of Rebekah in verse 23 performs a significant function in setting up subsequent narratives since Rebekah will be the wife of Isaac, who has already been introduced as Abraham's heir.[13] It is therefore plausible to consider chapters 23 to 25 within the structure of the Abraham narrative.

If we accept Abela and Sarna's observations, the Abraham narrative begins with Terah's genealogy (Gen 11:27–32) and ends with Nahor's genealogy (Gen 22:20–24), and the two genealogies have unmissable connections.[14] However, I am not convinced by Abela's argument regarding the introduction (Gen 11:27—12:9). Since there are strong connections between 12:1–9 and 22:1–19, Abela's outline should be modified to identify the introduction of the Abraham narrative at 11:27–32. We can thus summarize the structure of the *Toledot* of Terah as follows:[15]

A			11:27–32	Abram and his family
	B		12:1–9	God's calling to Abram
		C	12:10–20	Wife/Sister story
			D	13:1—14:24	Abram and Lot

12. Ibid., 79.

13. Ibid., 80. "The previous pericope closed with divine blessings and for these to be fulfilled Isaac must marry and found a family. The list therefore mentions Rebekah, Bethuel, Milcah, Nahor, and Aram as an intimation of Isaac's forthcoming marriage to Rebekah daughter of Bethuel son of Milcah of the city of Nahor in Aramnaharaim. In this way, its presence after the Akedah is purposeful, anticipating the events of ch. 24."

14. Rendsburg, *The Redaction of Genesis*, 29–30. Observing various connections between these two genealogies, Rendsburg concludes that these two genealogies function as "bookend" in the Abraham narrative.

15. For the further study, see Patterson, "The Righteousness and Survival of the Seed," 229–36.

			E	15:1–21	Covenant
				F 16:1–16	The birth of Ishmael
			E'	17:1–27	Covenant
		D'		18:1—19:38	Abraham and Lot
	C'			20:1—21:34	Wife/Sister story
B'				22:1–19	God's test to Abraham
A'				22:20—25:11	Abraham's family

Narrative Structure of the Toledot of Isaac

Unlike the two wife/sister stories in the Abraham narrative, the third wife/sister story appears in the *Toledot* of Isaac. Generally speaking, scholarly discussions on the extent of the *Toledot* of Isaac have led to more agreement concerning its beginning than its end. Most scholars agree that the *Toledot* begins with Gen 25:19, but there are multiple positions on the endpoint of the narrative. Fokkelman identifies 35:29 as the end of the Isaac *Toledot*, while Michael A. Fishbane points to 35:22 and Coats to 36:8.[16] In terms of overall structure, it is constructive to refer to Fishbane's remarkable observation, followed by Rendsburg and many others.[17]

A Oracle sought, struggle in childbirth, Jacob born (25:19–34)

B Interlude: Rebekah in foreign palace, pact with foreigners (26:1–34)

C Jacob fears Esau and flees (27:1—28:9)

D Messengers (28:10–22)

E Arrival at Haran (29:1–30)

F Jacob's wives are fertile (29:31—30:24)

F' Jacob's flocks are fertile (30:25–43)

E' Flight from Haran (31:1–54)

---

16. Fokkelman, *Narrative Art in Genesis*, 236; Fishbane, *Text and Texture*, 40–62; Coats, *Genesis*, 228.

17. Fishbane, *Text and Texture*, 40–62. His work was originally published in Fishbane, "Composition and Structure in the Jacob Cycle," 15–38; Rendsburg, *The Redaction of Genesis*, 53–54. In this work, the structure has been taken from Rendsburg. Mathews, *Genesis 11:27—50:26*, 377; Wenham, *Genesis 16–50*, 169–70.

D' Messengers (32:1–32)

C' Jacob returns and fears Esau (33:1–20)

B' Interlude: Dinah in foreign palace, pact with foreigners (34:1–31)

A' Oracle fulfilled, struggle in childbirth, Jacob becomes Israel (35:1–22)

One problem here is that Fishbane does not take the *Toledot* formula in 36:1 seriously and thus views 35:22 as the end of the narrative. We should also take note of John G. Gammie's observations. Focusing on the strife motif, Gammie analyzes the Isaac *Toledot* in terms of a concentric arrangement, starting with the genealogy of Abraham-Kedurah (25:1–11) and ending with the genealogy of Esau (36:6–9). Gammie, too, ignores the *Toledot* formulae in Genesis with no proper explanation. Along the same lines, he continually breaks up texts only to put them back together according to a structure he wants to present. For example, he places Gen 35:6–7 and 9–15 in C', but 35:8 and 16–29 in B'.[18] Referring to the basic structure of Genesis, it is natural to conclude the end of the Isaac *Toledot* comes at 35:29, because the next *Toledot* formula occurs again in 36:1.

The third wife/sister story corresponds to Gen 34, in which Jacob and his sons encounter foreigners, just like Isaac did in Gen 26. For Fishbane, these two chapters function as interludes. He suggests that "Genesis 26 serves as an interlude between the opening oracle of strife and tension and its fulfillment. And Genesis 34 serves as an interlude bridging Jacob's reconciliation with Esau and the denouement at Beth-el."[19] In some ways, Wenham attempts to modify Fishbane's analysis. First, he includes 26:34–35 not with chapter 26 but with 27:1—28:9. Second, he identifies 29:31—30:24 as the central scene, while Rendsburg and Fishbane locate two central scenes, F and F'. Finally, he distinguishes between 32:1–2 and 32:3–32, which Fishbane regards as a unit.[20]

From my perspective, the repeated expression "וְאֵלֶּה תּוֹלְדֹת" in Gen 25:19 and 36:1 make it clear that the Isaac *Toledot* extends from Gen 25:19 to 35:29. It is also clear that the Isaac *Toledot* has a concentric structure in

---

18. For details, Gammie, "Theological Interpretation by Way of Literary and Tradition Analysis," 118–24.

19. Fishbane, *Text and Texture*, 47. Following Fishbane, Rendsburg notes further similarities between Gen 26 and 34 with respect to theme-words. He also concludes, "they function in the same way within the Cycle, as important interludes craftly placed by our master compiler." Rendsburg, *The Redaction of Genesis*, 58–59.

20. Wenham, *Genesis 16–50*, 168–70; Rendsburg, *The Redaction of Genesis*, 53–69; Fishbane, *Text and Texture*, 40–62; Mathews, *Genesis 11:27—50:26*, 376–79.

which the two F and F' units are placed in the center. Most importantly, the third wife/sister story corresponds to Genesis 34 in terms of the encounter with foreigners. All in all, I agree with Rendsburg's analysis with the exception of his definition of A', which should be expanded to 35:29 based on the overall *Toledot* structure in Genesis.

Macrostructure of Genesis

At this point, it is necessary to examine the overall structure of the Book of Genesis. Given the fact that the wife/sister stories are not limited to Terah's *Toledot*, but also appear in Isaac's *Toledot*, we must now question why these stories are placed in different *Toledots* and what the stories' functions are.

Toledot

The apparent structure of the Book of Genesis is expressed by the phrase, "וְאֵלֶּה תּוֹלְדֹת," which generally means "and these are the generations of . . ." The *Toledot* formula appears ten times and functions to mark the book's main divisions (Gen 2:4a; 5:1; 6:9; 10:1; 11:10; 11:27; 25:12; 25:19; 36:1, (9); and 37:2). The term *Toledot*, which is derived from ילד (to bear, beget, or give birth), can be translated "generation, offspring, or descendant." We will now examine the basic features of the term *Toledot*.

The First Toledot

The *Toledot* formula is usually associated with the descendants of an individual identified by a proper name. In Gen 2:4a, however, this term comes not with the proper name, but with the heaven and the earth. Here it carries no biological meaning, but consider what follows: humanity as an offspring of the heaven and the earth.[21] Why, then, does this *Toledot* formula appear in Gen 2:4a rather than Gen 1:1? At this point, we need to note that the word *Toledot* usually indicates the presence of a main character in the subsequent narratives. The *Toledot* does not start with the birth of the main character, however; rather the main character will have already been introduced in the previous narratives. In this regard, the *Toledot* formula by nature presupposes the stories that precede it. Given the lack of a preceding narrative and the introduction of Adam and Eve as the first human beings, there is no need to use the formula at the very beginning of Genesis.

21. Thomas, *These Are the Generations*, 23–24.

THE WIFE/SISTER STORIES WITHIN THE CONTEXT

Toledot as Superscription

There have been many discussions of whether the *Toledot* formula is a superscription or subscription. Many scholars insist that the formula concludes the previous story. For example, Roland K. Harrison, who also argues that there are eleven tablets of *Toledot* in Genesis, believes that the formula functions as a colophon pointing back to the previous narratives.[22] If, however, we place the formula at the end of a narrative or genealogy, problems inevitably arise. Harrison divides Genesis into eleven units, placing each *Toledot* formula at the end of a unit. Through this process, he determines that the Joseph narrative cannot be placed in the original tablets of Genesis, so he simply puts it in a different category from the eleven tablets. As a result, there is no place for the Joseph story in his understanding of Genesis, and he deduces that the Joseph story is a supplement.[23] Furthermore, as Duane A. Garrett points out, the subscription theory cannot stand with the *Toledot* of Ishmael or that of Esau, as Gen 25:12 and 36:1 are not related to the Abraham and Isaac narratives that precede them.[24]

Other scholars think of the *Toledot* formula as a superscription, arguing that the *Toledot* formula relates to the sections that follow it, which continue the story from preceding sections.[25] Francis I. Anderson argues that when a sentence contains, זֶה, זֹאת, or אֵלֶּה, the verbless clauses—in which both subject and predicate are definite—function as a title.[26] In his book *These Are the Generations*, Matthew A. Thomas applies textlinguistic approaches (syntactic, semantic, and pragmatic) to the *Toledot* formulae. Syntactically, he identifies the *Toledot* formula in terms of verbless clauses that introduce the main character of the following narratives.[27] Most

---

22. Harrison, *Introduction to the Old Testament*, 547–53; on the formula as colophon, see von Rad, *Genesis*; Brueggemann, *Genesis*; Coats, *Genesis*; Sailhamer, "Genesis 1:1–2:4a," 73–82; Fokkelman, "Genesis," 41; Cotterell and Turner, *Linguistics & Biblical Interpretation*, 242; Westermann, *Genesis 1–11*.

23. Harrison, *Introduction to the Old Testament*, 548, 551–53; Garrett, *Rethinking Genesis*, 94–95.

24. Garrett, *Rethinking Genesis*, 95–96.

25. Thomas, *These Are the Generations*, 37–41. Also see Cassuto, *A Commentary on the Book of Genesis: From Adam to Noah*; Woudstra, "The Toledot of the Book of Genesis," 184–89; Cross, *Canaanite Myth and Hebrew Epic*, 301–5; Wenham, *Genesis 1–15*; Hamilton, *The Book of Genesis 1–17*; Garrett, *Rethinking Genesis*; Mathews, *Genesis 1—11:26*; Waltke, *Genesis*; Cotter, *Genesis*; McKeown, *Genesis*; Arnold, *Genesis*; Boda, *A Severe Mercy*, 16–18.

26. Andersen, *The Hebrew Verbless Clause*, 40. For details on the usage of independent declarative verbless clauses, see 59. Thomas, *These Are the Generations*, 37–38.

27. Thomas, *These Are the Generations*, 21–24, 123–25; Andersen, *The Hebrew Verbless Clause*, 52–99.

importantly, the *Toledot* formula, understood as a superscription, functions as a link to previous and subsequent generations. Textlinguistically speaking, the *Toledot* formula manifests continuity and discontinuity through all levels of Genesis. As Thomas rightly avers,

> The formula provides background information about the subject matter that is coming and reintroduces the progenitor whose offspring the narrative is about to turn to. In this way, the formula bridges the gap between the known progenitor (cohesion and continuity) and the unknown offspring (rheme, assertion, change of topic).[28]

If this is correct, the *Toledot* formula works well from the perspective of theme-rheme and type-scene approaches as well. The formula not only contains a given meaning, referring to a proper name that has already been introduced in the previous narratives (continuity), but also provides new information about the main character's offspring (discontinuity).[29]

Independent/Coordinate Toledot

It is important to note that two different syntactic formulae are present in the *Toledot* of Genesis. The two different clause forms observed in the *Toledot* are the independent and coordinate. These clauses can be identified by the absence or presence of the conjunction *waw*. Among the *Toledot* formulae, *waw* is absent in five independent headings (Gen 2:4; 5:1; 6:9; 11:10; and 37:2) and present in five coordinate headings (Gen 10:1; 11:27; 25:12; 25:19; 36:1). Syntactically, the independent clause indicates that there will be an addition of new information in subsequent narratives, while the coordinate clause shows that there will be a continuation of previously established information in subsequent narratives.[30] According to Thomas, the five independent clauses provide important signs for rebuilding the macrostructure of the Book of Genesis, as well as that of the Pentateuch. In his view, the five independent *Toledot*s form major headings, while the others function as "subheadings."[31] He thus divides Genesis into five major divisions with no *waw* (*Toledot* of the heavens and earth, Book of the *Toledot* of Adam, *Toledot*

---

28. Thomas, *These Are the Generations*, 31.

29. Ibid., 32–34.

30. Basically Thomas is heavily dependent Andersen's and Peter Weimar's analysis of the structure of Genesis. See Andersen, *The Hebrew Verbless Clause*; Weimar, "Die Toledot-Formel," 65–93.

31. Thomas, *These Are the Generations*, 124.

THE WIFE/SISTER STORIES WITHIN THE CONTEXT   49

of Noah, of Shem, and of Jacob) and five subsequent divisions with *waw* (*Toledot* of Shem, Ham, and Japhet, *Toledot* of Terah, *Toledot* of Ishmael, *Toledot* of Isaac, and *Toledot* of Esau).[32] This approach takes Thomas far away from the traditional understanding of the structure of Genesis as defined by ten *Toledot* formulae. His textlinguistic approach is insightful, but these different divisions should be considered with caution.[33] If Thomas's view is correct, we should first reconsider the beginning of the Patriarchal narratives in Genesis in relation to the *Toledot* of Shem.

Most scholars agree that the *Toledot* of Terah (Gen 11:27) marks the beginning of the Patriarchal narratives. For this reason, scholars have not given sufficient attention to the function of the *Toledot* of Shem.[34] As we have noted, however, the *Toledot* formula introducing Terah's genealogy—considered the beginning of the Patriarchal narratives—is, syntactically speaking, coordinated. This indicates that Terah's genealogy is not the main starting point of the subsequent narratives. Instead, the *Toledot* of Shem is primary. We should also note that it is a linear genealogy. It is clear, then, that Shem's genealogy should be regarded as the beginning of the Patriarchal narratives.

As Todd Patterson observes, the most basic pattern in the structure of the *Toledot* formulae is "[the] linear genealogy strand followed by narrative strand followed by segmented genealogy strand."[35] Wenham observes that these genealogies follow an alternating pattern of extended narratives for the mainline characters and short genealogies for characters not included in the mainline.[36] The alternating sequence is as follows:[37]

32. Ibid., 71–73.

33. To me, Thomas's chiastic structure to Genesis is not convincing. He places the *Toledot* of Noah as the center of Genesis, so that the central theme of Genesis is Noah's covenant. See ibid., 106–11.

34. Steinberg, "The Genealogical Framework," 42. Steinberg mentions that "neither scholar provides a convincing argument for the integrity of the priestly redactional technique which incorporates Gen 11:10–16 into the structural design of the book of Genesis."

35. Patterson, "The Righteousness and Survival of the Seed," 107–8. Patterson also distinguishes "Isaac Plexus" from "Terah Plexus" because he did not observe main and coordinate structure of *Toledot*. So I agree with his paradigm, except for his dissertation of the Isaac Plexus. I also prefer the term "Shem" to "Terah" following the biblical text (Gen 11:10).

36. Wenham, *Genesis 1–15*, 248.

37. This pattern is also observed in Gen 1–11.

1:1—2:3	The Creation of the Heaven and the Earth	Introduction
2:4—4:26	*Toledot* of the Heaven and the Earth	Narrative
5:1—6:8	*Toledot* of Adam	Genealogy

11:10–26	*Toledot* of Shem	Genealogy
11:27—25:11	*Toledot* of Terah	Narrative
25:12–18	*Toledot* of Ishmael	Genealogy
25:19—35:29	*Toledot* of Isaac	Narrative
36:1–37:1	*Toledot* of Esau	Genealogy
36:2—50:26	*Toledot* of Jacob	Narrative

As a linear genealogy, the *Toledot* of Shem is closely connected to the *Toledot* of Adam in Gen 5 in various ways.[38] Just as the *Toledot* of Adam links Noah to Adam, the *Toledot* of Shem links Noah to Abraham. As we assume, the coordinate genealogy is connected to the previous independent genealogy. For example, the *Toledot* of Noah's sons, which is a short genealogy, follows the *Toledot* of Noah, which contains extended narratives. Although the *Toledot* of Noah's sons contains the genealogy that is not included in the mainline, it is also a result of the previous narrative. That is, the *Toledot* of Noah's sons is the result of the Noahic covenant. Therefore, although these are different *Toledots*, it is clear that they should be understood as a sequence in the macrostructure of Genesis. On the same basis, the *Toledot* of Shem, which is a linear and independent genealogy, is followed by the series of coordinate genealogies of Terah, Ishmael, Isaac, and Esau. The *Toledot* of Shem connects Abraham to Noah, the new humanity after the flood. The coordinate genealogy series then clarifies who is and is not included in the mainline of the promise. In terms of theme, the *Toledot* of Shem and the following coordinate genealogies highlight God's promise to the patriarchs who encounter YHWH directly. This is clearly distinct from the *Toledot* of Jacob, which stresses the partial fulfillment of the promise.

While Naomi Steinberg's emphasis on the significance of the genealogy of Shem is insightful, the fact that the three genealogical superscriptions include the *Toledots* of Shem, Ishmael, and Esau is quite problematic.[39] Of course, these three are followed by important narrative genealogy, but it is necessary to note that the *Toledot* of Shem is quite different from the others. The *Toledot* of Shem is not only linear but also an independent genealogy, so it can function as a superscription. The genealogies of Ishmael and Esau,

6:9—9:29	*Toledot* of Noah	Narrative + Short Narrative
10:1—11:9	*Toledot* of Noah's Sons	Genealogy + Short Narrative

38. Mathews, *Genesis 1—11:26*, 487–91.
39. Steinberg, "The Genealogical Framework," 43–44.

on the other hand, are segmented and coordinated. In Genesis, linear genealogy is presented as a narrowing of genealogy from father to son, while segmented genealogy usually disregards lines that are not included in the mainline of promise.[40] It seems to me that Steinberg fails to properly distinguish between these two vastly different types of genealogy.

I contend that the Patriarchal narratives should be viewed as beginning with Shem's genealogy (11:10) and containing the narrative genealogies of Terah and Isaac and the segmented genealogies of Ishmael and Esau. This means that I disagree with scholars who argue that the second main part of the Book of Genesis begins with the Terah's *Toledot* (11:27).[41] Instead, we should consider Shem's *Toledot* as the beginning in the story of the patriarchs (11:10). It is worth examining Thomas's structure of Genesis here.[42]

0	Prologue		Gen 1:1
1	*toledot* of the heavens and earth	אלה תולדות . . .	2:4
2	Book of the *toledot* of Adam	זה ספר תולדות . . .	5:1
3	*toledot* of Noah	אלה תולדות . . .	6:9
	a *toledot* of Shem, Ham, and Japheth . . .	ואלה תולדות . . .	10:1
4	*toledot* of Shem	אלה תולדות . . .	11:10
	a *toledot* of Terah	ואלה תולדות . . .	11:27
	b *toledot* of Ishmael	ואלה תולדות . . .	25:12
	c *toledot* of Isaac	ואלה תולדות . . .	25:19
	d *toledot* of Esau	ואלה תולדות . . .	36:1
	e *toledot* of Esau (#2)	ואלה תולדות . . .	36:9
5	*toledot* of Jacob	אלה תולדות . . .	37:2

This observation gives us another way to answer the question I have raised. As we have seen, the wife/sister stories appear in two different *Toledots*. Based on the macrostructure of Genesis, however, we can conclude

---

40. Thomas, *These Are the Generations*, 79–82; Averbeck, "Factors in Reading the Patriarchal Narratives," 117–20; Koch, "Die Toledot-Formeln," 190–91; Scharbert, "Der Sinn der Toledot-Formel in der Priesterschrift," 45.

41. Turner, "Genesis, Book of," 350. Turner identifies the Shem's *Toledot* as concluding the first part of Genesis and Terah's as introducing the second part. To the best of my knowledge, most important commentaries agree with Turner's thought.

42. Steinberg, "The Genealogical Framework," 43, 47; Thomas, *These Are the Generations*, 72–73.

that each functions perfectly within its own *Toledot* structure. At the same time, we can observe that all three wife/sister stories belong to the same main genealogy—that of Shem—because the *Toledots* of Terah and Isaac both appear in the coordinate structure following the independent *Toledot* of Shem.

It is important to read each *Toledot* in relation to others because, as mentioned above, the *Toledot* formula requires us to regard the narratives in Genesis as connected to other *Toledot* sections. We can therefore assume that the first and second wife/sister stories in the Abraham narrative and the third in the Isaac narrative are connected and work together in both the *Toledot* of Shem and the Book of Genesis, because all three stories are located in the *Toledot* of Shem. Genesis 12–36 highlights YHWH's gifts to the patriarchs: His promises of the seed, land, and blessings to the nations. From this perspective, the three wife/sister stories work together to provide strong connections between the patriarchs and highlight the theme that YHWH keeps His promises in spite of the weakness of the patriarchs. In the following chapters, we will consider in detail how these stories are related, how they function within the Book of Genesis, and what the individual wife/sister stories highlight.

Linear/Segmented Toledot

As stated, the two types of *Toledot* in Genesis are linear and segmented (see Figure 1). The two types of genealogies can be illustrated as follows:[43]

---

43. Alternative terminologies may apply to this section. Kaminski adopts "main line" and "secondary line." Similary Malamat uses "horizontal" and "vertical" or "primary" and "secondary." See, Thomas, *These Are the Generations*, 55–58, 83–84; Kaminski, *From Noah to Israel*, 62; Malamat, "King Lists of the Old Babylonian Period," 183–86.

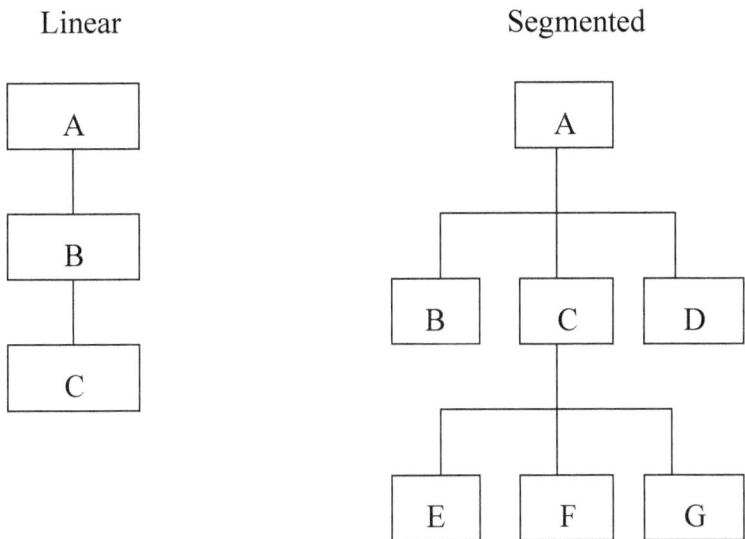

Figure 1: Types of Generation.

Robert R. Wilson has defined segmented and linear genealogies as follows.

> When a genealogy expresses more than one line of descent from a given ancestor, then it will exhibit segmentation or branching. We will refer to this type of genealogy as a *segmented genealogy*, and each of its component lines or branches will be called a segment. If the genealogy expresses only one line of descent from a given ancestor, then it will exhibit no segmentation, and we will refer to it as a *linear genealogy*.[44]

According to this definition, we can divide the *Toledot* formulae of Genesis into two types. Linear genealogy appears in Gen 5:1–32; 11:10–26; and 36:31–39. Segmented genealogy occurs in Gen 10:1–32; 11:27–30; 22:20–24; 25:12–18; 36:1–30; and 41–43.[45] In Genesis, segmented genealogies are mainly concerned with persons who are not main characters, such as Ishmael and Esau. Elimination is at the core of segmented genealogy.[46] Linear

---

44. Wilson, *Genealogy and History*, 8–10.
45. Averbeck, "Factors in Reading the Patriarchal Narratives," 117–20
46. It may at first appear that elimination does not play a role in the genealogy of the nation in Genesis 10. Of course, the basic purpose of this genealogy is to provide a full list of Noah's offspring. It is notable, however, that while the author normally lists Noah's sons as Shem, Ham, and Japhet (Gen 6:10; 9:18), in this genealogy the order is Japhet, Ham, and Shem. This is likely done to connect to the *Toledot* of Shem in Gen

genealogy, on the other hand, shows movement from creation to Adam, Adam to Noah, Noah to Abraham, and Abraham to the Israelites. It thus clearly emphasizes the mainline of promise.

The Function of Toledot

The function of the *Toledot*, both essential and foundational, is to emphasize the continuity of the narratives. The *Toledot* formulae connect all the narratives in Genesis, from creation to humanity, and from humanity to the Israelites. In this regard, the narratives in Genesis should be read as a whole. It is therefore necessary for us to read the Book of Genesis as a narrative plot developed intentionally by the author. Further, all of the named characters and nations we encounter in the narratives are interrelated through the *Toledot* formula. The use of *Toledot* thus highlights how all of humanity is made up of "the members of one extended family."[47]

The *Toledot* formula not only illustrates the continuity of the narratives but also defines the legitimacy of the descendants. That is to say, the *Toledot* significantly narrows down the line of seed. As our reading of Genesis progresses, the picture narrows from all of creation to the Israelites, and from the whole earth to Canaan and Egypt.

In summary, in linear genealogy the narrative focuses on the narrowing of the line of seed. In segment genealogy, the author simply ignores candidates who are not in the mainline of seed.

Thematic Approach

So far we have discussed the *Toledot* formula in terms of its roles within the general structure of Genesis and its thematic continuity and discontinuity. We will now examine in greater detail how this formula works with the themes present in Genesis. The themes of the Book of Genesis, and even the Pentateuch, have received ample attention, so in this work, we will focus only on the major themes of the Patriarchal narratives in Genesis.

11:10. After the table of the nations, Japhet and Ham disappear and the subsequent narratives only focus on Shem's offspring. To highlight this connection, Shem appears in the last part of the genealogy of the nation (Gen 10: 21–31). It is likely, therefore, that the *Toledot* of the nation (Genesis 10) serves to remove Japhet and Ham from our concern and focus our attention on the mainline of the seed. It is also worth noting that this generation is out of order with Gen 11:1–9. The order is reversed for the purpose of enhancing the connection to the subsequent stories.

47. Robinson, "Literary Functions of the Genealogies of Genesis," 601.

Seed

David J. A. Clines claims that it is hard to find a substantial plot line in Genesis, stating that "this book as a whole is no plotted story, but merely a chronicle or merely some incoherent collection of episodes."[48] Nevertheless, he sees that the Pentateuch as a whole has thematic coherence.

> The Theme of the Pentateuch is the partial fulfillment—which implies also the partial non-fulfillment—of the promise to or blessing of the patriarchs. The promise or blessing is both the divine initiative in a world where human initiatives always lead to disaster, and a re-affirmation of the primal divine intentions for man. The posterity-element of the promise is dominant in Genesis 12–50, the relationship-element in Exodus and Leviticus, and the land-element in Numbers and Deuteronomy.[49]

For Clines, a single theme—promise—becomes evident when the Pentateuch is read as a whole, with attention to the partial fulfillment of three major elements that can be found in every major narrative in Genesis: descendants, land, and relationship with God. These elements are ubiquitous throughout the whole narrative, and particularly influential in the plot and storyline of Genesis.[50]

According to Clines, the theme of posterity is found primarily in Genesis. Furthermore, James McKeown argues that the theme of descendants is the key theme and that the others, blessing and land, exist in relationship to it.[51] In fact, the word זֶרַע occurs 59 times in Genesis out of 229 total occurrences in the Old Testament, indicating that it is used comparatively frequently in Genesis. It is also noteworthy that the *Toledot* structure—one of the most obvious features of Genesis—and the presence of genealogies are closely linked to the concept of "seed." As mentioned, the word *Toledot* originates from the verb ילד, which means "to bear children." The use of the terms *Toledot* and "seed" effectively remind the readers about the main theme of Genesis. From this perspective, the whole narrative of Genesis consists of lineage, running from Adam to Joseph and

---

48. Clines, *What Does Eve Do to Help?*, 49. Clines argues that it should be the task of readers to make meaning, sense, and coherence of the Book of Genesis should be the task of the readers.

49. Clines, *The Theme of the Pentateuch*, 29.

50. McKeown, *Genesis*, 196.

51. Ibid., 197. Although Clines identifies the three themes as land, a relationship with God, and descendants, MeKeown replaces relationship with God with blessing, which is more related to Genesis itself. See Clines, *The Theme of the Pentateuch*, 34–35.

his brothers.[52] The concept of seed thus allows us to understand the Book of Genesis as a literary unity.

It is particularly clear that the theme of seed is crucial in the Abraham narrative. The main concerns in the Abraham narrative revolve around two questions: (1) "Can Abraham have a son, even though Sarah is barren?" and (2) "Who is the legitimate son of Abraham?" We are informed at the outset of the narrative that Sarah is barren, but this statement is immediately followed by God's promise of countless descendants to Abraham. If Sarah is barren, how will God's promise be fulfilled? This tension, the result of God's promise and Sarah's barrenness, gives way to the development of the following narratives, in which Abraham regards Lot, Eliezer, and Ishmael as his heirs. Finally, however, God gives Abraham a legitimate son, Isaac, through the womb of Sarah. In terms of structure, the whole Abraham narrative forms a chiasm with Gen 16 at its center. Consequently, we cannot miss the importance of seed while reading the Abraham narratives.

Land

The theme of seed is inseparable from the theme of land. God promises the land to Abraham's descendants (Gen 12:7–8), so the tension between the promise and reality continues: if Abraham does not have a son, then the promise of the land will also be lost. The calling and the blessing of Abraham (Gen 12:1–3) are presented as a turning point that orients the entire world toward the promise, and world history to Patriarchal history.

From the point of view of the land theme, the primeval history in Gen 1–11 develops important aspects of the land. First, there is a clear connection in the terminology of Adam (אָדָם) and land (אֲדָמָה); we are also told that human beings will revert back to dust after death (Gen 2:7; 3:19). Human beings have been disobedient to God, and as a result world history from Adam to Noah is the history of the loss of land. Adam is expelled from the Garden of Eden where he lived with the LORD, and becomes a tiller of the land; Cain kills his brother and has to wander the land with no rest. The land gradually becomes worse for human beings producing thorns and thistles for Adam after the Fall, and then failing to yield crops for Cain. When the violence of human beings is full in the land, God sends the flood and destroys everything on the land—the sins of human beings affect the condition of the land and eventually result in its loss. McKeown summarizes

---

52. For a general study on the seed in Genesis, see Alexander, "From Adam to Judah," 5–19; Alexander, "Genealogies, Seed and the Compositional Unity of Genesis," 255–70; Alexander, "Further Observations on the Term 'Seed' in Genesis," 363–67.

these features in primeval history: loss of fertility of land, expulsion from land, destruction of land, and dispersion away from the land.[53]

We see a radical change in Gen 12:1–3, when God calls Abraham to leave his homeland and move to a new land. This is striking, because up to this point the history of Genesis has been a history of expulsion. In contrast, in Gen 12:1 God first commands Abraham to leave his land but then shows him a new land and finally gives him the promises of seed, land, and blessings. Here it is probable that land is not used as a device for punishment but rather a symbol for covenantal blessing.[54] As Walter Brueggemann rightly points out, Abraham and his family can leave the history of dispersion and begin to live in the expectation of having the Promised Land.[55]

God does not give the promise of land in Gen 12:1–3, when Abraham builds up an altar and calls His name. His proclamation that this land will be given to Abraham's descendants comes instead in verse 7. He then confirms the promise of land to Abraham after Lot separates from Abraham (Gen 13:15–17). It is worth taking note of the developments between Gen 12:7 and Gen 13:15–17. In 12:7, God simply promises "this land" to Abraham's descendants, but in chapter 13 God reaffirms the promise with additional details, including the definition of the land and the fact that it will be given to Abraham and his descendants forever.[56] As the Abraham narrative progresses, the promise of land becomes increasingly explicit. At first, God's command is quite implicit, as seen in Gen 12:1. As the narrative continues, however, God includes Abraham's descendants in the promise of land (Gen 12:7) and explicitly adds Abraham to the narrative (Gen 13:15–17). In Gen 15:12–21 God reaffirms the promise of land with an oath and specifically includes His future plan and the boundary of the land. After passing the test of willingness to sacrifice Isaac, Abraham finally possesses a piece of land, which becomes the burial site for his wife. The theme of land continues in the subsequent narratives of Isaac (Gen 26:2–3) and Jacob (28:13–15; 46:1–4). Finally, the end of Genesis is filled with the expectation of the restoration of the Promised Land.

53. McKeown, *Genesis*, 242–47. McKeown's use of terms is thematic; to gain a better understanding, we need to define "the land." McKeown's phrase "explusion from land" normally refers to the place Adam and his descendants lost because of their sins.

54. McKeown, "The Theme of Land in Genesis 1–11, Part 1," 51–64; James McKeown, "The Theme of Land in Genesis 1–11, Part 2," 133–44.

55. Brueggemann, *The Land*, 16–18; McKeown, *Genesis*, 251–52. So, McKeown concludes, "[T]he call of Abraham represents a turning point. Beginning with the Abraham narratives the movement is towards a harmonious relationship with God in the promised land."

56. Rickett, "Rethinking the Place and Purpose of Genesis 13," 36–37; Wenham, *Genesis 1–15*, 298. I will deal with this issue in the following chapter.

Genesis describes the death and burial of Jacob and Joseph in extraordinarily detail, highlighting its theme by first describing Jacob and Joseph's last days and then emphasizing their burials with their forefathers in Canaan. In reality, it is very special to see that the author uses the last three chapters of Genesis to describe the last days of Jacob and Joseph as the conclusion of the patriarchs' story. For the author, however, the long procession of Jacob's burial and the strong expectation of Israel's future departure out of Egypt are the real climax of Genesis. Even though the theme of land is not the primary theme in Genesis, it can be considered as at least a secondary theme supporting the theme of seed. As Wenham summarizes, "through Jacob's dying words, the author of Genesis is able to sum up the theme of Genesis, to point to the fulfillment of the promises made to Abraham and Isaac about descendants and protection, and to reiterate the hope that one day Canaan will be theirs too, as the LORD had promised."[57]

Blessing

The term blessing (ברך) occurs more frequently in the Pentateuch than anywhere else in the Old Testament (Of 418 occurrences in the Old Testament, 161 appear in the Pentateuch—approximately 39 percent). It occurs 87 times in Genesis alone, representing approximately 55 percent of its occurrences in the Pentateuch. We can thus easily recognize that blessing is another important theme in Genesis and the Pentateuch as a whole.

Although the theme of blessing is clearly important in Gen 12:1–3, it appears even in the very first chapters of Genesis. Blessing in Genesis is very closely related to God's favor, so it is based primarily on the harmonious relationship between God and human beings.[58]

In the primeval narratives, humans enjoyed the blessings of God when they obeyed Him but were cursed and expelled from the land when they broke this relationship. God's original purpose was to bless the world, including human beings and all of creation. God created and blessed the world and at the climax of this creation, He created Adam and Eve in His image and commanded them to represent God Himself by ruling over the world, multiplying numerically, and filling the world with offspring. However, their failure brought sin into the world, and sin resulted in God's curse.

Clearly, the call of Abraham is the most important moment in Genesis. This is true in terms of blessing as well. The term ברך occurs five times in

---

57. Wenham, *Genesis 16–50*, 459.

58. Alexander, *From Paradise to the Promised Land*, 114–15; McKeown, "Blessings and Curses," 84–85.

Gen 12:1–3, and wordplay between this word and Abraham's name enhances the theme of blessing. McKeown states, "Since this is the first divine speech in the Abraham story, this pronouncement of blessing is extremely important. It gives the passage special significance, underscoring the importance of blessing since it is reiterated and emphasized by God himself."[59]

In terms of grammar, there are two commands in Gen 12:1–3. First, Abraham is commended to leave the land he had lived in for the land God will show him. Second, he is commanded to be a blessing. Abraham will be a blessing and as a result all the nations will find blessing through him. Abraham will first be a great nation, and then the destiny of all the nations will be decided in relation to how they react to Abraham.

The theme of blessing is also dominant in the patriarchal narrative. The wife/sister stories show us that foreigners can be either blessed or cursed according to their treatment of Abraham. In Gen 20:17, Abraham is considered a prophet, so when he prayers for Abimelech's household, God answers his prayer. God makes Abraham very rich (12:16; 13:5; 14:21–23), and makes Isaac greatly wealthy as well (26:12–13). Even though Jacob runs away from his brother with nothing, God even makes him very rich by the time he returns from Paddan Aram (32:3–21).

More importantly, the theme of God's blessing comes to a climax in the Joseph narrative, which shows how the descendants of Abraham, who bear the promise of blessing, will be a blessing to the nations. Indeed, the Joseph narrative shows "the gradual fulfillment of the promises made to Abraham in Gen 12:1–3."[60] We should also note that the author distinguishes Joseph from the three patriarchs, Abraham, Isaac, and Jacob. The Bible refers to the God of Abraham, Isaac, and Jacob, but not of Joseph. While the three patriarchs experienced direct divine interventions, Joseph did not. No speeches, no promises, no presences are directly addressed to Joseph—the only thing Joseph can do is trust in God's promises as they have been received and told by his fathers.[61] The Joseph narrative contributes to the patriarchal narrative in a different way, however. As Wenham points out, God's faithfulness in providing partial fulfillment is highlighted through the life of Joseph. Not only does Joseph bring reconciliation to Jacob and his sons, he also becomes a blessing to the Egyptians and all the nations who come before him to re-

---

59. McKeown, *Genesis*, 233. On the same basis, Wenham writes "By placing the promises to Abram right at the beginning of the patriarchal narratives the redactor is asserting their fundamental importance for the history of Israel and the world and indicating how the stories that follow ought to be understood." Wenham, *Genesis 1–15*, 271.

60. Wenham, *Genesis 16–50*, 344.

61. Mathews, *Genesis 11:27—50:26*, 929–30; Hamilton, *The Book of Genesis 18–50*, 709.

ceive food. In Gen 50:20 Joseph concludes, "You intended to harm me, but God intended it for good to accomplish what is now being done, the saving of many lives."

In sum, not only can we find these three major elements—seed, land, and blessing—within almost every narrative throughout the Book of Genesis, we can see them be developed and refined from promise to partial fulfillment. It is clear that the theme of seed deserves recognition as the primary focus in Genesis and that the other themes, land and blessing, can be closely connected to the seed theme. As noted, the land will be given to Abraham's descendants (Gen 12:7). At the climax of his life, Abraham passes God's test and finally receives reconfirmation, the promise of blessing, from God. Furthermore, if we compare Gen 22:16-18 to Gen 12:1-3, we may observe that the promise is expanded in the later passage, which highlights the blessing and is clearly connected to the seed of Abraham.[62] Indeed, Gen 22:16-18 emphasizes that all the nations of the earth will gain blessings through Abraham's seed. We can thus conclude that all three themes are dependent on each other.

Above all, we must keep in mind that the major themes can only be established within a close relationship to God because all the promises are given based on God's grace and faithfulness.[63] As McKeown writes:

> The interrelationship of the themes of blessing, land, and seed is very obvious in the patriarchal narratives. The blessing is to be channeled through one family line with which God has a close relationship. This emphasis on one family line focuses attention on the theme of seed. Furthermore, the line of chosen seed will become a great nation (goy) and, by definition, will require land. Therefore, all three themes are on the agenda for the remainder of chosen line through which it can be channeled to the world, and the chosen seed will have no influence in the world and will not appear blessed until they have land to occupy. Other nations will also have a share in blessing, seed, and land in a general sense, but this does not include a special relationship with God.[64]

We find these themes in every Genesis narrative, including the wife/sister stories. The author of Genesis emphasizes the major themes in the wife/

---

62. Wenham, *Genesis 16–50*, 111. The word is used several times in Genesis, but it is only used in infinite absolute form in 22:17 (כִּי־בָרֵךְ אֲבָרֶכְךָ וְהַרְבָּה אַרְבֶּה אֶת־זַרְעֲךָ כְּכוֹכְבֵי הַשָּׁמַיִם). Grammatically this form emphasizes the verb. For more on the usage of infinite absolute form, see Joüon and Muraoka, *A Grammar of Biblical Hebrew*, 390–401.

63. McKeown, *Genesis*, 218; Alexander, "Genealogies, Seed and the Compositional Unity of Genesis," 263.

64. McKeown, *Genesis*, 255.

sister stories using three similar motifs, and enhances and specifies the themes in turn. Furthermore, by emphasizing divine intervention within the wife/sister stories, the author enhances the concept that all things are accomplished through the gracious activities of God.

Conclusion

In this chapter I have attempted to draw a big picture showing the wife/sister stories in their context. First, I examined the larger context of the *Toledot* of Terah and the *Toledot* of Isaac, and showed that each story is well placed in harmony with the larger context. Second, I investigated the macrostructure of the book of Genesis, in which the *Toledot* formulae have been studied in detail. It is apparent that the term *Toledot* provides one of the most important means of clarifying the structure of the book of Genesis. This term is important for our study because if we accept the *Toledot* formula as a sign of division between sections, we need to answer the question of why the wife/sister stories are located in two different *Toledot* sections. I have therefore examined a potential new understanding of the *Toledot* formula. If we divide the formula according to independent and coordinate clauses, we can conclude that all three wife/sister stories are located in the *Toledot* of Shem, which is independent. Based on this analysis, the three wife/sister stories fulfill the important function of highlighting YHWH's faithfulness to keep His promises in spite of the patriarchs' weakness.

Finally, I explored the major themes of the book of Genesis. As Clines maintains, the dominant themes in Genesis are seed, land, and blessings to the nations. Although the theme of seed is primary, all three themes appear throughout the patriarchal narratives in Gen 12–36. Not surprisingly, these themes are also dominant in the three wife/sister stories. What I will attempt to show in the following chapters is that each story highlights a different theme. The textlinguistic and type-scene methods employed in this study will help clarify the major theme of each story.

An examination of the larger contexts and themes of the book of Genesis will help us explore the meaning of each story and understand how each makes a thematic contribution to the patriarchal narratives. Before synthesizing all the stories, however, we must examine each wife/sister story in greater detail. The next three chapters will be devoted to the texts in Gen 12:10—13:1; 20:1–18; and 26:1–11, respectively.

CHAPTER TWO

The First Wife/Sister Story

(Genesis 12:10—13:1)

THE PURPOSE OF THIS chapter is to examine the textlinguistic features of the first wife/sister story and to analyze it using literary type-scene methodology. Even though there are three wife/sister stories in Genesis, each closely connected to the others, we will first follow the presented order of the stories. Many scholars try to determine the function of the first wife/sister story (Story A) using clues from the later wife/sister stories. According to the narrative-critical approach, however, James Barr comments that, although similar stories are presented within the book of Genesis, this does not mean that each story has the same meaning. Therefore, before understanding the first wife/sister story in relation to the other stories, we need to examine it within the text itself and within its own context.

Delimitation of the Discourse Unit

Scholars have engaged in many discussions regarding the exact extent of Story A. There is not much controversy regarding the beginning of the story, but the end of the story has been debated extensively. We can divide most of the different views into three groups. First, most scholars think that Story A is contained in Gen 12:10–20.[1] Second, Petersen, following Gunkel

---

1. Arnold, *Genesis*, 136–38; McKeown, *Genesis*, 80–83; Jacobs, *Gender, Power, and Persuasion*, 73–102; Carden, "Endangered Ancestress Revisited," 1–14; Kessler and Deurloo, *A Commentary on Genesis*, 102; Waltke, *Genesis*, 210–15; Walton, *Genesis*, 395–410; Towner, *Genesis*, 140–42; Hoop, "The Use of the Past to Address the Present," 359–69; Hartley, *Genesis*, 137–41; Niditch, *A Prelude to Biblical Folklore*, 23–69; Turner, *Genesis*, 65–67; Westermann, *Genesis 12–36*, 159–68; Salanga, *Three Stories of the Endangered Wife*; Ronning, "The Naming of Isaac," 1–27; Biddle, "The 'Endangered Ancestress' and Blessing for the Nations," 599–611; Hamilton, *The Book of Genesis 1–17*, 379–88; Wenham, *Genesis 1–15*, 283–92; Coats, *Genesis*, 97; Brueggemann, *Genesis*, 126–30; Gibson, *Genesis 12–50*, 32–37; Vawter, *On Genesis*, 178–82; Van Seters, *Abraham in History and Tradition*, 169–70; Kidner, *Genesis*. Speiser, *Genesis*, 89–94; Maly, "Genesis 12:10–20; 20:1–18; 26:7–11," 255–62.

THE FIRST WIFE/SISTER STORY 63

and Koch, argues that Gen 13:1 should be the end of the first story because "(1) Gen. 13:2 is yet another initial disjunctive clause; (2) 13:1 includes the phrase *hû' wᵉ' ištô* which is central to the tale; and (3) the travel agenda is necessary to deposit Abraham back in the Negeb."[2] Lastly, Cassuto considers Gen 13:4 to be the end of the story.[3]

It is clear that the previous unit (Gen 12:1–9) ends with a recapitulation, as verse 9 again introduces Abraham's journey to Negev. In this description, no further information or sequence of action is given; it therefore functions only as closure of the unit.[4] Then we see the phrase וַיְהִי רָעָב בָּאָרֶץ. There are several indications of discontinuity in the biblical narratives. D. W. Baker presents the following as signs of discontinuity: change of time, change of subject, genealogical list, change of venue, formal literary structures, and some rhetorical devices.[5] Among them, וַיְהִי is a clear device showing discontinuity of time, even though it is presented with the *waw-consecutive*, which usually denotes the sequence of actions and events in the biblical narratives.[6] We can therefore conclude that the first wife/sister story begins with verse 10.

It is more difficult to locate the end of Story A. As previously mentioned, most scholars see verse 20 as the end. In biblical narratives, if a narrative begins with someone's leaving and going into a new place, the narrative tends to end with that person's departure or return home.[7] Following this observation, some scholars prefer verse 20 as the ending for this narrative.[8] However, we need to note that, on the same basis, 13:1 and even 13:4 could be the ending of the narrative. So, this criterion may not be a good standard. Also noteworthy is the fact that both 12:20 (וַיְצַו עָלָיו פַּרְעֹה אֲנָשִׁים) and 13:1 (וַיַּעַל אַבְרָם מִמִּצְרַיִם) start with the *waw*-consecutive, which usually

---

2. Petersen, "A Thrice-Told Tale," 33–34; Also see Patterson, "The Righteousness and Survival of the Seed," 247–51; Mathews, *Genesis 11:27—50:26*, 122–30; Cotter, *Genesis*, 91–93; Brodie, *Genesis as Dialogue*, 217–18; Wallace, "On Account of Sarai," 32–41; Roop, *Genesis*, 103–4; Pappas, "Deception as Patriarchal Self-Defense in a Foreign Land," 35–50; Alexander, "A Literary Analysis of the Abraham Narrative in Genesis," 37–38, 136–37.

3. Cassuto, *A Commentary on the Book of Genesis, Part 2*, 334–35; Sailhamer, *Genesis*, 157–60; Gunkel and Biddle, *Genesis*, 168–72. Also there are some other views like 12:9–20, 12:9—13:1 and so on. In my opinion, broadly speaking, those views can be added to the three views that I presented.

4. Zeelander, *Closure in Biblical Narrative*, 62.

5. Baker, "Diversity and Unity in the Literary Structure of Genesis," 197–215.

6. *GKC*, 111f and g.

7. Zeelander, *Closure in Biblical Narrative*, 96–97; Bar-Efrat, *Narrative Art in the Bible*, 130.

8. Bar-Efrat, *Narrative Art in the Bible*, 132; Wenham, *Genesis 1–15*, 285–86.

denotes the continuity of the mainline of the narrative. Wenham observes that the change of subject occurs in 13:1. Pharaoh is the subject of 12:20, whereas in 13:1 the subject is Abraham. Because of this, Wenham argues that the new subject indicates the beginning of the new episode.⁹ It seems to me, however, that referring to Abraham as a new subject is not indicative of a new episode; this change in subject from the previous subject, "they (וַיְשַׁלְּחוּ אֹתוֹ וְאֶת־אִשְׁתּוֹ וְאֶת־כָּל־אֲשֶׁר־לוֹ)" is not significant.

Second, we need to note that the repetition in 13:1 is also seen in 12:20. The phrase הוּא וְאִשְׁתּוֹ וְכָל־אֲשֶׁר־לוֹ is almost identically repeated. This repetition functions as a recapitulation, connecting it to the phrase in 12:20 and indicates the end of the unit. Zeelander states, "Repetitions can also be a natural sign of ending . . . Repetition in the Genesis narratives is closural when descriptive repetitions occur after the causal actions are over and there is a new equilibrium in a plot. Repeated statements at that point add to the stability or finality of a story as it ends."¹⁰

Third, in terms of the use of הַנֶּגְבָּה in 12:9 and 13:1, we may see the same conclusion repeating the same place name. This reiteration shows that 12:1–9 and 12:10—13:1 are closely connected to each other. If we conclude that moving toward the Negev is a narrative conclusion, 13:1 is likely the conclusion of the first wife/sister story. The narrator suddenly places Lot on the stage not to indicate the start of the next unit, but to introduce a main character for the subsequent unit. Linguistically speaking, the narrator establishes connectivity by repeating the same phrase (theme) and providing new information by introducing a new character (rheme) who is about to take on an important role.

Lastly and most importantly, we see that 13:2 starts with a disjunctive *waw* with the subject (וְאַבְרָם כָּבֵד מְאֹד). Usually this syntax functions to introduce a new episode in Genesis and to provide background information for the following story.¹¹ In this regard, it is worth noting that 13:5 (וְגַם־לְלוֹט הַהֹלֵךְ אֶת־אַבְרָם הָיָה) has the same disjunctive *waw* with the subject. By using this, it manifests that Lot appears as one of the main characters in the Abraham-Lot narrative in Gen 13:2–18. We may thus see a kind of gram-

---

9. Wenham, *Genesis 1–15*, 286.

10. Zeelander, *Closure in Biblical Narrative*, 62.

11. Merwe, "Discourse Linguistics and Biblical Hebrew Grammar," 29–34. A few examples are 3:1, 4:1, 14:18, 19:24, 20:4, 16, 26:26, 27:5, 31:47, etc. Some of the functions of the *waw-X-Qatal* form are noteworthy. It is often a marker of discontinuity denoting background information, change of topic, initial, or final. For example, Gen 20:4 reads "וַאֲבִימֶלֶךְ לֹא קָרַב אֵלֶיהָ." Here Abimelech's action is not in sequence, rather it refers to the prior situation. So, it provides background information using the *waw-X-Qatal* form.

matical connection through the use of the word גַּם.¹² As a consequence, 13:1 may be considered as the conclusion of the first wife/sister story.

Textlinguistic Analysis

From the above analysis, we have come to conclude that Story A covers Gen 12:10—13:1. We now need to examine the text using the textlinguistic approach.

Story A within the Surrounding Narratives

Before proceeding with a detailed discussion of the text itself, it is necessary to look at the story within the surrounding narratives. Form critics generally argue that Gen 12:20—13:1 is loosely connected to the surrounding narratives, indicating that Story A might have been inserted into its current place at a late date. First, according to form critics, even though Lot is an important character in Gen 12:1–9 and 13:2–18, he has no role in Gen 12:10—13:1. Second, Abraham makes a great decision in moving into the Promised Land, so it is odd that Abraham decides to leave the land right after this decision. For these reasons, Koch concludes, "A could quite simply be taken out of the context. Indeed, if this were done, the description of Abram's journey through the Promised Land in chapters xii and xiii would flow more easily."¹³ However, it is very important to understand the story within the broader literary context, for surely we must acknowledge that no proper understanding of the story can come without its context.

First, the previous narratives (Gen 11:27–32 and 12:9) function as the most important interpretive keys to Story A; and this is true even for Stories B and C. The tension developed in the previous narratives appears in two different ways. First, we have already perceived that Sarah is barren (Gen 11:30); second, God has promised descendants, land, and blessings to Abraham (Gen 12:1–3). God reiterates, and thus emphasizes, his promise to Abraham that "this" land will be given to Abraham's seed. Obviously, the promises of land and blessing will make no sense if Abraham has no son. If Sarah is barren, then, how will all these promises be fulfilled? Will Abraham have a son? Will Abraham's descendants inherit the Promised Land? These questions constitute the entire background of Story A.

---

12. Wenham, *Genesis 1–15*, 286. From this observation, Wenham rejects arguments that the first wife/sister story may extend to 13:4.

13. Koch, *The Growth of the Biblical Tradition*, 116–17; See Pappas, "Deception as Patriarchal Self-Defense," 37; Brueggemann, *Genesis*, 126–27.

Second, there are clear geographical connections between Story A and the surrounding narratives. In fact, chapters 12 and 13 share the journey motif. In chapter 12, Abraham travels to Canaan, obeying the word of God, and continues to journey within this land. In Story A, the narrative follows Abraham's journey to Egypt. Then, just like chapter 12, Gen 13:2–18 introduces Abraham's journey to, and within, Canaan. In terms of the names of places where Abraham moves, when he comes into Canaan, he firstly stays at the site of the great tree of Moreh at Shechem (v. 6). He then moves to the hills with Bethel on the west and Ai on the east (v. 8). After that he continues to travel to the Negev. After coming up from Egypt, in chapter 13 Abraham moves from the Negev to the place between Bethel and Ai (13:3), which the text refers to as the place "where his tent had been earlier." We see that Gen 13 reminds us of Gen 12:7–8. In terms of geographical information, DeRoche illustrates the structure of chapters 12–13 as follows:[14]

I. Introduction, 12:5

II. The Journey, 12:6—13:18

  a. Oak of Moreh (Shechem), 12:6-7

    b. a mountain between Ai and Bethel, 12:8

      c. the Negeb, 12:9

        d. Egypt, 12:10-20

      c'. the Negeb, 13:1-2

    b'. the mountain between Ai and Bethel, 13:3-17

  a'. Oaks of Mamre (Hebron), 13:18

As we have seen, Story A marks the center of chapters 12 and 13. If we assume that Story A was added by a later redactor and remove Story A from its current place, we are left with a serious gap between 12:1–9 and 13:2–18.

Third, there are some literary connections between Story A and the surrounding narratives. First, Gen 12:1 and 19 include strong commands issued by YHWH and pharaoh. In Gen 12:1, God commands Abraham to go into the land of Canaan (לֶךְ־לְךָ), and in verse 19 we see a similar command

---

14. DeRoche, "The Dynamics of Promise," 127–31; Kennedy, *Seeking a Homeland*, 53–54. DeRoche states, "The chiasmus not only binds the stages of the journey together as a unit but suggests that the second half constitutes some sort of reversal of the first half . . . By fleeing to Egypt Abram thus abandons his original goal, but returns to it when Pharaoh expels him from Egypt and he returns to Canaan. Appropriate to its position in the centre of the chiasmus the Egyptian sojourn is the journey's pivotal episode, and effectively divides it into two parts."

from Pharaoh, which makes Abraham return to the land at the beginning and the end of chapter 12. Also, a couple of grammatical patterns are similar throughout chapters 12 and 13. The use of directive-h is especially dominant, occurring thirteen times in Chapter 12 and 13 (12:5 [x2], 8, 9, 10, 11, 14, 13:1, 14[x4]). An important keyword, הלֹךְ, is also used throughout the chapters (12:1, 4[x2], 5, 9, 19, 13:1, 5, 17).[15]

Finally, Story A shares thematic connections with its surroundings. In particular, chapters 12 and 13 are directly related to the theme of land. As seen above, these chapters have a symmetrical structure in terms of their geographical place. It is also important to observe that all the narratives in this section raise the issue of land. In Gen 12:8, for example, God promises that this land will be given to the descendants of Abraham; in Gen 13:15, God provides a more specific promise to Abraham and his descendants. At the center of these narratives, Story A begins with the departure from the land (v. 10) and ends with the return to the land (13:1). It thus clearly displays a departure-return pattern, stressing the promise of land throughout Genesis (Gen 12:10—13:1; 42:3–26; 43:20—44:24; for going down or going up, Gen 39:1; 42:38; 43: 4, 5, 7, 15, 20; 44: 21, 23, 26, 33–34; 45:25; 46:3–4; 50:24).[16] In terms of thematic connections, Alexander maintains that Story A highlights the divine fulfillment theme found in the previous narrative: "In actual fact the exact opposite occurs; instead of a description of their fulfillment we are given a picture of their non-fulfillment."[17]

Structure

So far, we have examined the place of Story A within its surrounding narratives, and I have shown that Story A should be considered as a part of a unified story along with the surrounding passages. Now we must examine the structure of Story A, itself. Most importantly, it is necessary to observe the uses of וַיְהִי, which occurs four times in verses 10, 11, 14, and 16. As mentioned above, וַיְהִי, which represents change of time and space, often signals the introduction of a new unit-but not always. The last occurrence is somewhat different. It seems to me that, in verse 16, וַיְהִי does not lead to a new

---

15. For more analysis, DeRoche, "The Dynamics of Promise," 128–30.

16. Kennedy, *Seeking a Homeland*, 56–58. Extended discussion for the promise of land as the main theme will be presented below.

17. Alexander, "A Literary Analysis of the Abraham Narrative in Genesis," 37. Although he calls this "non-fulfillment," he modifies Goldingay's terminology. Goldingay suggests calling this "anti-fulfillment." See Goldingay, "The Patriarchs in Scripture and History," 3.

unit; but only explains the increase of Abraham's wealth. Furthermore, it is important to note that verse 16 contains both the *We-X-Qatal* form (וּלְאַבְרָם הֵיטִיב בַּעֲבוּרָהּ) and וַיְהִי. It is clear that וַיְהִי denotes circumstantial change as usual. In this regard, we can clearly see that the mood of the scene changes radically between 10–16 and 17–20. In the first part, Abraham's plan seems to be very successful and he gains wealth as a result (v. 16). In the subsequent part, however, Abraham's plan is revealed and rebuked. On top of this, we can see that after a series of the *Wayyiqtol* forms, the *We-X-Qatal* form in verse 16 functions as a kind of climax by adding a background storyline. So, the *We-X-Qatal* form functions as the end of the unit.[18]

From these observations, we may conclude that Gen 12:10—13:1 consists of two major parts. The first is verses 10–16, divided by וַיְהִי in verses. 10, 11, and 14. Verse 10 informs us of a change of time and space, as Abraham begins to go down to Egypt. In verse 11, the circumstance changes: Abraham is about to enter Egypt very soon. Verses 11–13, therefore, describe what will be happening in the land of Egypt. Finally, verse 14 indicates that Abraham is actually entering Egypt. By recapitulating the previous subunit, verse 14 functions as the start of a new unit; this is enhanced by the following series of the *Wayyiqtol* form.[19] It is also enhanced by the parallels of similar expressions that appear in 11–13 and 14–16, but not 17–20: Sarah's beauty (11, 14), Egyptians (12, 14), "And they saw" (12, 15), and "on account of her (you)" (13, 16). These clear parallels highlight how Abraham's plan is accomplished in reality.

The second part of the story, verses 17–20, shows that Abraham's plan to deceive is radically revealed by God. In verse 17 a very important change of subject occurs. The initial action is made by YHWH Himself, which creates a turning point for the narrative. As Petersen rightly observes, "the narrative switches from a history under the control of Abraham's plan, 12:10–16, to a history under the control of YHWH's plan, verses 17–20. YHWH takes the initiative by plaguing Pharaoh because of Sarah, Abraham's wife."[20] Here we need to go one step further. It is noteworthy that the change of subject occurs again in verse 18. Also, verses 18–19 clearly reflect verses 11–13 by using the direct speech of Pharaoh. While verse 17 strongly emphasizes God's intervention, verse 18 focuses only on Pharaoh's speech

---

18. Wenham, *Genesis 1–15*, 285; Niccacci, "On the Hebrew Verbal System," 123–28; Andersen, *The Sentence in Biblical Hebrew*, 80–82. Andersen provides some examples denoting episode-final circumstantial clauses. In this case, v. 16 should be the episode final because v. 16 recapitulates the previous unit and v. 17 is under the sequence of the *Wayyitol* until v. 20.

19. Gropp, "Toward a Discourse Grammar," 16.

20. Petersen, "A Thrice-Told Tale," 37.

and action, which occur as a result of verse 17. We may therefore further divide this section between verse 17 and verses 18–20.

Mathews summarizes the overall structure of this narrative as follows:[21]

A Descent of Abram and Sarai (12:10)

B Abram instructs Sarai (12:11–13)

C Pharaoh kidnaps Sarai and the Lord intervenes (12:14–17)

B' Pharaoh instructs Abram and his men (12:18–20)

A' Ascent of Abram

Wenham also sees a chiastic structure:[22]

A Exposition: Entry	10
B 1st scene: Abram's speech	11–13
C 2nd scene: Fulfillment of Abram's fears	14–17
B' 3rd scene: Pharaoh's speech 18–20	
A' Conclusion: Exit	

These two suggested structures offer good insights, but we need to reconsider them in light of the preceding analysis. First, as recognized by Mathews and Wenham, we need to think of the two instructions made by Abraham and Pharaoh. We should also emphasize the major turning point in verse 17, which is the most important moment in this story.[23] Unlike Wenham, we should consider 13:1 as a conclusion that recapitulates the story. From these observations I would outline the structure of Gen 12:10—13:1 as follows:

A Abraham's Departure: Going down to Egypt	10
B Abraham's Speech (Plan)	11–13
C Fulfillment of Abraham's Plan	14–16
C' YHWH's Intervention	17
B' Pharaoh's Instruction	18–20
A' Abraham's Return: Going up to Canaan	13:1

---

21. Mathews, *Genesis 1—11:26*, 126.

22. Wenham, *Genesis 1-15*, 286.

23. Pratt, "Pictures, Windows, and Mirrors," 156–67. Even though he connects v. 17 to v. 16b, I am not sure if v. 16b should be linked to v. 17 or not.

Textual Analysis

We have examined the structure of Story A. Now we need to explore each unit in detail. The textual analysis of Story A will become an important basis for our study of Stories B and C, which are closely related to it.

A. Abraham's Departure (12:10)

By using וַיְהִי, which indicates the beginning of the unit, verse 10 begins Story A. In contrast to God's promise, there is a severe famine in the land of Canaan. Just as Abraham's wife is barren, the land is also barren. In contrast to the great faith he displayed in Gen 12:1–9, here in Gen 12:10—13:1 Abraham is depicted as an unfaithful and anxious man. Although not all such occasions were a result of God's judgment, famine was often used for the fulfillment of God's purpose.[24] The present text gives no reason for the famine, but it is clear that God will protect and fulfill His promise to Abraham, even though Abraham fails to be faithful. Clauses 10a and 10b are independent, while 10c is subordinate; 10c provides a reason for 10b. Westermann argues that 10b and 10c are original while 10a was added at the beginning of the verse in order to stress the theme.[25] In terms of stylistic analysis, however, 10a and 10c correspond to each other, forming a chiastic structure. The following is the structure of verse 10:

וַיְהִי רָעָב בָּאָרֶץ

וַיֵּרֶד אַבְרָם מִצְרַיְמָה לָגוּר שָׁם

כִּי־כָבֵד הָרָעָב בָּאָרֶץ׃

Cassuto maintains that the expressions "רָעָב" and "בָּאָרֶץ" give verse 10 a well-consisted symmetrical form.[26] Through this repetition, "the famine in the land" is given meaning, while the word כָּבֵד is added. Thus, כָּבֵד has an important role here. The severe famine is associated with the Patriarchs' lives (12:10; 26:1; 47:13) and is sufficient reason for leaving the land. In the case of Isaac, God clearly prohibits going down to Egypt while God allows it for Jacob. With Abraham, however, there is no explicit mention of God's prohibition or permission.

On the one hand, by emphasizing the severity of famine in the land, we may consider Abraham to be free of responsibility for his choice to leave

---

24. Shea, "Famine," 2:769–73.
25. Westermann, *Genesis 12–36*, 163.
26. Cassuto, *A Commentary on the Book of Genesis, Part 2*, 346.

the Promised Land, since the text does not explicitly evaluate Abraham's departure from the land. Also, it is noteworthy that at this point Abraham still has a very abstract promise of the land. After YHWH commands Abraham to go to the land he will show, YHWH promises land to Abraham's descendants: "To your offspring I will give this land" (12:8). Abraham then receives a more explicit promise of land after Lot departs from him: "All the land that you see I will give to you and your offspring forever" (13:15).[27]

On the other hand, there are some suggestions of condemnation regarding Abraham's departure. For example, "going down" is sometimes understood as a negative moral term, indicating spiritual depravity.[28] Further, Mathews argues that Gen 12:10—13:1 parallels the Eden story. Based on this, we may acknowledge that the characterization of Abraham in Story A is implicitly negative. Genesis 13:10 compares the plain of the Jordan to the garden of the LORD and the land of Egypt. This verse allows us to connect Story A with the garden of LORD (the Garden of Eden) and the land of Egypt. However, it is not necessary to conclude that Abraham's departure should be rebuked based on the fact that Abraham's characterization is negative and that there are a number of similarities in the use of words and expressions in Story A and the Eden story.[29]

Since we have no strong evidence indicating the proper evaluation of Abraham's departure, we may conclude that Abraham's action in going down to Egypt is open to either negative or positive evaluation, especially from Abraham's point of view. It is an understandable decision because, as the text mentions, the famine is severe; Abraham may have had no other option.

One more issue needs to be addressed here. The text says that Abraham goes down to sojourn in Egypt. The term "sojourn" is used of one who separates oneself from his home and places himself in a place where one is unknown by other people. The most frequent reason for sojourning in the Old Testament is famine, as in Gen 12:10 and 26:1, and the cause of famine in the land of Canaan was usually drought. Although the term is used to indicate a temporary residence, we cannot exactly define the length of time spent sojourning, because this term is employed in various contexts. For instance, in Gen 23:4 Abraham describes himself as "an alien and a stranger" in Canaan, after spending over fifty years there. In this case, the term should be understood to describe a long period (cf. Ruth 1:4). As Mathews

27. Wenham, *Genesis 1–15*, 287; Kidner, *Genesis*, 115–16; Turner, *Announcements of Plot in Genesis*, 97–98; Hamilton, *The Book of Genesis 1–17*, 379–80.

28. In relation to the story of Judah and Tamar, the term ירד suggests both geographical and spiritual descent. See Waltke, *Genesis*, 509; Mathews, *Genesis 11:27—50:26*, 666.

29. Mathews, *Genesis 11:27—50:26*, 123.

mentions, however, the term "sojourn" only indicates that a person lives among people who do not know him and lives without full legal rights.[30] Thus, we cannot confirm how long Abraham stayed in Egypt by examining the terminology itself.

Not surprisingly scholars have various suggestions regarding the length of Abraham's sojourn in Egypt. Wenham suggests that this term refers to a long-term settlement, while Casutto believes it describes a shorter and more temporary dwelling.[31] In order to decide the length of time spent in Egypt, we need to look into Gen 16:3: "So after Abram had been living in Canaan ten years, Sarai his wife took her Egyptian maidservant Hagar and gave her to her husband to be his wife." Abraham was seventy-five upon entering Canaan and eight-six when he begot Ishmael. Therefore, ten full years are required between Gen 12 and 16, a period which included Abraham's time in Egypt, the international warfare described in chapter 14, and the Abrahamic covenant seen in chapter 15. If we define Abraham's life in Canaan as spanning only ten years, as the text mentions, we need to reduce the length of time spent in Egypt. If so, we should be careful in defining sojourning as a long-term journey.

B. Abraham's Plan (12:11–13)

The second scene takes place right before Abraham and Sarah enter Egypt. This new scene begins with the term וַיְהִי, which indicates the beginning of a unit, as in verse 10. In this scene Abraham devises a plan to protect his own life from the Egyptians. The whole section is formatted as speech, and it is Abraham's monologue here that provides a balance to the later speech from Pharaoh (vv. 18–20).[32] Although Sarah is Abraham's main counterpart and his address is directed to her, she surprisingly does not speak at all. Abraham is unnecessarily afraid of the Egyptians: he assumes that if they see the

---

30. Ibid., 127; For the legal status of sojourner, see Kellermann, "גּוּר," in *TDOT*, 448.

31. Wenham, *Genesis 1–15*, 287; Cassuto, *A Commentary on the Book of Genesis, Part 2*, 346; Wacholder, "How Long Did Abram Stay in Egypt?," 43–56. Jewish traditions have seen the significance in Abraham's sojourn, positing that the Egyptians learned sciences like astrology from Abraham. In order to account for this, Jewish traditions such as the Genesis Apocryphon and the Book of Jubilee set up a long period for Abraham's stay in Egypt. Genesis Apocryphon and Jubilee explain that Abraham stayed for seven years in Egypt; Also see, Avigad and Yadin, *A Genesis Apocryphon*; Fitzmyer, *The Genesis Apocryphon of Qumran Cave I*. See, *Jubilee* 13:10–15.

32. Westermann, *Genesis 12–36*, 166. Westermann argues that the speeches of Abraham and Pharaoh are highpoints of the story.

beauty of a wife, they will kill the husband in order to take the beautiful wife away, because they do not fear God. As the story progresses, however, it becomes clear that Abraham's fear is lacking in substance and demonstrates a lack of trust in God's protection.[33] Some might think that since Sarah is taken by Pharaoh in verses 14–16, Abraham's action can be justified. However, in verse 18, Pharaoh asks why Abraham did not identify Sarah as his wife. In fact, because we do not have further explanation of this, we cannot confirm whether Abraham spoke the truth and Pharaoh would take her to his harem like Abraham expects. Rather, from Pharaoh's accusation, we may assume that taking someone's wife is regarded as wrong by the Egyptians. In the three wife/sister stories, the crisis always arises not because of the truth, but because of the Patriarchs' lies.

As mentioned above, if we read the text to this point it is clear that while God has promised Abraham a descendant, Sarah is barren (11:30). Abraham does believe that God's promise will be achieved, but he does not know the specific way in which it will be executed. From his understanding of the promise, Abraham is not sure of the possibility of Sarah as the vessel of God's fulfillment because of her barrenness. His interpretation of the promise of YHWH should be noted in order to properly understand the text. To rebuke Abraham's departure is to bring our awareness of future events in Abraham's story to our understanding of the current text. Even though the stories are connected to each other, we should be cautious in taking ideas from Gen 20 or 26, or even the Exodus motif, and relating them to Gen 12.[34] When we read Gen 20:11–13, we learn that Abraham's ruse was his regular practice when moving to a foreign land as a sojourner. However, we need to think about why the author does not mention this at the very beginning of the wife/sister stories. Based on our understanding on Gen 20:11–13, we cannot confirm whether Story A represents the first occurrence of this action or not, and we might even assume that Abraham lied in this way more than three times during his life. The author intentionally chose not to give us this information in Story A, and the author decides to record only three wife/sister stories in the book of Genesis. Therefore, the fact that Story A does not explicitly mention their decision to lie to a foreign ruler indicates that Story

---

33. Waltke, *Genesis*, 213. Waltke claims that Abraham's mistake is a lack of trust in God's promise, but it is not evident that Abraham does not believe in God's promise itself. Generally speaking, his fear reflects his lack of trust in God's protection. It does not automatically indicate his unfaithfulness to the promise but may rather expose his misunderstanding of God's recent promise.

34. Turner, *Announcements of Plot in Genesis*, 63–65; Clines, "The Ancestor in Danger," 67–84. Clines suggests reading "each tale strictly in the light of the Genesis story so far" (69).

A does not focus on the reason for Abraham's lie. This is an example of how the author leads readers to understand the text.

In order to carry out his plan, Abraham strongly requests Sarah to participate in the deception. The Hebrew expression נָא is used twice in this scene (vv. 12 and 13). Furthermore, it comes with the word הִנֵּה, which calls for special attention. Strictly speaking this is not a command, but a strong request. However, Sarah may have had no other option. Surprisingly, she does not speak at all in this scene, which may mean that she accepted Abraham's plan because she had no power to refuse her husband's request or it made good sense to her.

It may seem strange that Abraham was so concerned about Sarah's beauty, since at this point in the story she is at least sixty-five years old.[35] How beautiful can a woman be at sixty-five? Scholars have proposed various solutions. First, because Sarah died at 127, it is possible to consider sixty-five as roughly her middle age. Kidner thinks that the life span of the patriarchs was nearly double ours by the special providence of God (Deut 34: 7). He argues that Sarah's age of sixty-five may have corresponded to our thirties or forties.[36] Similarly, Calvin mentioned her sterility as a means of the preservation of her beauty.[37] Interestingly, Wenham suggests a good reason for the perception of Sarah's beauty. He argues that "it should be borne in mind that ideas of feminine beauty in traditional societies differ from ours; well-endowed matronly figures, not slim youthful ones, tend to represent their ideal of womanhood. By such criteria, Sarai might well count as very beautiful even at her age."[38] Even today, intercultural encounters may reveal different views on beauty, and most people have difficulty guessing the ages of people from other races. For example, a missionary in Ethiopia has commented to me that, although she is in her mid-fifties, Ethiopians rarely guess here to be older than her thirties. This is probably because of differences between cultures, environmental situations, and individuals' tendency to seek skin-improving treatments, and so forth.[39] We can recognize, then, that there are

---

35. Abraham came to Canaan when he was seventy-five years old. Since Sarah was ten years younger than Abraham (Gen 17:17), she was sixty-five years old at that time. We do not know the exact time of the incident in Egypt, but we can confirm that Sarah was at least sixty-five.

36. Kidner, *Genesis*, 116–17; Avigad and Yadin, *A Genesis Apocryphon*, 43. In fact, Genesis Apocryphon describes Sarah's beauty in detail. "And all maidens and all brides that go beneath the wedding canopy are not more fair than she. And above all women is she lovely and higher is her beauty than that of them all, and with all her beauty there is much wisdom in her . . ."

37. Calvin, *Genesis*, 101.

38. Wenham, *Genesis 1–15*, 288.

39. I would like to personally thank a Korean missionary, Mrs. Eun Hye Chang, for

various possible solutions to the question of Sarah's beauty. We may need to reconsider approaches to this text that propose the presence of different sources and be open to other possible solutions, since there is no clear mention of why people thought Sarah was so beautiful.[40]

We also need to evaluate Abraham's suggestion at this point. Many scholars try to either defend or criticize Abraham's action. Following Speiser, some scholars have tried to justify Abraham's action from the perspective of ancient Near Eastern culture.[41] From an ancient point of view, Gunkel argues the lie was not serious: "If no particularly foul intention is associated with it, it was not considered dishonorable."[42] Gunkel praises Abraham's cleverness in predicting exactly what will happen and handling it the way he does.[43] Even if his act was not considered dishonorable, however, what remains is that the text defines Abraham's action as deception. Abraham is reproached by the voice of Pharaoh (vv. 18–20). His character is clearly described; here he has chosen to lie. Even though we do not clearly know if Abraham, from the beginning, expects to put his wife in Pharaoh's hand, it is evident that he has lied. It seems to the readers that he acts very selfishly and would choose to abandon his wife to save his own life. It is therefore worth noting Westermann's conclusion. Even though Westermann also acknowledges that there may have been no other option but the ruse, he maintains that Abraham's ruse has to be judged: "He does not think of an intervention of God; he does not appear here as a man of faith. Faced with the threat of death, he surrenders what he ought not surrender."[44]

Did Abraham really hope to get some benefit by passing his wife off as his sister? Did he act this way while realizing that someone else might take his wife away? Beyond these questions, we need to learn from the text itself what Abraham really wanted. In the story, Abraham is clearly and primarily concerned about staying alive in Egypt. In verses 11–12, Abraham's speech concerning his life is repeated. In order to stress his concern, verse 12b has

---

this observation. She holds a PhD degree in the area of intercultural studies from TEDS.

40. Cassuto deals with the source critical issue on this passage. According to this view, since all chronological data belong to P, while this story is attributed to J, there is no relationship between this story and Sarah's age. Cassuto, however, questions this in terms of the role of redactor who combines P and J into the present form. See, Cassuto, *A Commentary on the Book of Genesis, Part 2*, 347; Wenham, *Genesis 1–15*, 288.

41. We already have discussed at "Social-Historical Study" in Introduction.

42. Gunkel and Biddle, *Genesis*, 169–70.

43. Ibid., 169.

44. Westermann, *Genesis 12–36*, 164. He enhances his argument by comparing the last words of Pharaoh in vv. 18–20. "It (Pharaoh's reproach) shows at once that the narrator does not approve of Abraham's conduct and attributes a clear conscience to the Pharaoh. The reproach is justified and puts Abraham to shame" (166).

a chiastic structure (וְהָרְגוּ אֹתִי וְאֹתָךְ יְחַיּוּ). This expression occurs again in verse 13 (וְחָיְתָה נַפְשִׁי בִּגְלָלֵךְ). Verse 13 raises another question. At a glance, the expression "לְמַעַן יִיטַב־לִי בַעֲבוּרֵךְ" seems to again reveal Abraham's desire for benefit. If this so, Abraham had the vile intention of obtaining wealth by exposing his wife to danger. Even though a similar expression occurs in verse 16, in relation to wealth, we should first consider it within the context of verse 13. As we see, יִיטַב־לִי in 13b parallels to וְחָיְתָה נַפְשִׁי in 13c. We can surmise from this parallel that "it may go well" does not automatically relate to wealth; rather, it is related to Abraham's life.[45]

אִמְרִי־נָא אֲחֹתִי אָתְּ[46]

לְמַעַן יִיטַב־לִי בַעֲבוּרֵךְ

וְחָיְתָה נַפְשִׁי בִּגְלָלֵךְ

We can thus confirm that Abraham's main concern at the outset is his own life. Why, then, does Abraham want to keep his life? As mentioned above, from the preceding narrative we know that Abraham is aware of three things: the promise of his descendant, the barrenness of Sarah, and the company of Lot. The solid fact for Abraham at this point is that God will keep his promise through him. He is not, however, aware of the role of Sarah. At this point, from the context, it is likely that Abraham believes Lot, his nephew, to be a possible option for the fulfillment of God's promise. For this reason, he is willing to sacrifice himself for Lot. In contrast to his treatment of Sarah in Gen 12:10—13:1, in chapter 13, Abraham appears unselfish in relation to Lot-he would concede his right so that Lot can choose the land he wants. Also, because he assumes that Lot is his seed, Abraham, who endangered Sarah in Egypt, is willing to put his life in danger for Lot in chapter 14.[47]

In light of these narratives, Turner concludes:

---

45. Cassuto, *A Commentary on the Book of Genesis, Part 2*, 347–52. Cassuto argues that if benefit is the concern here, it is more natural to switch the order of 13b and 13c. If his life cannot be spared, he can have no benefit from the gifts.

46. It is interesting to note the modification of the LXX. Although the Hebrew text says, "you are my sister," the LXX clearly says, "εἰπὸν οὖν ὅτι Ἀδελφὴ αὐτοῦ εἰμι" ("Say, therefore, that I am his sister"). There is a change of the subject. By making this change, the LXX tries to reduce Abraham's responsibility for the lie. The use of "therefore" and the emphatic word order ("his sister I am") are also noticeable. The Samaritan Pentateuch also adds "עמו ולוט."

47. Helyer, "The Separation of Abram and Lot," 78–79; Turner, *Announcements of Plot in Genesis*, 66–70.

We must ask ourselves whether Abraham would risk his life for Lot, when in Egypt he had been unwilling to risk his life for Sarah, if the responsibilities of kinship were the only ruling factor. I can only conclude that in Abraham's eyes his nephew is of more value to him than his wife. This reinforces my point that on Abraham's present understanding of the nation promise, Sarah is expendable, but Lot is crucial."[48]

It is clear for me that in this story Abraham believes in God's promise, but simply does not know how God will fulfill his promise. We can conclude, then, that (1) Abraham has sinned by deceiving Pharaoh and the Egyptians, (2) he wants to believe in God's promise even in the present dangerous situation, and (3) he does not understand the way of fulfillment of God's promise. From Abraham's perspective, at this point, the danger is not in Sarah, but in Abraham himself.[49] So, Abraham, as a bearer of the promise, plunges God's promise into the greatest crisis by passing his wife off as his sister.[50] As we see, ethical evaluation of Abraham's behavior is not the main focus of this story, so we should not overanalyze his action to the point that the true focus is overshadowed. Rather, we are to see why Abraham does things the way he does and what Abraham wants to keep in Egypt.

It is interesting to note that Sarah has no voice in this story. This parallels Abraham's silence in verses 18–20. In fact, Sarah, the most important character, is the most frequently referenced character (including by name, pronoun, and status) throughout the story (vv. 11 [x2], 12 [x3], 14 [x2], 15 [x4], 17 [x2], 18, 19 [x4], 20, and 13:1). It is also important that Sarah's name is rarely used here: she is instead mentioned as "the woman" or "the wife." Surely "the woman" is a *leitwort* in the story.[51] We also need to look at how the text mentions Sarah. Sarah is only depicted in terms of her beauty and her relationship with her husband. Thus, while Sarah plays the most important role in this story, the author does not intend to portray her as an independent character. In this regard, the fact that Sarah has no voice is a device used to stress her fragile situation. Therefore, it is not necessary to assume that her silence represents her approval of Abraham's plan.

---

48. Turner, *Announcements of Plot in Genesis*, 69.

49. Clines, "The Ancestor in Danger," 68; Turner, *Announcements of Plot in Genesis*, 65–67.

50. Von Rad, *Genesis*, 169.

51. Peleg, "Was the Ancestress of Israel in Danger?," 197; Salanga, *Three Stories of the Endangered Wife*, 37–39. It appears ten times.

C. Fulfillment of Abraham's Plan (12:14–16)

The third וַיְהִי indicates the beginning of a new scene. The appearances of וַיְהִי in verses 10, 11, and 14 denote different phases of Abraham's journey to Egypt, which takes him from Canaan, to the border of Egypt, and finally into the land of Egypt. This new scene takes place in the land of Egypt and shows that what Abraham feared actually occurs. Just as Abraham assumed, the Egyptians see Sarah's beauty and praise her before Pharaoh. Just as Abraham expected, he is well on account of Sarah. The motif leading the narrative is Sarah's beauty. Verse 14 stresses her beauty by adding the adverb "very" in comparison to verse 11. In fact, this scene parallels to the previous scene in many ways. First, the introduction of the time and space of the scene in verse 14a syntactically parallels 11a.

11a וַיְהִי כַּאֲשֶׁר הִקְרִיב לָבוֹא מִצְרָיְמָה

14a וַיְהִי כְּבוֹא אַבְרָם מִצְרָיְמָה

Second, the expression for Sarah's beauty in verse 14 is adopted from 12a. As mentioned above, however, by adding "very" the text subtly enhances the meaning. Third, 14b and 15a use words from 12b and 12c, such as הַמִּצְרִים and יִרְאוּ.

14b וַיִּרְאוּ הַמִּצְרִים אֶת־הָאִשָּׁה

15a וַיִּרְאוּ אֹתָהּ שָׂרֵי פַרְעֹה

12b כִּי־יִרְאוּ אֹתָךְ הַמִּצְרִים

12c וְאָמְרוּ אִשְׁתּוֹ זֹאת

Finally, 16a clearly repeats the expression in 13b.

16a וּלְאַבְרָם הֵיטִיב בַּעֲבוּרָהּ

13b לְמַעַן יִיטַב־לִי בַעֲבוּרֵךְ וְחָיְתָה נַפְשִׁי בִּגְלָלֵךְ:

In addition to this parallelism, the narrative also contains verse 16b, which introduces a subtle development of the storyline. This kind of development appears in the use of "the woman" as well. In verse 11, אִשְׁתּוֹ refers to Abraham's wife, but in verse 14 הָאִשָּׁה simply means "the woman." We can see here that the meaning of "the woman," as a *leitwort*, is changing. Also, we can easily notice a good parallel in the three phrases of verse 15. Each phrase begins with the same grammatical verbal form and ends with the same word (Pharaoh). Also in the middle, the object of the verb indicates Sarah. The change of the verb also expresses the progression of the story (see-praise-take). The verb form in 15c represents the only difference, as the passive form is used. This change is associated with the change of subject. The fact that it would be more natural not to change the subject at this point indicates that the phrasing is meant to stress that the subject has changed. The subject ("the woman") is an impersonal expression referring to Sarah. By using this term, the storyline implies that Sarah is mistreated as an object and that she plays only a passive role.[52]

וַיִּרְאוּ אֹתָהּ שָׂרֵי פַרְעֹה

וַיְהַלְלוּ אֹתָהּ אֶל־פַּרְעֹה

וַתֻּקַּח הָאִשָּׁה בֵּית פַּרְעֹה:

We need to observe the word order first in verse 16. By placement of וּלְאַבְרָם at the beginning causes us to realize that all the benefit described in 16b is especially for Abraham. By repeating the same words used in verse 13, verse 16 also highlights that Abraham's plan has been fulfilled. The story now reaches the climax of its first scene, in which Abraham's plan appears likely to be successful

The *We-X-Qatal* form, followed by the series of the *Wayyiqtol* forms, indicates that verse 16 provides background information, which constitutes the end of the previous unit. Also, 16b lists what Pharaoh provided to Abraham on account of Sarah. Does Abraham's wealth derive from Pharaoh? This narrative implies that Pharaoh enriches Abraham because of his wife, Sarah. However, I am not convinced that Abraham's wealth came from Pharaoh alone.[53] On the one hand, Gen 12:5 indicates that Abraham had already accumulated possessions from Haran. In Gen 13:2 silver and gold in particular are included in Abraham's wealth, yet they are not mentioned in 12:16 and 13:5. With this in mind, Sarna argues that the reference to Abraham's wealth in Gen 12:5 serves to confirm that his wealth does not derive from Pharaoh's gift.[54] The character of the gift is also problematic. Can the Pharaoh's gift be considered a marriage portion? It appears doubtful to me that the wealth is God's blessing. Polzin points out that the wealth itself does

---

52. Waltke, *Genesis*, 214; Wenham, *Genesis 1–15*, 289; Salanga, *Three Stories of the Endangered Wife*, 32.

53. The antecedent of the verb הֵיטִיב in verse 16 is not clear. Wenham suggests that it is impersonal, but not Pharaoh because of the passive form in the previous clause. He therefore translates, "Meanwhile Abram was well treated . . ." Wenham, *Genesis 1–15*, 285; See also, Cassuto, *A Commentary on the Book of Genesis, Part 2*, 354.

54. Sarna, *Genesis*, 90; idem, "The Anticipatory Use of Information," 76–82; Cassuto also observes that the story itself does not indicate that Abraham's wealth was only from Egypt, although it possibly increases Abraham's wealth in cattle. See, Cassuto, *A Commentary on the Book of Genesis, Part 2*, 354–55.

not indicate God's blessing; rather, it needs to be in a certain condition, like connection to progeny. For instance, Ishmael and Esau were very rich, but they were not included in a mainline of the promised seed. In this sense, their wealth is not the same as that of Isaac's.[55]

There are a couple of controversial issues in this passage that cause scholars to argue that the text was written in a later period added to the earlier narrative. First, male servants and female servants are introduced between he-asses and she-asses. Gunkel argues that even though male and female servants are considered as the owner's property, these words might be a later addition because their place disrupts the he-asses and she-asses.[56]

On the other hand, it is possible to understand the order of the text from a different perspective. Waltke argues that the order here is simply following the order of moving in an actual caravan. Since male donkeys have strong sexual drives toward females' scents, this arrangement is necessary in order to separate male and female donkeys by placing male and female servants who can manage the animals in between the two groups.[57] Furthermore, in the light of other occurrences in Genesis, it is natural for us to see the mixed order. For example, Gen 24:35 and 30:43 list male and female servants between animals or silver and gold. We thus do not need to accept the proposal of later addition to account for this ordering of the list. Instead, we recognize that this order faithfully reflects the characters' actual concerns when moving a caravan, or simply reflects their own understanding of servants as their property.

Second, Van Seters thinks the mentions of camels (Gen 12:16, 24:10–64, 30:43, 31:17, 34, 32:7, 15, 37:25) as evidence of anachronism, for while there is some evidence for limited domestication of camels in the third millennium B.C., there is no evidence for their widespread domestication at this time. According to Van Seters, camels were common in the seventh and eighth centuries.[58] William Foxwell Albright also acknowledges that camels were not domesticated before 1200 B.C., so he assumes that

---

55. Polzin, "'The Ancestress of Israel in Danger' in Danger," 88–89.

56. Gunkel and Biddle, *Genesis*, 170. The Samaritan Pentateuch recognizes this issue, so it modifies the text to "צאן ובקר מקנה כבד מאד ועבדים ושפחות וחמרים ואתנות וגמלים." Here, the Samaritan Pentateuch adds "very much livestock" ("מקנה כבד מאד") and puts וחמרים after ושפחות. The LXX, however, follows the MT. The MT is more difficult to read. So, it is not necessary to modify this text; rather, we have alternative interpretations of this.

57. Waltke, *Genesis*, 214; Sarna, *Genesis*, 96; Cassuto, *A Commentary on the Book of Genesis, Part 2*, 355. Cassuto simply mentions that the male and female servants can manage Abraham's possessions.

58. Van Seters, *Abraham in History and Tradition*, 17.

Abraham was using donkeys for the caravan.⁵⁹ Following these conclusions, Sarna offers the following summary: "All available evidence points to the conclusion that the effective domestication of the camel as a widely used beast of burden did not take place before the twelfth century B.C.E., which is a long time after the patriarchal period."⁶⁰ However, as Kenneth A. Kitchen shows, there have been numerous discoveries of camels' remains from Egypt, Byblos, Canaan, and north Syria, and even references to them in Sumerian lexical work.⁶¹ According to Kitchen, the domesticated camel occurs in the area of *Alalaḫ*in eighteenth century B.C. Also, in Egypt camel skulls have been found and dated to 2000–1400 B.C., which is related to the Patriarchal and Moses period.⁶² There is thus no reason to think of the existence of camels in the narratives of the patriarchs as an anachronism. Rather, we need to consider Sarna's idea as a possible solution. Sarna concludes that camels were found originally in Arabia and that the domestication of camels was slow to spread, so in the Patriarchal times only very wealthy people could obtain camels, which they used for the purpose of ornament, rather than for transportation.⁶³

C'. Fulfillment of God's Plan (12:17)

The divine name YHWH appears here for the first and only time in this narrative. YHWH's appearance marks a turning point for the entire story. In the previous scene, Abraham's plan is fulfilled as he predicted except Sarah has been endangered in the house of Pharaoh. YHWH's intervention stands in clear contrast to the previous scene and emphasizes that Abraham's plan is not out of God's control. Finally, YHWH intervenes in the situation and saves both Sarah and Abraham. Paronomasia is used in verse 17 as a stylistic device, using the same verbal root in order to strengthen YHWH's plague on Pharaoh (וַיְנַגַּע יְהוָה אֶת־פַּרְעֹה נְגָעִים גְּדֹלִים).⁶⁴ Significantly, Sarah is now identified as Abraham's wife rather than just "the woman."

---

59. Albright, "Abram the Hebrew," 38; For extended discussion, see William Foxwell Albright, "Historical Framework of Palestinian Archaeology," 12–18.

60. Sarna, *Genesis*, 96.

61. Kitchen, *On the Reliability of the Old Testament*, 338–39; Davis, "The Camel in Biblical Narratives," 141–52; Horowitz. "Sweeter Than Camel's Milk," 1–9; Heide, "The Domestication of the Camel," 331–84.

62. Kitchen, "Camel," 160–61.

63. Sarna, *Genesis*, 96; Speiser, *Genesis*, 90; Waltke, *Genesis*, 215.

64. For the general study and usage of Paronomasia in the Old Testament, see, Glück, "Paronomasia in Biblical Literature," 50–78; Guillaume, "Paronomasia in the Old Testament," 282–96; Casanowicz, "Paronomasia in the Old Testament," 105–67.

YHWH's intervention changes Sarah's status and saves Sarah, Abraham and, ultimately, the promised seed.

We are not sure whether Abraham expects Pharaoh to take Sarah to the Pharaoh's harem at the outset. Since he is about to sojourn in Egypt during the famine, it is more reasonable to infer that Abraham only intends to keep himself safe through the deception, not expecting his wife to be taken away. In verses 14–16, Abraham's plan succeeds. The sequence of the *Wayyiqtol* form stresses the fulfillment of Abraham's plan. The result of the deception, however, is outside his control, and does not follow Abraham's intentions.

At any rate, YHWH radically changes the situation through His intervention, which makes verse 17 the climax of the story. Pharaoh immediately knows the reason for the plague, although the story does not mention how he comes to know it, whether he learns the truth from God, the Egyptian diviners, or their gods.[65] We need to be cautious in attempting to determine the reason for Pharaoh's knowledge based on later narratives. The reason for discovery in the other wife/sister stories is divine intervention (Gen 20) and chance (Gen 26), but there is no clear explanation in this story. We are simply told that YHWH sends a serious plague and Pharaoh at once knows that it is related to Sarah. It is plausible to assume that Pharaoh acknowledges YHWH's intervention because he neither punishes Abraham, who deceived him, nor asks him to return the gifts he provided.

We are also unable to confirm what happened to Sarah in the Pharaoh's harem. Cassuto strongly argues, "Undoubtedly the Bible intends us to understand that these plagues were inflicted on Pharaoh and his house before the king was able to approach the patriarch's wife."[66] However, we must keep in mind what the text says and what the text does not say. The author intentionally omits what happened to Sarah in Pharaoh's harem in the first wife/sister story, whereas the issue is addressed in the second story. We can at least acknowledge that Sarah's sexual intercourse is not a main issue here, though it is in Gen 20. There is no crisis brought upon the promised seed in Gen 12 because we already know that Sarah is barren from Gen 11:30. The question of whether Sarah was defiled by Pharaoh does not affect the storyline itself, particularly in the first wife/sister story.[67] Nevertheless, we need to consider why YHWH punished Pharaoh and his household in

---

65. Gunkel and Biddle, *Genesis*, 171; Koch, *The Growth of the Biblical Tradition*, 123; Petersen, "A Thrice-Told Tale," 37.

66. Cassuto, *A Commentary on the Book of Genesis, Part 2*, 356–57.

67. Turner, *Announcements of Plot in Genesis*, 66; Peleg, "Was the Ancestress of Israel in Danger?," 198–99.

relation to Sarah's status.[68] YHWH clearly sent serious plagues because of Sarah, the wife of Abraham, as a punishment.[69] It is also clear that Pharaoh did not know Sarah's real marital status when he took Sarah as his wife. What, then, is Pharaoh's sin?

In Gen 20:6, God protects the honor of both Sarah and Abimelech. Since Abimelech does not approach Sarah, he is innocent. Of course, God brings diseases to Abimelech and his household to prevent Sarah from any defilement in Story B. By the same token, if Pharaoh had not approached Sarah in Story A, we might find Pharaoh not guilty. Although we must be open to the possibility of YHWH's making the first move in order to protect Sarah from any defilement, as He does in Story B, we must keep in mind that the text does not mention it, so it could only be implied. On the contrary, if we consider three stories from the development of characterization, theme, and plot, YHWH's involvement develops from implicit to explicit as the stories go on. Therefore, we might conclude that Story A does not make the innocence of Pharaoh and Sarah clear. For this reason, we do not need to make an effort to keep Sarah's honor in Story A.[70] Furthermore, verse 19 indicates that Pharaoh takes Sarah as his wife. The Hebrew expression "take her as a wife" is used in a marriage situation (Gen 4:19, 11:29, 20:2, 24:3, 25:20; Exo 6:20–25).[71] This may indicate that Pharaoh takes Sarah through a legal process and may have had a sexual relationship with her.[72] Therefore, although the text itself has no clear mention of what happened to Sarah in

---

68. The BHS suggests that the phrase וְאֶת־בֵּיתוֹ might be added based on the same expression in Gen 20:17. Because the MT, the LXX, and the Samaritan Pentateuch keep this phrase in the text, we do not need to regard it as a later insertion. See Wenham, *Genesis 1–15*, 285.

69. Sarna, *Genesis*, 96; Wenham, *Genesis 1–15*, 290. Wenham argues that the nature of plagues is skin disease. Actually, the term נגע is mostly used for skin disease in Lev 13–14, in which the noun form occurs 61 times. On the other hand, Sarna sees that the nature of plagues might be "temporary sexual impotence induced by some severe inflammation or acute infection of the genital area." Sarna's argument is right in the second wife/sister story in Gen 20, but we cannot confirm the same in Story A. Again, we need to acknowledge the fact that the brevity of the first wife/sister story also leaves this issue unanswered.

70. Peleg, "Was the Ancestress of Israel in Danger?," 206–7. Peleg maintains that if we keep Sarah's honor in Story A, we cannot keep YHWH's honor. If so, YHWH punishes an innocent Pharaoh. However, this is a little conceptual. In reality, God punishes Abimelech in order to prevent any defilement of Sarah's honor in Story B. It is clear from the perspective of the development of characterization that Abimelech places greater value on morality than Pharaoh does.

71. Ibid., 202–5; Seebass, "לָקַח," 19; Salanga, *Three Stories of the Endangered Wife*, 36.

72. Koch, *The Growth of the Biblical Tradition*, 125; Polzin, "'The Ancestress of Israel in Danger' in Danger," 83; Coats, *Genesis with an Introduction to Narrative*, 111.

the house of Pharaoh, we might think about her status in light of Pharaoh's actual punishment and the integrity of God's character.

B'. Pharaoh's Instruction (12:18–20)

Like the second scene (vv. 11–13), this scene consists of Pharaoh's direct speech, during which Abraham, the conversation partner, has no words. Here again, Abraham's silence is closely connected to Sarah's silence in verses 11–13. As Sarah's silence implies her agreement, Abraham's silence also indicates his acknowledgement of his guilt.[73] This scene consists of two parts. The first part contains Pharaoh's three questions (18b–19) following the narrator's introductory statement (18a). The second shows Pharaoh's action (v. 20). The first question that Pharaoh raises begins with the Hebrew expression מַה־זֹּאת. The interrogative pronoun usually denotes exclamations of wonder or indignation; especially with the demonstrative pronoun זֹאת, it emphasizes vividness.[74] In the first question, Pharaoh strongly and vividly expresses his indignation against Abraham.

The second accusation is expressed in לָמָה לֹא־הִגַּדְתָּ לִּי כִּי אִשְׁתְּךָ הִוא. Like מָה, לָמָה expresses a rebuke against someone (cf. Exo 2:20). It is used as a way of introducing an alternative.[75] So, in this second question, Pharaoh develops his accusation against Abraham by adding new information to the given meaning of the first question. Now, Abraham has to answer something else, which is not mentioned in Pharaoh's second accusation.

Whereas the second question is negative, the third question is expressed in a positive way. Since it also adds new information, Pharaoh's three questions are closely connected to each other from a linguistic perspective. The sentences, consisting of only four short words, are emphatic: Pharaoh's anger is clearly stressed: וְעַתָּה הִנֵּה אִשְׁתְּךָ and קַח וָלֵךְ.[76] The first sentence calls for our special attention. Sarah's status is restored when Pharaoh calls her, Abraham's wife. The series of imperatives express what Pharaoh is feeling and his decisive determination to restore Sarah. Most importantly, these two imperatives remind us of the first command of YHWH in chapter 12.[77]

---

73. Wenham, *Genesis 1–15*, 188–89; Sarna, *Genesis*, 97; Cassuto, *A Commentary on the Book of Genesis, Part 2*, 361.

74. *GKC*, § 148 a, b and §137 c; *IBHS*, 18.3.a and b.

75. *IBHS*, 18.3.c.

76. The LXX adds "ἐναντίον σου" ("before you") after "your wife," but the MT and the Samaritan Pentateuch keep the same wording. It is not necessary to add this as the LXX does.

77. Turner, *Announcements of Plot in Genesis*, 106; Kuruvilla, *Genesis*, 167.

v. 1	And YHWH said to Abraham
	Go forth (לֶךְ־לְךָ)
v. 4	And Abraham went
v. 19	And (Pharaoh said to Abraham)
	Take! Go! (קַח וָלֵךְ)
v. 13:1	And Abraham went up

It is interesting to note the fact that Pharaoh only rebukes; he does not act in revenge nor does he try to get back what he has provided to Abraham. Although he expresses his anger very strongly, he does not focus on Abraham's deception, but acknowledges a divine protection over Abraham. So, he decides to remove Abraham from his surroundings.[78] Just as God commanded Abraham to go to the land that He would show him, now Pharaoh commands Abraham to go back to that land. Furthermore, Pharaoh also commands his officers to send Abraham away. At this point, Abraham has no other option but to return to the land of Canaan. In this way, verses 19–20 emphasize the theme of the return to the land.

A'. Abraham's Return: Going up to Canaan (13:1)

Abraham returns to Canaan. Since the brief description is an evident feature in the story, 13:1 leaves the reader with many unanswered questions about subjects such as the condition of the famine in Canaan and how Abraham and Sarah feel and communicate with each other after the event. Simply by repeating the expression in verse 20 (אֹתוֹ וְאֶת־אִשְׁתּוֹ וְאֶת־כָּל־אֲשֶׁר־לוֹ), this verse functions as a recapitulation, so the basic intention of this repetition is to connect verse 1 to verse 20. Genesis 13:1 thus functions as an ending of the whole narrative.

It is important to observe what is added in this verse: Lot is suddenly reintroduced. We have not been told whether Lot went down to Egypt with Abraham.[79] Gunkel argues that this verse referring to Lot is a gloss because even though it is the conclusion of 12:10–20, Lot is not mentioned in Gen

---

78. Cassuto, *A Commentary on the Book of Genesis, Part 2*, 360–61; Wenham, *Genesis 1–15*, 290. Wenham insists that Abraham's deception to Pharaoh deserves the death penalty throughout the Ancient Near East.

79. The LXX includes the phrase "καὶ Λωτ μετ' αὐτοῦ" ("and Lot with him") in the last part of v. 20. According to the LXX, Lot clearly accompanies Abraham to Egypt. This addition assimilates to Gen 13:1, but it is not necessary.

13:1.[80] It is not plausible, however, that the absence of Lot in the narrative of 12:10–20 can confirm his actual absence. As Nicol mentions, his absence in the narrative hardly answers whether or not he was present with Abraham in Egypt.[81] We should instead infer that Abraham brings Lot from his father's house and finally goes into the land of Canaan with him. Apparently, Abraham thinks of Lot as an heir who will inherit God's promise-there is therefore no reason for Abraham to leave Lot behind during his journey. Furthermore, when Abraham and Lot have to be separated, Lot chooses the plain of Jordan because it looks like the land of Egypt. This certainly implies that Lot has experienced the land of Egypt. Based on Gen 13:1 and 13:10, then, we can conclude that Lot accompanied Abraham during the journey to the land of Egypt.

Why, then, does the author not mention Lot in 12:10–20 but choose to mention him in 13:1? First of all, Lot is closely related to the theme of seed. In the first chapters of the Abraham narrative, Lot appears in relation to Abraham's heir. However, 12:10–20 places the focus on the theme of land, though the theme of seed is still in the narrative, so the author intentionally did not include Lot in this particular story. The reason for the reference to Lot in 13:1 is different, however. As mentioned above, 13:1 functions as a conclusion to 12:10–20. What is more, 13:1 creates a connection to the following narrative by introducing the main character of chapter 13, namely Lot. In this regard, as Waltke mentions, 13:1 is a *janus* between the preceding and following narratives. It forms as an *inclusio* with 12:10 and provides a setting for the following narrative.[82]

One more thing we need to consider is the order of the list. Lot is placed after Abraham's possessions in the list. In Gen 11:31, Lot appears between Abraham and Sarah, but in 12:5 he comes after Sarah. Finally, in 13:1, Lot appears after Abraham's possessions. This seems to imply the subtle change of the importance of Lot. Sarna states, "By placing him last in the list, after Abram's possessions, the text hints at a degree of estrangement."[83]

---

80. Gunkel and Biddle, *Genesis*, 172; Westermann, *Genesis 12–36: A Commentary*, 174. However, Westermann thinks that v. 1 is a constituent part of the itinerary (vv. 1–5).

81. Nicol, "Story-Patterning in Genesis," 225.

82. Waltke, *Genesis*, 210n31; Also see Sarna, "The Anticipatory Use of Information," 76–82. Applying to Sarna's notion of the anticipatory use of information, Lot has no important function in the narrative, but he will have important role in the subsequent narrative. Nicol, "Story-Patterning in Genesis," 225.

83. Sarna, *Genesis*, 97.

Type-Scene Analysis

In the previous section, we analyze the linguistic features of the first wife/sister story and deal with the scholarly issues. By definition, type-scene analysis involves repetition of similar stories. The type-scene model allows us to recognize the similarities and variations. Previous studies have mainly focused on figuring out the fixed patterns of scenes. However, I will examine them in terms of the following three areas, which occur throughout the stories: characters, theme, and plot. The analysis of the first wife/sister story (Gen 12:10—13:1) will prove very important as we consider similarities and variations, because the following stories are related to the first both explicitly and implicitly. In this section, therefore, we will focus only on Story A.

Characterization

Characters and their characterizations are important devices to the author because they show his or her intent. No narrative can stand without its characters, and the author is the one who puts textual themes into the mouths of the characters. The author chooses characters and characterizes them in order to make the author's perspective on the story clear. R. Alan Culpepper defines characterization as "the art and techniques by which an author fashions a convincing portrait of a person within a more or less unified piece of writing."[84] If characters and characterizations are an important means of manifesting authorial theme in a narrative, it is worth questioning the reason for the existence of particular characters in the narrative.

E. M. Forster proposed two types of characters: flat and round. These two-dimensional distinctions have been dominant in literary criticism.[85] However, recent scholarly discussions on the types of characters vary. As Alter states, the various references of characters show the authors intention, which is closely related to the narrative's theme. These characteristics include the actions, appearances, gestures, postures, costumes, direct and indirect speeches, inward speeches, feelings, attitudes, and the narrator's statements.[86] It is crucial to analyze the characters throughout each of the wife/sister stories, since their characterizations are repeated by the author.

---

84. Culpepper, *Anatomy of the Fourth Gospel*, 105.

85. Forster, *Aspects of the Novel*, flat character keeps a single quality, whereas round character is more complicate showing multiple traits. See Harvey, *Character and the Novel*, 56, suggests four types: the protagonist, the card, the choric, and the ficelle. Berlin, *Poetics and Interpretation of Biblical Narrative*, 23–24, sees it as three types: full-fledged character, the type, and the agent.

86. Alter, *The Art of Biblical Narrative*, 116–17.

Narrator

We should start with the existence of a narrator in the story. In a narrative, the narrator provides everything we see, hear, and feel.[87] This story begins with the voice of the narrator in verse 10 and ends with the explanation of the narrator in verse 13:1. The narrator in biblical narratives should be regarded as being guided by the Holy Spirit in writing the narratives. For this reason, the narrator is essentially omnipresent and omniscient.[88] The narrator offers the background information that forms the setting of the story, informing readers of the existence of a famine, and highlighting the gravity of the situation in verse 10. As an observer, the narrator explains Abraham's travel toward Egypt in verses 11–13. He freely listens to the private dialogue between Abraham and Sarah. Through direct speech, the narrator lets us know what Abraham thinks, fears, and devises. As the location changes from Canaan to Egypt, the point of view of the narrator also changes. Whereas the narrator sees through Abraham's eyes in verses 11–13, he sees through the eyes of the Egyptians in verses 14–16.[89] The narrator shows how the Egyptians feel when they see Sarah and what they do for Pharaoh, and in verse 16, he exposes the reason why the Egyptians treated Abraham well.

The activity of the narrator is noticeable in verse 17; he again appears to be omniscient. Verse 17 introduces YHWH, the most important character in the story, for the first time. YHWH sends great plagues, and the narrator reveals that the plagues striking the house of Pharaoh are from Him. The narrator even knows YHWH's intention, as demonstrated by the addition of עַל־דְּבַר שָׂרַי אֵשֶׁת אַבְרָם. In verses 18–20, the narrator simply reports the character's feelings, fears, and actions by means of speech, corresponding to the first dialogue (vv. 11–13). Finally, in 13:1, the narrator concludes the story by reporting Abraham's journey to the Negev as an observer.

---

87. Bar-Efrat, *Narrative Art in the Bible*, 13; Berlin, *Poetics and Interpretation of Biblical Narrative*, 44.

88. Bar-Efrat, *Narrative Art in the Bible*, 17–23; Sternberg, *The Poetics of Biblical Narrative*, 84–86; Alter, *The Art of Biblical Narrative*, 155–57; Berlin, *Poetics and Interpretation of Biblical Narrative*, 44. Berlin says, "The biblical narrator is omniscient in that everything is at his disposal; but he selects carefully what he will include and what he will omit. He can survey the scene from a distance, or zoom in for a detailed look at a small part of it. He can follow one character throughout, or hop from the vantage point of one to another."

89. Tolmie, *Narratology and Biblical Narratives*, 29–38. Tolmie would use the term "focalization" than "point of view." According to Tolmie, the movement in a narrative can be perceived through the change of focalized objects without change in narrator. He mainly follows Gerald Genette's argument. Genette, *Narrative Discourse*, 189–94.

As we see, the narrator rules over everything throughout the story. We see what the narrator intends to show, we listen to what he wants us to hear, and we perceive and share perspectives with the narrator, even in the description of YHWH.[90]

Abraham

The first important figure in this narrative is Abraham. We see him everywhere in the story. It is clear that Abraham is a round character who has feeling and opinion, although his character is not fully developed throughout the story. As a round character, Abraham acts dominantly. He makes assumptions about what is going to happen in Egypt and suggests deceiving the Egyptians. He is one of only two characters who speak in the story. As Alter mentions, direct speech is the most important instrument for revealing character and a character's relationships.[91] Through this direct speech, which reveals both the actual words that Abraham says and the unspoken thoughts of Abraham, the author characterizes Abraham.[92]

Before considering the content, it is important to consider the position of Abraham's direct speech. We see the speech at the beginning of the story (vv. 11–13), which requires us to give special attention to it. According to Alter, "In any given narrative event, and especially, at the beginning of any new story, the point at which dialogue first emerges will be worthy of special attention, and in most instances, the initial words spoken by a personage will be revelatory, perhaps more in manner than in matter, constituting an important moment in the exposition of character."[93] In the case of the first wife/sister story, the short narration providing background information of the story is followed by the speech of Abraham.

In his speech, we can discern Abraham's character. First of all, Abraham's main concern is not to save his wife, but his own life. An important motif of Abraham's characterization is fear. He is afraid that the Egyptians may kill him for the sake of his wife, Sarah. His second concern is to be treated well by the Egyptians. Although he has YHWH's promises (12:1–3, 7), from his speech we see that Abraham is clearly afraid for his life. So, the

---

90. For a comparison of the narrator with God, see Sternberg, *The Poetics of Biblical Narrative*, 153–59. The omniscient narrator knows everything as much as God does, in the story, but the narrator goes beyond or parallel to God's viewpoint without challenging its authority (see esp. 154).

91. Alter, *The Art of Biblical Narrative*, 66.

92. Ibid., 68.

93. Ibid., 74–75.

speech itself reveals his unfaithfulness to the promise of YHWH. As a result, in contrast to YHWH's promise regarding the nations, Abraham brings a curse, not a blessing to Pharaoh and his house. On the same token, the text implies that Abraham's enrichment is not a consequence of YHWH's blessing. Though he appears in every verse except 15, Abraham's character does not change over the course of the first wife/sister story. From the outset, he fears, plans to deceive, and puts his deceptive plan into practice when he enters Egypt. Strangely, he does not say a single word when his lie is detected. The author may have intentionally left out what Abraham said in order to keep his character unchanging.

Sarah

Sarah is also presented in every scene, with the exception of verse 10, where the background of the story is explained. The most significant thing to note about Sarah's character in this story is that her voice is not heard. Furthermore, most of the time she is not called by her own name but referred to as "the woman" or "wife," which sets her in relation to someone else. This is striking when we consider the fact that Sarah has a central role in the story. Generally speaking, a person who remains unknown in biblical narratives is seen as non-prominent or downplayed.[94]

It is important to recognize that Sarah has no voice here. Even in some situations where she could have spoken up, Sarah does not speak. We would naturally expect her to say something when Abraham asks her to call herself his sister, or when she is taken to the house of Pharaoh, but in these situations, she is silent. Here we need to recognize that the absence of speech is a means of characterization. Alter states, "When someone's silence is actually isolated for narration, we may infer that the refusal or avoidance of speech is itself a significant link in the concatenation of the plot."[95] We may therefore conclude that, although Sarah plays a central role in this story, she plays a passive role as a flat character. We need to keep in mind, however, that she is not always passive in the Abraham narrative. Elsewhere she actively raises issues and argues with Abraham, and she requires him to take action in the matter of Hagar (Gen 16 and 21). The fact that she is silent here, then, is a result of characterization by the author. By keeping her nameless and voiceless in most cases, the author gives us the impression that she is being manipulated by others, including her husband, and that her social location is always dependent on others.

94. Reinhartz, *"Why Ask My Name?,"* 5; Revell, *The Designation of the Individual*, 51.
95. Alter, *The Art of Biblical Narrative*, 79.

Pharaoh

Abraham's fear originated with his assumption that Pharaoh and the Egyptians might be evil. Just as Abraham expects, Pharaoh takes Sarah into his house as a wife. It is clear, however, that this is not Pharaoh's fault, because he is told that Sarah is a sister to Abraham. From Pharaoh's perspective, taking Sarah as a wife is a natural process. He even gives great gifts to Abraham on account of Sarah. The crisis comes not because of Pharaoh's sin, but because of Abraham's deception. It is clear to see, therefore, that Pharaoh is in a higher moral position than Abraham. What is more, it is significant that Pharaoh's speech serves as the counterpart to Abraham's speech in verses 11-13. As mentioned, speech is a major part of plot and of characterization of this story. Through a person's speech, we can discern his character. Pharaoh's speech shows us that Abraham's fear is not true, or at least exaggerated.

Pharaoh's repeated accusations emphasize his innocence and clearly show that he would not have taken Sarah if he had known that she was the wife of another man. This implies that Pharaoh follows a higher moral standard than Abraham, at least at this point. Nevertheless, the text indicates that Pharaoh and his house fell under God's punishment. Although Pharaoh did not have access to the full truth of Sarah's status, his action in taking her constitutes mistreatment of Abraham. As YHWH promised earlier, blessing and curses will be given to the nations according to their relationship with Abraham (Gen 12:3). In this regard, by declaring great plagues on Pharaoh and his house, the author confirms YHWH's faithfulness to His promises.

YHWH

If we acknowledge that the book of Genesis is a great Theo-Drama, it is natural to see YHWH as the central character of the entire narrative of Genesis. Although we feel that YHWH is almost absent from the first wife/sister story, YHWH plays the central role in the story. It is noteworthy that God's roles differ significantly between 12:1-9 and 12:10—13:1. In 12:1-9, God initiates, speaks actively, and makes a plan for the future, while God neither speaks nor acts directly in Gen 12:10—13:1. God only acts once in this passage, using the narrator's voice (v. 17).[96] Since there is no clear reference to the character of God, we need to infer God's character from the text. Even though YHWH does not rebuke or confirm Abraham's departure from the Promised Land, the reduction of his initiative implies that

---

96. Humphreys, *The Character of God in the Book of Genesis*, 86-87.

Abraham's departure does not please YHWH. The role of YHWH is the smallest of all the characters in this story, but the appearance of YHWH makes the story's turning point of the story. Richard L. Pratt provides a useful chart showing the appearances of each character in the story. This chart illustrates how all the characters are recalled to the stage, centered around YHWH's appearance. [97]

Table 4: Occurrence of the Characters in Story A

Genesis 12	10	11	12	13	14	15	16	17	18	19	20
Abraham	x	x	x	x		x		x	x	x	x
Sarah		x	x	x	x			x	x	x	x
Officials			(x)	(x)	x			x			x
Pharaoh			(x)	(x)	x			x	x	x	x
Possessions							x				x
YHWH								x			

In this regard, although it is apparent that YHWH reduces his appearance in this story and is therefore little mentioned, YHWH is the most important character, who reverses the situation in one sweep.

Minor Characters

Minor characters also play a part in the plot of this story. Minor characters usually play a secondary role in relation to the major characters, contributing to the background of the main storyline and assisting the main characters.[98] In this story, the Egyptians and Lot can be considered minor characters. The Egyptians, first, appear in Abraham's speech. They are depicted as evil characters in Abraham's mind, but this is not actually true. More specifically, the Egyptians are called officials (v. 15). The narrator both describes how they see Sarah's beauty and gives them their own voice. Surely, they play the role of a mediator, introducing Sarah to Pharaoh. So, although they are very much secondary, these minor characters play an important role in the development of the plot.

---

97. Pratt, "Pictures, Windows, and Mirrors," 161–62.
98. Bar-Efrat, *Narrative Art in the Bible*, 86–88.

The male servants and female servants observed in v. 16 also have no role in the narrative plot. We might assume, however, that Hagar—who will play a crucial role later in the narratives—might be among them.

Finally, Lot is totally absent until the entire story ends. Compared to his importance within the first chapters of the Abraham narrative, his absence here is striking. The author intentionally makes no reference to Lot while the narrative moves to the area of Egypt, but when Abraham comes back to the land of Canaan, Lot appears again. His appearance does not actually serve this story itself but helps prepare for the next story. As a character, his role in this narrative is only to connect the wife/sister story to the following narrative.

Themes

The author develops his thematic intentions through characterization, so we need to watch for the appearance of themes in the various speeches and actions of the characters. Since one of the most important aspects of type-scene analysis is the examination of repetitions and variations in the stories, examining the continuity and discontinuity of themes is crucial for an understanding of the whole picture of each story and even the three wife/sister stories, as well. Particularly, type-scene creates meaning without explicitly stating such meaning. The meaning in the type scene model appears between the lines, not within them.

As mentioned earlier, the major themes of the entire book of Genesis-seed, land, and blessings-are seen in YHWH's promises to Abraham (Gen 12:1–3). These themes occur in the almost every narrative throughout Genesis including the wife/sister stories. We can clearly see these three themes in each wife/sister story, but the weight of themes is different within each story. Polzin, however, sees that these three stories share the same theme throughout. He states,

> All three versions of our story help to develop the same theme along the larger story-line of the narrative. This theme may be stated in two ways, both amounting to the same thing: "When in fact is a man blessed by God?" or "how does one know that a certain man is blessed by God?" The answer of our three stories is, "when a man in fact correctly possesses both progeny and wealth."[99]

---

99. Polzin, "'The Ancestress of Israel in Danger' in Danger," 95; Biddle, "The 'Endangered Ancestress' and Blessing for the Nations," 602–4. Biddle sees the theme of the three stories as the promise of blessing to the nations. However, although it appears in

In this regard, although he examines the relationship between wealth, progeny, and blessing, Polzin focuses on "ill-begotten wealth" concerning the theme of the first wife/sister story.[100]

David J. A. Clines points out that the dominant element of the patriarchal narratives is posterity. He summarizes this theme through the following questions: "[w]ill there be even one son, let alone a posterity?" "Once the son is born, will he survive to produce a posterity?"[101] Clines argues that the three wife/sister stories should be read with these questions in mind. The other themes function secondarily. However, since each story is set within a different context, the three stories should play different roles within their own surrounding context.[102]

Seed

The theme of seed is the most prominent theme in the entire book of Genesis. It plays an especially central role in the patriarchal narratives, which means we can see it in every moment of these stories—including, naturally, the first wife/sister story. Verse 17 clearly states that YHWH sent serious plagues on account of Sarah. Broadly speaking, the crisis of Sarah is related to that of the seed, because she is the one who will deliver the promised seed. However, as mentioned above, when we look at the scene according to the text so far, there is no reason to think of a crisis of the seed in Gen 12:10—13:1.[103] Even though Abraham has YHWH's promise from 12:1-3 and 7, YHWH does not designate the woman who will deliver the seed until Gen 17:15-19. For this reason, after waiting for ten years Abraham and Sarah try to fulfill the promise of the seed through a surrogate, Hagar (Gen 16:1-3). It is clear that Abraham is confident in Ishmael as his seed—he laughs in his mind when God reveals His plan to give Abraham a son through Sarah and says, "if only Ishmael might live under your blessing" (Gen 17:17-18). As we know, Gen 11:30 tells us that Sarah is barren. It is natural, then, to think that Abraham does not understand how YHWH will fulfill His promise of the seed through Sarah, his wife.

---

the stories, it is not plausible to see all the stories only in terms of the blessing theme.

100. Polzin, "'The Ancestress of Israel in Danger' in Danger," 96; Patterson, "The Righteousness and Survival of the Seed," 214-15. Patterson argues that the first wife/sister story also should be read with the question of Abraham's seed.

101. Clines, *The Theme of the Pentateuch*, 48.

102. Waltke, *Genesis*, 211-12.

103. See chapter 4, n33.

Still considering the theme of the seed, we can also look at the scene in a different perspective. It is clear that Abraham, who believes in YHWH's promises, keeps the promises in mind through every moment of the Abraham narrative. Because he does not think of Sarah as a part of the fulfillment of the promised seed, he plots the deception using Sarah. In Abraham's mind, putting Sarah in crisis is a way to protect both himself and Lot, who is a candidate of the seed, from the crisis of the seed.[104]

Lastly, the absence of Lot in this story helps us see that the seed is not the primary theme here. There is no doubt that for Abraham, Lot is the most strongly supported candidate. In the subsequent narratives in chapters 13 and 14, Lot is a very important character and plays a specific role in relation to Abraham. According to 13:10, when Lot sees the whole plain of the Jordan from which to choose his land, he feels that the land he decides upon is like the garden of YHWH and like the land of Egypt. Therefore, we may infer that Lot was in Egypt with Abraham. However, the author gives him no role in 12:10—13:1. It seems to me that the author intentionally avoids referring to Lot because the seed is not the main focus of the story. Therefore, we can conclude that while the theme of the seed is present in this story, and while it is primary and ubiquitous in the entire book of Genesis, the prominent issue in Story A is not that of the seed.

Blessings

The theme of blessing, like that of the seed, is not prominent until chapter 14, even though it is very important in the larger story. YHWH promises blessing to Abraham, commands him to be a blessing, and confirms that all peoples on earth will be blessed through him (12:2–3). All nations will

---

104. Turner, *Announcements of Plot in Genesis*, 68–70. Turner observes that in this way we can understand the event in Gen 14, in which Abraham, who put Sarah in risk for the sake of his own life in Egypt, would risk his life for Lot. Therefore, we may conclude that Abraham is always thinking of the seed issue in Gen 12 and throughout the whole Abraham narrative. For him, family solidarity cannot satisfactorily explain Abraham's participation in the international war in Gen 14, when we compare to the first wife/sister story. Here Turner disagrees with Sarna and Westermann. Clines, "The Ancestor in Danger," 69–70; Sarna, *Genesis*, 108, 379–80; Westermann, *Genesis 12–36*, 199; Sweeney, "Form Criticism," 28–29. Even Sweeney raises the following question: "Will their descendants be Egyptian, whether born to Sarah or to Abraham?" The first wife/sister story answers this question but this is not the case at this point. Similarly Alexander does not distinguish Story A from Story B, so that he concludes, "12:10—13:1 recounts how the birth of an heir to Abraham is placed in jeopardy by Pharaoh's abduction of Sarah." However, this is not the case so far. See Alexander, "A Literary Analysis of the Abraham Narrative in Genesis," 20–21.

be blessed or cursed based on how they treat Abraham (v.3). In Story A, however, Abraham does not seem to be a blessing. Even though Pharaoh does display a higher moral character than Abraham expected, Abraham's deception provokes serious plagues onto the house of Pharaoh. Walter Brueggemann points out:

> When Abraham acts faithlessly, as he has obviously done, curse is released in the world. The faith and/or faithlessness of Israel matters not only to Israel. It is decisive for the nations. In this strange way, Israel has the capacity to impact the affairs of nations. That is anticipated in the programmatic promise of 12:3b and now demonstrated in this narrative.[105]

As Polzin observes, Abraham's enrichment by Pharaoh in Egypt does not indicate the result of YHWH's blessing.[106] Wealth itself may not be evidence of blessing in the biblical narratives; it should be evaluated in context. In terms of the blessing theme, we can conclude that Abraham clearly recognizes that the blessing of the nations is directly related to their treatment of Abraham and his family. By deceiving Pharaoh and his family, Abraham conveys not his blessing, but a curse.

Land

The call of Abraham begins with a call to the new land that YHWH will show him (Gen 12:1), and the first wife/sister story ends with Abraham returning to the Promised Land. In 12:7, YHWH promises "this land" to Abraham's seed, but an unforeseen event takes place in "the land"—there is a severe famine. The possible questions raised in Abraham's mind include: Is this land really the Promised Land? Can I possess this barren land?

We must begin by acknowledging that the reference to famine in the land is basically a premise for a crisis of the land. As McKeown comments, "famine is incompatible with the promise that Abram would be blessed in the land that Yahweh would show him."[107] What is Abraham to do in this unexpected situation? He has to choose whether or not to stay in the land, and under the pressure of the severe famine, Abraham unfortunately decides to depart from it. Abraham's departure introduces more tension to

---

105. Brueggemann, *Genesis*, 128–29; McKeown, *Genesis*, 82–83; McKeown, "Blessings and Curses," 83–87.

106. Polzin, "'The Ancestress of Israel in Danger' in Danger," 88–89. See, n53 in chapter 4.

107. McKeown, *Genesis*, 80. On the same basis, Gen 20 does not mention famine, because the second wife/sister story is not concerned with the crisis of the land.

the promise of the land. In this regard, it is worthwhile to note Waltke's observation that "the three scenes, which transcend the acts of Genesis, are also linked thematically. Viewed as a unity they represent a triple threat to the holy seed. However, since they are isolated from one another, within each act they function differently. In this act, Scene 2 is the first of three scenes of conflict related to the issue of land."[108]

As we have observed, there is a strong connection between Pharaoh and YHWH's commands. In 12:1, YHWH commands Abraham to go into the land that He will show to him. The expression is highlighted (לֶךְ־לְךָ). Pharaoh's command in verse 19 is expressed in very simple words (קַח וָלֵךְ), which are stressed as well. So, Pharaoh's command reminds us of YHWH's original command to Abraham. Pharaoh expels Abraham from Egypt, commanding his officers to escort Abraham away from Egypt and into the land of Canaan, the Promised Land. From this textual analysis, we can conclude that the first wife/sister story is mainly wrapped up in the theme of the land: the crisis within the story is about the land. By departing from the Promised Land, Abraham and his family are put in danger. Faithful YHWH, however, removes this danger from Abraham by causing Pharaoh to expel Abraham from Egypt and by allowing Abraham to go back to the land.

As the central theme in the first wife/sister story, the theme of the land is also closely connected to the surrounding narratives. First, there is a clear geographical connection between chapters 12 and 13. In order to highlight the return to the land, 13:1 refers to the same place mentioned in the last scene before Abraham's departure from the land (12:9). By connecting Negev to Negev, the text implies that the story restores itself to its original point.[109] Furthermore, we should observe that there is a clear development of the land theme throughout chapters 12 to 14. All the stories in chapters 12 and 13 are about the land. Gen 12:7 indicates that "this land" will be given to the seed of Abraham. The separation of Abraham and Lot is also related to the land, because after their separation YHWH promises land directly to Abraham and declares that He will give all the land he sees and walks on to Abraham and his descendants (Gen 13:14–18). We should take note of this development of the land theme: although Abraham stays in the land of Canaan in Gen 12, the promise of the land in Gen 13 is to be more specific.

In conclusion, according to this analysis, we can confidently conclude that (1) the three wife/sister stories share important themes, (2) since each

---

108. Waltke, *Genesis*, 211–12.

109. DeRoche, "The Dynamics of Promise," 130–32. For the chiastic structure, see the textlinguistic analysis provided above.

story is located within a different narrative situation, each story should contain its own dominant theme, and (3) from this thematic analysis, the first wife/sister story is mainly about the crisis and the restoration of the Promised Land. Having established the characterizations and themes in the story, now we can analyze the plot of the story.

Plot

In the previous sections, we analyzed characterization and themes. Now, in order to complete our analysis of the story, we must consider the plot. As a type-scene, the wife/sister stories as a type-scene contain similar plot progressions. As his first principle of poetics, Aristotle asserted that a story should have a plot consisting of an arrangement of a beginning, a middle, and an end. So, well-organized stories should have these elements.[110] A story is well organized and must function as a whole. If any part of the whole is displaced or removed, the story will become something different.[111] As for the structure of biblical narratives, Tremper Longman III suggests a more complex analysis and provides a helpful diagram of one plot.[112] A basic plot-line typically moves toward its climax from conflict to resolution. Almost every story has its own plot, including the beginning, the conflict generated, the resolution, and the conclusion.[113]

Beginning

The setting provides a temporal and spatial background behind the characters featured in the narrative. Two important causes of narrative crisis are introduced. First, there is severe famine (v. 10), which causes Abraham and his family to go down to Egypt. This means that Abraham might be exposed to an unknown hostile situation. Second, Abraham thinks that his life may be endangered in Egypt because of his wife, Sarah, who is extraordinarily beautiful. While Sarah does not actually speak within the passage, the dialogue in Gen 12:11–13 introduces Abraham's voice. Abraham's plan is (1) to present the relationship between himself and Sarah as one of siblings, (2) to

---

110. Aristotle, *Poetics*, 30.
111. Ibid., 31–32.
112. Longman III, *Literary Apporaches to Biblical Interpretation*, 92–93.
113. Ibid.; Bar-Efrat, *Narrative Art in the Bible*, 93–94; Coats, *Genesis*, 110–12. Coats divides the plot of Gen 12:10—13:1 into four categories like exposition, complication, resolution, and conclusion.

be well treated by the Egyptians for the sake of Sarah, his wife, and finally, and (3) to preserve his life.

Middle

In the beginning of the middle section of the plot, the tension suggested at the start of the story is increasing. At first, events occur just as Abraham had expected. The Egyptians praise Sarah's extraordinary beauty to Pharaoh, and for her sake do well to Abraham. However, the story is beyond Abraham's expectation. Sarah is taken to the house of Pharaoh as his wife. Even though Abraham becomes richer, Sarah is endangered in the foreign land: Sarah is taken, and Abraham can do nothing but let her go.

At the end of the middle part of the plot, resolution comes from YHWH, not from Abraham. The text itself does not inform the reader how Pharaoh came to know the identity of Sarah, but it is clear that YHWH did something to Pharaoh and his house and that Pharaoh understood what was going on. So, the story comes to a dramatic turning point with the intervention of YHWH in verse 17. YHWH sends great plagues to Pharaoh's house because of Pharaoh's sin of adultery, and Pharaoh begins to fix the problem. First, he summons Abraham and asks a series of accusatory questions. He then restores Sarah to her real husband, Abraham. Again, Sarah becomes Abraham's wife after being Pharaoh's. Finally, Pharaoh orders the officials to expel Abraham from the land of Egypt. The intervention of YHWH changes everything and restores Abraham and Sarah to the original place that YHWH has promised.

End

The story comes to a conclusion by reporting Abraham's return to the land of Canaan, even though it takes the form of an expulsion by Pharaoh. The crisis and tension established in the beginning of the plot have been removed.

The plotline of Story A can be captured as follows:[114]

---

114. I am indebted to Tremper Longman and Sydney Greidanus for this diagram. Longman III, *Literary Approaches to Biblical Interpretation*, 92; Greidanus, *Preaching Christ from Genesis*.

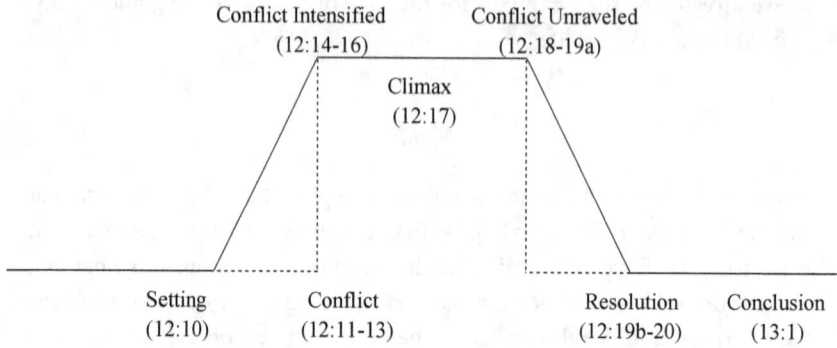

Figure 2: The Plotline of Story A.

Conclusion

In this chapter, we examined the first wife/sister story in Gen 12:10—13:1. Adopting a textlinguistic point of view after deciding the extent of the passage, we examined the story's broad contextual function within the surrounding narratives, its textual structure, and the textual meaning of its small literary units. The literary place of the story fits the surrounding stories in terms of linguistic indicators such as structure, key words, and thematic progressions. From a type-scene perspective, we focused on the three categories of characterization, theme, and plot, seeking to discover how these three elements function within the story. This approach differs from that of previous scholarly discussions of the type-scene, in which scholars tended to focus on the similar form of the wife/sister stories.

An important premise of this study is to study the text itself "so far." The characters in this story do not know about chapters 20 and 26, so we need to limit our view to what, from their perspectives, had already happened. When we come to Gen 20 and 26, however, this first story will be crucial to our understanding, because the author develops the plot of each story in relation to previous ones. Because of its relationship to the other stories, the first wife/sister story is briefly described, leaving many unanswered questions. With respect to the ambiguity in the story, we will need to investigate how these unanswered questions work together in the following stories and why the author creates these kinds of ungratified curiosity. In the following two chapters, we will examine how the next stories are related to the previous ones, how they are dissimilar from one another, how they function differently within their own literary contexts, and how they progress through type-scene variation.

CHAPTER THREE

The Second Wife/Sister Story

(Genesis 20:1–18)

THE SECOND WIFE/SISTER STORY (Story B) appears in Gen 20:1–18. In this narrative, Abraham deceives Abimelech, the king of Gerar, by saying that Sarah is actually his sister. This situation is perplexing because in Story B, unlike Story A, Sarah is well advanced in years and her age of childbearing has already passed (Gen 18:11). Furthermore, according to the Word of the LORD (Gen 18:10), she might be pregnant, and will give birth in less than a year. These background situations raise the necessity of a closer examination of Story B.

In the previous chapter, we examined Story A (Gen 12:10—13:1). From the viewpoint of literary type-scenes, Story B should be read in relation to Story A. The purposes of this chapter, therefore, are to analyze Story B from the textlinguistic point of view and to develop a better understanding of Story B, including the whole wife/sister story, by investigating textual similarities and variations through type-scene analysis.

Delimitation of the Discourse Unit

Compared to the wife/sister stories in Gen 12 and 26, there is considerable agreement among scholars on the extent of Story B. Gen 20:1 starts with the *Wayyiqtol*. The *Wayyiqtol* mainly expresses a sequence, yet it seems that 20:1a does not follow the previous clause. There are some important distinctions between Story B and the previous chapters: most importantly, Story B introduces a totally new time and space. In this case, then, the *Wayyiqtol* may function as an initial clause.[1] The use of the *We-X-Qatal* form also makes it clear that Gen 21:1 marks the beginning of a new story. The story itself contains different episodes as well as a different time and place from

---

1. Heimerdinger, *Topic, Focus, and Foreground*, 156–57. "This example shows that a vayyiqtol clause may also be used as the initial clause in a new section, reintroducing a semi-active referent."

the previous narrative. Therefore, regarding the extent of Story B, we can easily define the extent of Story B as Gen 20:1–18.

Some scholars consider Story B along with Gen 21.[2] Looking at chapters 20 and 21 together provides additional insight into their relationship to Gen 26. If we compare chapters 20–21 with 26, we see that it is not only the wife/sister stories that are connected to each other, but the other stories as well. The following elements appear in both places: the wife/sister story, Abimelech and Phicol, dispute over the well, treaty, and naming Beersheba. Furthermore, we see the expression, וַיָּגָר בִּגְרָר in 20:1c, which is stylistically paronomasia, and the expression, וַיָּגָר בְּאֶרֶץ in 21:34a. It appears that the word "sojourn" forms an envelope for chapters 20 and 21. Therefore, although Story B is confined to Gen 20:1–18, we must understand it in relation to the subsequent stories in Gen 21.

Generally speaking, source critics assign Gen 20 to the E source, which has its first appearance in the book of Genesis. According to this theory, Gen 20 is the beginning of the E source because we do not know where Abraham and Sarah came from.[3] Scholars also assign 1a to the work of redactor of JE. Furthermore, the geographical information is repeated in 1b and 1c, so these scholars suggest that ישׁב and גור denote two different sources.[4]

Verse 18 is more problematic in this regard. Because the divine name YHWH, considered strong evidence of the J source, is used, source critical scholars tend to conclude that verse 18 does not originally belong in Gen 20.[5] As Alexander points out, however, different names do not automatically indicate the presence of different sources; to assume that they do represents a "purely mechanical application," of source critical method.[6] Clearly the two different divine names are interchangeable and can be used differently in different contexts. While YHWH is a personal name, Elohim is a common name. In Gen 20 the personal name, YHWH, would not be used in conversation with the foreign ruler.[7] Similarly, the serpent in Gen 3 only

---

2. Brueggemann, *Genesis*; Sarna, *Genesis*; Walton, *Genesis*.

3. Friedman, *The Bible with Sources Revealed*, 61. Scholars have different positions on the source issues of the three wife/sister stories. See Introduction for more details.

4. Westermann, *Genesis 12–36*, 320–21; Speiser, *Genesis*, 148; Wagner, "Literary Analysis of Gen 12–36," 72–73.

5. Van Seters, *Abraham in History and Tradition*, 173; Wagner, "Literary Analysis of Gen 12–36," 73–74; Westermann, *Genesis 12–36*, 328. The Samaritan Pentateuch reads "God" instead of "YHWH," while the MT, the LXX, and Targums keep "the LORD."

6. Alexander, *Abraham in the Negev*, 91.

7. Ibid., 92–93; Whybray, *The Making of the Pentateuch*, 67, who argues, "God is called sometimes Yahweh and sometimes Elohim, as though the two names were interchangeable. These are not passages where a non-Yahwist is speaking (as in Exod. 18.13–23), nor is Elohim used descriptively: it is used as a name of God"; Cassuto, *The*

uses the common name, Elohim, because the author does not want to put the personal name, YHWH, in the mouth of the serpent.

We should also recognize that the two divine names are occasionally used in the same narrative unit. For example, in Gen 4:25–26, Elohim and YHWH appear in the same context. Verse 25 uses with the name Elohim: "Adam had relations with his wife again; and she gave birth to a son, and named him Seth, for, she said, 'God has appointed me another offspring in place of Abel, for Cain killed him.'" Right after this, however, verse 26 reads with the name of YHWH: "To Seth, to him also a son was born; and he called his name Enosh. Then men began to call upon the name of YHWH (NIV)." Here, we can see that divine names can be used interchangeably. In the Abraham narrative, the two different divine names occur in a same unit in a similar way. Genesis 20–22, which is generally assigned to the E source, contains the personal name, YHWH, in Gen 20:18; 21:1, and 21:33. Alexander observes,

> While the author of Abraham narrative is reluctant to associate the divine name Yahweh with those outside of the chosen line, he is prepared to insert the epithet Yahweh at the beginning and conclusion of episodes, which predominantly use the name Elohim (e.g., 17:1; 20:18; 21:1; 21:33). In this way he leaves the reader in no doubt that Elohim is none other than Yahweh.[8]

Therefore, when determining the extent of Story B, we have no need to eliminate verse 1 or verse 18.

Textlinguistic Analysis

From the above analysis, we conclude that the extent of Story B can be limited to Gen 20:1–18. We must now examine the text from a textlinguistic approach.

Story B within the Surrounding Narratives

In terms of its relationship with the surrounding narratives, Story B has two important features. First, it is usually assigned to the E source, whereas chapters 18–19 are assigned to the J source. Second, Story B shares its motif with the other two wife/sister stories (12:10—13:1; 26:1–11). For

Documentary Hypothesis, 40.
   8. Alexander, *Abraham in the Negev*, 100.

these reasons, scholars tend to view Story B as only loosely connected with its context.

It is necessary, however, to look at the unique features of each wife/sister story by observing it in its own surrounding context. In fact, Story B and its context share many similarities in terms vocabulary, theme, and narrative pattern.[9] For example, the story pattern of the Sodom narrative in chapters 18 and 19 is similar to that of Story B. First, both stories are similar in the ways in which they treat foreigners, as well as sexual issues. In the Sodom narrative, Lot receives the angels, who are foreigners, into his house (19:1); in Story B, Abimelech receives Abraham and Sarah into his land (20:1-2). Second, in both stories, the major crisis is related to women and sexual desire. In the Sodom narrative, Lot provides his own daughters to the angry people of Sodom in order to protect his male guests. Similarly, in Story B Abraham provides Sarah to Abimelech in order to keep his own life. So, both stories are about men who hand over women in order to save male lives. Third, there is a prayer theme in both stories, in which Abraham prays for Sodom (18:23-33) and Abimelech (20:17-18). Through this intercessory prayer, both stories reveal Abraham as a prophet (20:7). Fourth, both stories contain the theme of judgment by God. In the Sodom story, YHWH actually destroys Sodom and Gomorrah, whereas in Story B, God offers a warning by sending diseases to Abimelech and his land. Fifth and most importantly, both stories concern the crucial concept of righteousness. In fact, Abraham's prayer in 18:25 and Abimelech's speech in 20:4 convey similar ideas. Abraham and Abimelech raise questions about God's righteousness and His ability to protect righteous people. So, here we see the important theme of God bringing righteousness and justice (18:19; 20:6).[10]

Above all, we need to observe 20:1a, "וַיִּסַּע מִשָּׁם אַבְרָהָם אַרְצָה הַנֶּגֶב." Linguistically speaking, the word, מִשָּׁם, clearly serves as a device to connect Story B to the previous story. Although it is hard to clarify the exact location, the word "there" presumes that the readers already know the place. For all these reasons, we can confidently conclude that Story B is closely connected to the previous stories. Moreover, Story B takes into account the events of the previous stories.[11]

Finally, we must observe the connection of Story B to the subsequent stories. Gen 21:1-21 is connected not to Story B, but to Gen 16; but Gen

---

9. Hamilton, *The Book of Genesis 18-50*, 58.

10. See, Mathews, *Genesis 11:27—50:26*, 246-49; Hamilton, *The Book of Genesis 18-50*, 58-59; Sykes, "Patterns in Genesis," 97-99.

11. In this regard, the Documentary Hypothesis should be reconsidered. In this passage, at least, separating sources is untenable. See, Alexander, *Abraham in the Negev*, 48-50.

21:22–34 is clearly connected to Story B. Genesis 21:22 begins with the words "at that time," and the character Abimelech presents himself again. This presupposes that the readers already know Gen 20:1. More importantly, geographical indications in 20:1 and 21:34 function as an envelope for the whole story of Gen 20–21. Matthews argues that the mention of Abraham's sojourn in the beginning and conclusion serves to bind Gen 20 and 21 as a whole.[12] We may also note that in this covenantal treaty, Abimelech surprisingly asks Abraham not to deal falsely with him. This reminds the reader of Abraham's deception in Story B.[13] Based on this observation, it is clear that Gen 20 and 21 are closely connected to each other.

In terms of structure, Gen 20:1–18 and 21:22–34, intended to be understood together, frame the story of Isaac's birth (Gen 21:1–21). In this regard, Mathews observes that these two Abraham-Abimelech accounts function as bookends to the story of the birth of Isaac.[14] If we follow the natural flow of stories from chapter 17 to 21, the theme of the promise-fulfillment of the seed is dominant in Gen 21:1–11. Story B enhances this theme by demonstrating how God protects His promise of the seed. It is natural to expect the birth narrative after God's promise of seed (Gen 18). Story B, however, is located between the birth narratives. Through this arrangement, the author underscores the crisis of the promise of God.

Here, again, we see the theme of God's faithfulness and humankind's unfaithfulness. According to Waltke, "By revealing Abraham's weaknesses in the midst of these significant events, the narrator captures the magnitude of Abraham's obedience and also inspires the readers' own faith struggles. The disclosure of Abraham's failures also confirms God's sovereignty and power."[15] Although he had surely heard that the promise of seed would be fulfilled in about a year's time, Abraham becomes a deceiver in Story B. Because of this, he brings another threat to the promise of seed. Although Abraham was unfaithful to God's promise, God shows His faithfulness through Isaac's birth narrative. Afterwards Abraham recovers his role as one who is to be blessed and to be a blessing to the nations in both Story B and Gen 21:22–34. In Story B, Abraham prays for Abimelech and his household to recover from the plague; in Gen 21:22–34 Abraham makes a covenant with Abimelech, who acknowledges God's presence with Abraham and asks Abraham to act kindly.

---

12. Mathews, *Genesis 11:27—50:26*, 275.

13. Wenham, *Genesis 16–50*, 187. As Wenham notes, there are also significant similarities between Genesis 20–21 and Genesis 26. We will deal with this issue in chapter 4.

14. Mathews, *Genesis 11:27—50:26*, 275.

15. Waltke, *Genesis*, 284.

For all these reasons, we can conclude that Story B is closely connected to Gen 18–19 and Gen 21 in terms of vocabulary, theme, and the flow of the storyline. This means that—contrary to the opinion of critics who argue that Story B fits only loosely in its current place—Story B actually functions well in its present location and should be understood in light of the context before and after.

Structure

We have examined the place of Story B within the surrounding narratives. Through this, we have argued that Story B is well-placed within its current context and should be understood in relation to the surrounding stories. We are now ready to investigate the structure of Story B.

One of the most important tasks in discerning the literary structure of Story B is to distinguish direct speech from the narrator's voice. We clearly see the narrator in verses 1–2, 8, 14, and 17–18, where the author recounts the development of the event in the form of narration. Amid the narrations, there are three dialogues between God, Abimelech, and Abraham. Observing these dialogues, Peter Weimar proposes the following structure:[16]

Exposition (20,1.2): Abraham-Abimelek

   I. Szene (20, 3–7): Elohim-Abimelek

      1. Rede Elohims (im Traum) (20, 3. 4a)

      2. Rede Abimeleks (an Elohim) (20, 4b.5)

      3. Rede Elohims (im Traum) (20,6.7)

   II. Szene (20, 8.9a. 10–12): Abimelek-Diener-Abraham

      1. Handlung (+Rede) Abimeleks (Diener) (20.8)

      2. Rede(n) Abimeleks (an Abraham) (20,9a. 10)

      3. Rede Abrahams (an Abimelek) (20,11. 12)

   III. Szene (20, 14–18): Abimelek-Abraham-Sara

      1. Handlung Abimeleks (Abraham) (20,14)

      2. Reden Abimeleks (an Abraham und Sara) (20,14)

---

16. Weimar, *Untersuchungen Zur Redaktionsgeschichte Des Pentateuch*, 70–72; also see, Brueggemann, *Genesis*, 177–78.

3. Handlung (Fürbitte Abrahams+ Heilung durch Elohim
(20, 17. 18)

Other scholars, however, tend to divide the story into two major parts. Mathews argues that the story consists of two main scenes, of which one takes place at night in a dream, and the other of which takes place in the morning. The following is the summary of his analysis:[17]

1–2 Introduction

3–7 God-Abimelech encounter (night dream)

8–16 Abraham-Abimelech encounter (morning)

17–18 Conclusion

There is a clear chiastic structure in verses 3–7, as Mathews and Alexander argue, while the structure of the second main scene (8–16) is "less obvious." Mathews suggests the following structure for verses 3–7:[18]

A v. 3 you are as good as dead

  B v. 3 the woman you have taken

    C v. 4 Abimelech had not gone near her

      D v. 4 will you destroy an innocent nation?

        E v. 5 with a clear conscience

          F v. 6 God said to him in a dream

        E' v. 6 with a clear conscience

      D' v. 6 I have kept you from sinning

    C' v. 6 I did not let you touch her

  B' v. 7 return the man's wife

A' v. 7 you will live . . . if you do not . . . you and all yours will die

It is necessary to examine the structure of the second main unit to see if it can be divided into two scenes, as Weimar suggests. Verse 14 uses the narrator's voice. There is a sequence of the *Wayyiqtol* form in 14a. The speaker in 15a is Abimelech, while the speaker in verses 11–13 is Abraham. So, this *Wayyiqtol* form can be considered the main independent clause and a new beginning. In the broad context, however, the dialogue still continues

---

17. Mathews, *Genesis 11:27—50:26*, 249-50; Alexander, *Abraham in the Negev*, 38-39.

18. Mathews, *Genesis 11:27—50:26*, 250; Alexander, *Abraham in the Negev*, 39.

between Abraham and Abimelech throughout verses 8–16 even though there is a change in speaker. So, verse 14 can be seen as part of the second main scene. Based on this observation, we can now suggest the following structure for Story B:

A Introduction: Abraham's Deception and Crisis 1–2		Narrative
B God and Abimelech 3–7		Speech
God 3		
Abimelech 4–5		
God 6–7		
B' Abraham and Abimelech 8–16		Speech
Abimelech (to his people) 8		
(to Abraham) 9–10		
Abraham (to Abimelech) 11–13		
Abimelech (to Abraham) 14–15		
(to Sarah) 16		
A' Conclusion: Abraham's Prayer and restoration 17–18		Narrative

Textual Analysis

Now that we have examined the structure of Story B, we need to investigate each unit in detail. When it comes to the textual analysis of Story B, it is important to keep Story A in mind, since Story A and B are closely interrelated as a type-scene.

Introduction: Abraham's Deception and Crisis

As seen, the appearance of the *Wayyiqtol* form as a thematic initial verb signals a new beginning in verse 1. Also, clauses 1a–c basically consist of the sequence of the *Wayyiqtol* forms. So, this sequence also shows us the sequence of the mainline of the story. On the other hand, clause 2a indicates the direct speech formula. Both the speaker and the addressee appear. According to Longacre's analysis, this clause refers to the initiation of dialogue and introduces two participants in the following lines. 2b is a non-verbal clause that simply provides a background situation. 2c begins with the *Wayyiqtol* form as a mainline of the discourse. So, it forms part of the sequence to the previous clause (2a). As a result, 2c is related to 2ab. According to Longacre's analysis, it seems that local reciprocities are present as Abraham's action in 2ab results in Abimelech's action.[19] Finally, 2d is a coordinate clause, since it continues at the same syntactic level. We can therefore see that the syntactic function of 2c is also continuing—that is, 2d also functions as a result of 2ab.

1a וַיִּסַּע מִשָּׁם אַבְרָהָם אַרְצָה הַנֶּגֶב

1b וַיֵּשֶׁב בֵּין־קָדֵשׁ וּבֵין שׁוּר

1c וַיָּגָר בִּגְרָר:

2a וַיֹּאמֶר אַבְרָהָם אֶל־שָׂרָה אִשְׁתּוֹ

2b אֲחֹתִי הִוא

2c וַיִּשְׁלַח אֲבִימֶלֶךְ מֶלֶךְ גְּרָר

2d וַיִּקַּח אֶת־שָׂרָה:

Verse 1 introduces the spatial background of Story B. Abraham again journeys from "there" to the land of Negev and dwells in Gerar, which is placed between Kadesh and Shur. The geographical information is, first of all, connected to Story A through its reference to Negev and its use of the words, נָסַע and גור (see Gen 12:9–10). Unlike Story A, Story B adds new information in verse 1: Gerar is located between Kadesh and Shur.

Kadesh appears two other times in Genesis (Gen 14:7; 16:14). First, it is mentioned during Chedorlaomer's campaign into southern Canaan. In Gen 14:7, Kadesh is identified with En-Misphat. In Gen 16:14, Kadesh is again referred to as a place near Beer Lahai Roi. According to 16:7, Kadesh is on the way to Shur. In Num 13–14, Moses sends spies from Kadesh and the Israelites begin to wander for forty years due to their lack of faith. We can therefore conclude that Kadesh is located near the southern border of Canaan.[20] Shur, meanwhile, is traditionally considered the southwestern border of Canaan. When Hagar flees to Shur from the hand of Sarah in Gen 16:7, she is most likely about to enter Egypt, her homeland. So, Shur is closer than Kadesh to Egypt.[21] Gerar, the place where Abraham sojourns, is thus near the southern border of Canaan.

---

19. Longacre, *Joseph: A Story of Divine Providence*, 72–73. "Local reciprocities may occur anywhere along the storyline. That is, we have a situation in which A does something and B in return performs an action. Usually the conditions are specific enough lexically that the change of subject need not be formally marked."

20. Wenham, *Genesis 16–50*, 69; Manor, "Kadesh," 759.

21. Hummel, "Shur," 1217.

Abraham dwells in Gerar, but where he came from is not clear. Verse 1 simply mentions "from there," presumably referring to a place previously mentioned. The problem is that there is no immediate antecedent. Scholars have therefore held different views on the identity of "there." Westermann argues that we do not know the exact place because "it is a stereotyped phrase," and concludes that this expression only reveals its origin in a different source, namely, an older tradition.[22] Most scholars, however, argue that "there" refers to Mamre (Gen 18:1). As Sarna observes, the expression "from there" is used twice more in close context (Gen 18:16 and 22), and both occurrences point to Mamre in Hebron. According to the context, the place to which Abraham returned in verse 33 is also Mamre.[23] So, he lived in the oaks of Mamre, and "from there" he moves to where he can look down on Sodom (Gen 18:16 and 22). He returns to his place after speaking with God (v. 33). Within this context, in Gen 20:1, Abraham again journeys to Gerar "from there." It is therefore natural to understand that "from there" refers to the place referred to in Gen 18:1.

Unlike Stories A and C, Story B does not clearly describe the reason for Abraham's move to Negev. Although the famine theme is an important motif in the wife/sister stories, the fact that Story B does not mention it is a variation on the other stories. In Story A, Abraham goes down to Egypt because of severe famine, while in Story C there is a famine driving Isaac to go to Gerar, which indicates that it is different from Story A.

The author very briefly describes the process of the ruse in verse 2. In Story A, the author aims to reveal Abraham's feeling and his intention to protect himself. Consequently, Story A describes both Abraham's ruse and its exposure in detail (12:11–16). Story B, however, intentionally avoids this issue and summarizes it only in verse 2. According to Van Seters, this is a "blind motif," in which the later version shortened the previous idea.[24] Those who read Story B can only assume and fill in the gaps from the previous account, which is a more detailed story. Methodologically, there is no doubt that Story B cannot be properly understood without knowledge of Story A.

Again, we see that not all of the information was given in Story A. Abraham's intention for the ruse, which is absent from Gen 20:2, is provided when he reveals his plan in verses 11–13, where Story B even adds new

---

22. Westermann, *Genesis 12–36*, 320.

23. Sarna, *Genesis*, 141; also see Sailhamer, *Genesis*, 203; Hartley, *Genesis*, 193; Wenham, *Genesis 16–50*, 254; von Rad, *Genesis*, 226; however, Hamilton points that we can choose either the immolation of Sodom (Gen 19:28) or Mamre (Gen 18:1). See Hamilton, *The Book of Genesis 18–50*, 59.

24. Van Seters, *Abraham in History and Tradition*, 162–63.

information not provided in Story A. We cannot conclude, therefore, that due to the blind motif, Story B simply avoids being the same as Story A. Rather, from the type-scene motif, it is more plausible that the author intentionally provides information from a different angle, so that the readers can understand a different emphasis in theme. Textlinguistically speaking, Story B leaves unanswered gaps in the introduction. Through this, the author increases suspense in the text. As the story goes further, these gaps will be filled and the suspense will be turned into surprise. According to Meir Sternberg, the text does not initially explain why Abraham uses the ruse or why Abimelech does not approach Sarah because the author, using gaps and gap-filling methods, adds suspense and surprise to Story B. This shows how Story B is an elaborately woven, continuous narrative that highlights, not how Abraham deceives the foreign rulers, but how God reveals Abraham's evil plan and its results.[25] So, the consequences of verse 2 are remarkably emphasized in the dialogue between God and Abimelech (vv. 3–7).

While famine was a very common reason for leaving one's land in the ancient Near East, we do not need to presume that famine is Abraham's reason for moving to Negev. Verse 2 only summarizes 12:11–13. There is no reason for Abimelech to take Sarah. When Abraham and Sarah come into Gerar, Abimelech brings Sarah to him. When Sarah is taken to Abimelech, she is eighty-nine (Gen 17:17). Regarding her age, some assume that Sarah is much younger than ninety.[26] It may be hard to accept Sarah's extraordinary beauty when she is nearing her nineties. It is not possible to pinpoint when Story B actually happens. Regardless, we need to focus on the chronology of the narrative. Story B itself clearly suggests that the events occur sometime before Sarah is actually ninety years old. From the context, not only does she receive a promise to give birth to a son in one year's time, but she is also already worn out due to her age (Gen 18:11–13). Furthermore, unlike Story A, Story B includes no clear mention of Sarah's beauty. There may have been other reasons for Abimelech to take her. Mathews, for example, assumes that Abimelech's motive is related to "forging an economic relationship with the Abraham clan."[27]

---

25. Sternberg, *The Poetics of Biblical Narrative*, 309–16. Sternberg states, "[T]he production of surprise depends on the reader's being lured into a false certitude of knowledge. In structural terms, therefore, the discontinuities in chronology, especially between cause and effect, must assume here the appearance of continuities, so that the gap will surface only at the moment of its filling . . . In short, the dynamics of recognition is characterized by a sequence where imperceptible disordering sets us up for unpredictable reordering (309)."

26. Von Rad, *Genesis*, 227.

27. Mathews, *Genesis 11:27—50:26*, 251. On the same basis, Hoffmeier suggests "a diplomatic or legal connection" for the Abimelech's plan. Hoffmeier, "The Wives' Tales

In short, for some unknown reason, Abimelech takes Sarah into his household. Now Abraham's ruse falls into crisis and affects not only Abimelech and his houses, but also Sarah and, most importantly, Abraham's promised seed. In order to untangle the knot of crisis, God has to intervene in the narrative.

God and Abimelech

This unit is constituted by the dialogues between God and Abimelech. The changes of speaker and addressee are as follows:

Table 5: The Change of Speaker and Addressee in Gen 20:3–7

Verse	Speaker	Addressee
3	God	Abimelech
4–5	Abimelech	God
6–7	God	Abimelech

God's Speech (20:3)

Genesis 20:3a begins with the *Wayyiqtol* expressing the sequence of the mainline. However, it introduces a new participant, God. We can therefore understand Gen 20:1a–2d as an introduction that provides background for the following section. Verse 3, a main clause, proceeds as a foreground, and 3b introduces a speech expressing a continuing dialogue. Verse 3b has an introductory participle. It can commonly take "הִנֵּה," and frequently the subject of the participle is placed right after הִנֵּה.[28] The participle in this clause stresses an impending future. Here, the declarative statement is followed by a causal form. In 3d, the relative pronoun + the *Qatal* form provides background information with no influence on the mainline. Since it does not influence the mainline, as a subordinate clause it can be understood as a present perfect form. It also functions as a flashback, which can indicate previous events without any chronological sequence.[29] The *Waw+X+passive participle* form appears in 3e, which also provides a background situation.

---

of Genesis 12, 20, and 26 and the Covenants at Beer-Sheba," 81–99.

28. Longacre, *Joseph: A Story of Divine Providence*, 76.
29. Ibid., 79.

3a וַיָּבֹא אֱלֹהִים אֶל־אֲבִימֶלֶךְ בַּחֲלוֹם הַלָּיְלָה

3b וַיֹּאמֶר לוֹ

3c הִנְּךָ מֵת עַל־הָאִשָּׁה

3d אֲשֶׁר־לָקַחְתָּ

3e וְהִוא בְּעֻלַת בָּעַל׃

God, the main character, appears in Abimelech's dream.[30] It is noteworthy to see the divine name adopted here. As noted, the difference in usage of the divine name is not evidence of different sources. Therefore, it suffices here to mention that the divine name, God, is used in place of YHWH, especially when used by foreigners or those related to them.[31] In a dream, God declares a death sentence to Abimelech because of Sarah. God's voice takes the form of Hinneh + Participle, which stresses an impending judgment. We do not know why Abimelech takes Sarah, how long he has her, or what happens to her afterward.[32] God only reveals that Abimelech's taking of Sarah deserves death as a consequence. Compared to Story A, God's presence is clearer in Story B. In Story A, God sent great plagues, whereas in Story B God appears in a dream and speaks to Abimelech. This shows that God's intervention is more dominant in Story B. From Abraham's point of view, however, God's intervention is still implicit, because God has no direct contact with Abraham.

Abimelech's Speech (20:4–5)

The word order of 4a constitutes the *We+X+Qatal*. This form shows the typical formula used for a background situation. Thus, 4a describes the circumstance of the main clause. We can translate it as a pluperfect ("Now Abimelech had not drawn near to her"). Verse 4b, with a sequential *wayyiqtol* form, introduces a direct speech. Verses 4c–5e give additional information using the *Qatal* and non-verbal clause.

4a וַאֲבִימֶלֶךְ לֹא קָרַב אֵלֶיהָ

4b וַיֹּאמַר

---

30. For a dream in the Ancient Near East, see, Walton, *Genesis*, 495; Lipton, *Revisions of the Night*, 52–55; Oppenheim, "The Interpretation of Dreams in the Ancient Near East," 184–307.

31. Waltke, *Genesis*, 258.

32. We can assume, from the use of definite article for the night, הַלָּיְלָה, that God's intervention occurred the night Abimelech took Sarah.

4c אֲדֹנָי הֲגוֹי גַּם־צַדִּיק תַּהֲרֹג׃

5a הֲלֹא הוּא אָמַר־לִי

5b אֲחֹתִי הִוא

5c וְהִיא־גַם־הִוא אָמְרָה

5d אָחִי הוּא

5e בְּתָם־לְבָבִי וּבְנִקְיֹן כַּפַּי עָשִׂיתִי זֹאת׃

What is more, גַּם in 5c indicates a coordinate narrative.[33] It usually occurs in a second clause in order to express an equal verbal rank.[34] The interrogative in 5a, and as a result 5c, leads the clause, because 5c is connected to 5a by a conjunction. Also, גַּם makes it possible to see juxtaposition.[35] By using גַּם, 5b and 5d express corresponding terms, brother and sister. גַּם also appears in 6b. In this case, it is used rhetorically, and it can be translated as "even, yes!"[36]

Abimelech's response is followed by the background information provided in the *We-X-Qatal* form. At this point, we do not know why Abimelech does not approach Sarah; Story B does not give us any hints. Although we cannot identify the exact reason, verses 17–18 are surprising. If Sarah was already taken to the house of Abimelech, but Abimelech experienced God's judgment, then we might think that Abimelech did not approach Sarah, but could not approach her.[37] This is plausible because Abimelech restores Sarah as Abraham's wife in the early morning right after God's intervention in his dream and we hear in verse 18 that God has already sent judgment on Abimelech's house. Therefore, we may consider that when God shows Himself in Abimelech's dream, judgment has already been imposed on Abimelech and his house.

---

33. The LXX, Syriac, and Vulgate read καὶ αὐτή, but the Samaritan Pentateuch reads וגם היא and BHS suggests reading וגם היא. It is difficult to decide which of these is original but it seems that most variants and translations have tried to make it smooth. Since the MT, the LXX, and the Samaritan Pentateuch preserve different variations, there is no need to emend the MT. Furthermore, as David. F. Payne points out, it is possible that the MT includes a kind of idiomatic expression. The difficult reading is to be preferred, so at this point, the MT is preferred. See Payne, "Old Testament Textual Criticism: Its Principles and Practice," 112.

34. Longacre, *Joseph: A Story of Divine Providence*, 100; Andersen, *The Sentence in Biblical Hebrew*, 154.

35. Andersen, *The Sentence in Biblical Hebrew*, 160.

36. For the rhetorical use, see Williams and Beckman, *Williams Hebrew Syntax*, 138; Merwe, Kroeze, and Naudé, *A Biblical Hebrew Reference Grammar*, §41.4.5.2.1c.

37. Sternberg, *The Poetics of Biblical Narrative*, 315–16.

It is important to notice that v. 18 is in the *Qatal* form and thus presents itself as background information. Through this device, the author lends the readers a new understanding of the preceding narrative. In this case, after reading verse 18, we come to know that Abimelech could not approach Sarah because of God's plague. Tzvi Novick argues based on this observation that Abimelech committed a great sin just like Pharaoh in Story A, but is trying to hide his sin and pretend to be righteous. Therefore, according to Novick, by exposing Abimelech's impotence in verse 18, the narrator makes him a fool.[38] I agree with Novick's observation on the flashback function of verse 18, but I doubt that this makes Abimelech as great a sinner as Pharaoh in Story A. First, there is no clear evidence that God's judgment against Abimelech was related to his impotence. Second, what the narrator wants to emphasize is the fact that Sarah, who bears Abraham's seed, is protected by God's intervention and that Abimelech did not touch her, no matter the reason. God's judgment prior to speaking to Abimelech enhances God's intervention and protection, not Abimelech's injustice.[39] We should note that the text itself stresses the fact that Abimelech argues his innocence and that God acknowledges Abimelech's clear conscience (vv. 4–6). By delaying the information until verse 18, the author highlights Story B's distinct theme compared with Story A: fertility and infertility are in the hands of God.[40]

It is surprising to note what Abimelech says to God. In verse 4, he pleads with God, questioning God's justice: "Lord, will you destroy an innocent nation?" This statement reminds us to return to the preceding narrative, in which Abraham asks the same question of YHWH. First of all, in Gen 18:18, YHWH remarks to Abraham that, "Abraham will surely become a great and powerful nation, and all nations on earth will be blessed through him." Abraham then appeals to YHWH, in 18: 23 and 25, "Will you sweep away the righteous with the wicked? Will not the Judge of all the earth do right?" Consequently, Abimelech's appeal to God is also a linking device to Abraham's appeal.[41]

This parallel may help us think about Abimelech's use of the expression "nation (גוי)." Since this Hebrew word usually means "nation," some scholars have concluded that it represents an emendation. For example, BHS sees

---

38. Novick, "'Almost, at Times, the Fool,'" 277–90. Novick suggests that Abimelech in Story B is a comic figure who exaggerates his righteousness and is finally exposed in his impotence.

39. Ibid., 278–89; Alter, *Genesis*, 96.

40. Alter presents v. 18 as "a lovely piece of delayed narrative exposition." See, Alter, *Genesis*, 96. This theme will be explored in more detail when we look at verse 18.

41. Ibid., 93; Hamilton, *The Book of Genesis 18–50*, 61–62; Novick, "Almost, at Times, the Fool," 283.

הֲגוֹי גַּם as a dittography of הגם.⁴² However, this word has been utilized in order to parallel Abraham and the promise of blessing that flows to all the nations through Abraham. Matthews aptly states:

> The appearance of "nation" (*gôy*) is a reflex of the promissory blessing recited in 18:18 ("nations" cf. 22:18). The patriarchal promises make Abraham and his legacy an important factor in the future blessing of "all peoples" (12:3). In microcosm the treatment of Abraham and Sarah by the Philistine presages the divine blessing that Abraham as mediator will afford the peoples of the world.⁴³

Furthermore, God's punishment on Abimelech is not only for him, but also for his people (v. 9). It is plausible for Abimelech to think that the punishment will threaten both him and his nation. Therefore, we do not need to emend the text.

What Abimelech depends on is his innocence. By using a metaphor of "clear conscience and clean hands," he tries to show that he has no evil intention and committed a sin without knowing it.⁴⁴

God's Speech (20:6–7)

The roles of the speaker and addressee are swapped in verse 6. It begins with the *wayyiqtol* form, which begins with a main independent clause. In this case, unlike in 3a, the speaker is identified by name, but the addressee appears only in the pronoun form. This means that the speaker is dominant in this dialogue. The *wayyiqtol* form in 6a is changed to the *Qatal* form in 6b and 6c, which provide background information. In particular, 6c is connected to 6b by a כִּי clause, so it is dependent. Then 6d-e begins with the *wayyiqtol* form. There is thus a sequence from 6b to 6d-e.

6a וַיֹּאמֶר אֵלָיו הָאֱלֹהִים בַּחֲלֹם

---

42. Gunkel and Biddle, *Genesis*, 220; Speiser, *Genesis*, 149; Westermann, *Genesis 12–36*, 318. Regarding BHS's suggestion, if one can see גם as an emphatic expression, it is not necessary to emend the text. On top of this, to establish dittography, commentators have tried to emend הֲגוֹי first. Because גוי usually indicates a territorial concept, the more suitable term here is העם. Targum Onkelos simply emends this and Pseudo-Jonathan tries to explain it, adding a long sentence ("O LORD, a gentile who has not sinned, who is even worthy of being declared innocent in judgment, shall he be put to death?"). The LXX adds "ἔθνος ἀγνοοῦν καὶ" to clarify. There is no reason to emend the MT text.

43. Mathews, *Genesis 11:27—50:26*, 253; also see Alter, *Genesis*, 93.

44. See Hamilton, *The Book of Genesis 18–50*, 62–63.

6b גַּם אָנֹכִי יָדַעְתִּי

6c כִּי בְתָם־לְבָבְךָ עָשִׂיתָ

6d וָאֶחְשֹׂךְ גַּם־אָנֹכִי אוֹתְךָ

6e מֵחֲטוֹ־לִי

In the dream, God acknowledges Abimelech's sincerity by adding an expression almost identical to Abimelech's in 6c: בְתָם־לְבָבְךָ עָשִׂיתָ זֹאת. God prevents Abimelech from sinning against Him by not allowing him to touch Sarah. Even though there are some unanswered questions, we clearly see that God had already done something to Abimelech, before showing Himself in his dream, in order to protect Sarah. As Hamilton observes, the reason that Abimelech did not touch Sarah is not his high value of morality, but God's active intervention.[45] What God has done to Abimelech is unclear, but we can grasp the larger truth of what has happened in Gen 20:18. According to verse 18, God had already closed up every womb in Abimelech's household. Thus, strictly speaking, the truth is not that Abimelech *did not* touch Sarah; it is that he *could not* touch Sarah. This is somewhat different from what we see in Story A. In Story A, YHWH sent great plagues to Pharaoh and his house. This was clearly a punishment for his adultery. In Story B, however, God intends not to punish Abimelech, but to prevent him from committing adultery. Since Abimelech took Sarah with clear hands and an innocent heart, there is no reason for him to be punished. Because of this difference, in this scene Story B does not follow the flow of Story A.

The use of the word נָגַע in verse 6 is significant. This word is used in all three stories (Gen 12:17; 20:6; 26:11), but used differently in detail. Even though the term has a different meaning in each story, it is clear that the author intentionally uses this specific term in the wife/sister stories. Moreover, this term has mostly conveyed a negative meaning in Genesis. The first appearance of this term is in Gen 3:3, where Eve uses it when she distorts the command of YHWH God. It appears three times in the wife/sister stories (12:17; 20:6; 26:11), once more in the context of Story C (26:29), and then again when a man who wrestles with Jacob at the ford of Jabbok strikes the socket of Jacob's hip (vs. 25, 32). There is an exception in Gen 28:12, where the term simply means "reach."

When it comes to the wife/sister stories, in Story A, God strikes (נָגַע) Pharaoh because of Sarah. Here, "to strike" means to aggressively send great plagues. In Story B, on the other hand, the word is applied to Abimelech's approach to Sarah. Here, the word conveys a sexual relationship. In Story

---

45. Ibid., 63; Mathews, *Genesis 11:27—50:26*, 254.

C, the word is applied to both man and woman and can refer to both an aggressive treatment and a sexual relationship.[46]

Verse 7a begins with a new initial form by expressing "And now (וְעַתָּה)" and changing first person indicative to second person imperative. There is the sequence of imperatives in 7a, d, and f. We may consider 7c as a purpose. It is common to find a sequence of imperative clauses with the conjunction *waw* (see Gen 12:1–2; 17:1). So, 7b, e, and g are all subordinate clauses providing background information (7b), condition (7e), and result (7g). Verse 7 is clearly connected to verse 3 as an *inclusio* through its reference to God's death sentence. This stylistic device allows us to consider verses 3–7 as one unit.

7a וְעַתָּה הָשֵׁב אֵשֶׁת־הָאִישׁ

7b כִּי־נָבִיא הוּא

7c וְיִתְפַּלֵּל בַּעַדְךָ

7d וֶחְיֵה

7e וְאִם־אֵינְךָ מֵשִׁיב

7f דַּע

7g כִּי־מוֹת תָּמוּת אַתָּה וְכָל־אֲשֶׁר־לָךְ׃

Here we see the term נָבִיא for the first time in the Bible. Abraham, as a prophet, will pray for Abimelech. In terms of Abraham's intercessory prayer, we are immediately reminded of Abraham's prayer for Sodom and Gomorrah in Gen 18. Since source critics consider Gen 18 as belonging to the J source, they do not recognize a connection between Gen 20: 7 and Gen 18. However, it is hard to miss that Gen 18 and 20 have the theme of Abraham's intercession in common. Biddle rightly avers that the fact that in Gen 20, "the patriarch fills an intercessory role ought, perhaps, best be understood as an echo of the same theme in Gen 18 (J). These phenomena call the supposed

---

46. Van Seters, *Abraham in History and Tradition*, 181; also see 173. Van Seters expresses it as "ingenious double entendre." Furthermore, Van Seters sees that Story B can be a possible answer to the questions left behind in Story A regarding the reason for God's punishment, the way of knowing Sarah's identity, and so forth. However, to find an answer to a question from an earlier narrative in a later one is not possible in a narrative sense. Also, there is no reason to assume that both Story A and B are developing the same storylines. Therefore, it is necessary and natural to follow each story's own narrative flow. Furthermore, it is not plausible to see Genesis 20 as an answer or a theological reflection on Story A. Story B does not resolve some of the questions raised in Story A, and it even raises another moral issue by mentioning that Sarah is Abraham's half-sister. See Lipton, *Revisions of the Night*, 45–47; Hamilton, *The Book of Genesis 18–50*, 63; Alexander, *Abraham in the Negev*, 45–46.

independence of J and E into question."⁴⁷ As mentioned above, in order to connect this passage with Gen 18:18, verse 4 utilizes the term גּוֹי for Abimelech and his household. On the same basis, therefore, we can conclude that Abraham's intercessory role in Story B is surely related to his function with regard to Sodom and Gomorrah in Gen 18. The role of Abraham as a prophet is a fulfillment of God's promises to bless the nations (Gen 12:1–3). Abimelech is left with no option except to return Sarah to Abraham.

Abraham and Abimelech (20:8–16)

In this unit, the dialogue shifts from God and Abimelech (vv. 3–7) to Abraham and Abimelech (vv. 8–16). The dialogue begins with Abimelech's quick response to the previous night's warning from God. Verses 8–16 consist of three units of dialogues, two of which are initiated by Abimelech (8–10 and 14–16). Abimelech's speeches are interrupted by Abraham's speech (11–13). The units contain Abimelech's rebuke, Abraham's explanation, and Abimelech's resolution, respectively.

ABIMELECH (20:8–10)

Abimelech's speech can be divided into two parts: speech to his people (v.8) and to Abraham (vv. 9–10). There is a clear sequence from 8a to 9b. The only change that one needs to observe is the change in 8d, where the sequence of third person masculine singular suddenly shifts to third person masculine plural. In this case, although the subject is changed from Abimelech to the men, the role of Abimelech as a subject is continued to verse 10. Therefore, the change of a subject in 8d does not indicate a thematic initial, but "a thematic participant."⁴⁸

Abimelech summoned all his officials early the next morning, which means that he immediately acted, obeying God's command. When he told them everything he heard in his dream, all the officials were afraid.⁴⁹ Their prompt response to God's command reminds us of two things from

---

47. Biddle, "The 'Endangered Ancestress' and Blessing for the Nations," 611.

48. Longacre, *Joseph: A Story of Divine Providence*, 70–71. Longacre argues, "When the implied reciprocity is sufficient to indicate the switch without an overt noun phrase and the latter occurs anyway, then the motivation for the occurrence of the noun phrase is to mark a thematic participant in some stretch of the discourse."

49. The Samaritan Pentateuch, the LXX, and the Vulgate add כָּל before הָאֲנָשִׁים. This variant may intend to harmonize with the previous phrase (כָּל־הַדְּבָרִים). But it is not necessary to emend the text. The shorter reading is to be preferred.

its context. First, in relation to the Sodom narrative (Genesis 18–19), the phrase "in the early morning" reminds us of Abraham's viewing of Sodom and Gomorrah (19:27) and contrasts with Lot's hesitation when he heard God's plan to destroy Sodom (19:16). Second, their quick response clearly highlights Abraham's wrong assumption that there is no fear of God in the land of Gerar (v. 11).

There is a change of addressee in verse 9, which introduces the direct speech denoting dialogue initial. However, 9b only indicates the addressee with a pronoun, which is a common signal of the sequence of dialogue. In 9c and 9d there is apposition. The function of the second clause is to specify explicitly some general information from the first clause.[50] The question in 9c is simply related to Abraham's ruse itself, while 9d refers specifically to Abraham's act of bringing great sin onto them.[51] Verse 10a introduces direct speech again. In this case, even though 10a appears in the sequence of direct speech and there is no change of speaker or addressee, it refers again to the speaker and the addressee. Since the dialogue's initial form reappears in the sequence, it denotes redirection of the dialogue. This repetition of the speaker and addressee creates the feeling of a fresh beginning. 10b and 10c are the content of the speech. Finally, the syntactic function of 10c is to convey a result.

9a וַיִּקְרָא אֲבִימֶלֶךְ לְאַבְרָהָם

9b וַיֹּאמֶר לוֹ

9c[52] מֶה־עָשִׂיתָ לָּנוּ

9d וּמֶה־חָטָאתִי לָךְ

9e כִּי־הֵבֵאתָ עָלַי וְעַל־מַמְלַכְתִּי חֲטָאָה גְדֹלָה

9f מַעֲשִׂים אֲשֶׁר לֹא־יֵעָשׂוּ עָשִׂיתָ עִמָּדִי׃

10a וַיֹּאמֶר אֲבִימֶלֶךְ אֶל־אַבְרָהָם

10b[53] מָה רָאִיתָ

---

50. Andersen, *The Sentence in Biblical Hebrew*, 47.

51. The LXX emends first person singular to first person plural (μή τι ἡμάρτομεν εἰς σέ). The LXX may harmonize with the previous phrase, but this is not necessary. The MT naturally works well.

52. BHS proposes the Syriac reading: *'bdt lk* ("what have I done to you"). The LXX reads Τί τοῦτο ἐποίησας ἡμῖν ("what is this you have done to us"). Emendations may try to harmonize with the following phrase (וּמֶה־חָטָאתִי לָךְ).

53. BHS proposes an emendation to מָה יָרֵאתָ following Gen 26:7. The MT, the LXX, and Targum translations keep the same expression. Therefore, it is not necessary to emend as BHS does.

10c כִּי עָשִׂיתָ אֶת־הַדָּבָר הַזֶּה:

Abimelech now rebukes Abraham's deception. His rebuke contains three questions, which are similar to Pharaoh's questions to Abraham in Story A.

Table 6: Pharaoh's Questions in Stories A and B

Gen 12:18-19	Gen 20:9-10
מַה־זֹּאת עָשִׂיתָ לִּי	מֶה־עָשִׂיתָ לָּנוּ
לָמָה לֹא־הִגַּדְתָּ לִּי כִּי אִשְׁתְּךָ הִוא	וּמֶה־חָטָאתִי לָךְ כִּי־הֵבֵאתָ עָלַי וְעַל־מַמְלַכְתִּי חֲטָאָה גְדֹלָה מַעֲשִׂים אֲשֶׁר לֹא־יֵעָשׂוּ עָשִׂיתָ עִמָּדִי
לָמָה אָמַרְתָּ אֲחֹתִי הִוא	מָה רָאִיתָ כִּי עָשִׂיתָ אֶת־הַדָּבָר הַזֶּה:

The first question in each story is rhetorical, since everyone already knows what is happening. The questions in Story A and B are nearly identical; the only difference is shown in the change of the first pronoun from singular to plural. This difference implies that whereas Pharaoh is only concerned about himself, Abimelech cares for his people. In his second question, Abimelech mentions his kingdom again. Compared to Pharaoh, who only asks the reason for Abraham's lie, Abimelech's ask is, "How have I wronged you that you have brought such great guilt upon me and my kingdom?" Abimelech's second question clearly reveals his higher level of morality.[54]

Unlike the first two questions, which are rhetorical, the third question—"What was your reason for doing this?"—is intended to give Abraham a chance to defend himself. In order to distinguish this question from the previous ones, verse 10 again introduces the speaker and the addressee. As Alter mentions, verse 10 implies that Abraham does not know what to say concerning Abimelech's strong rebuke in verse 9. Abimelech therefore repeats his question in shorter form to hear Abraham's reason for his deception.[55] This naturally connects to the defense of Abraham that follows in verses 11–13.

---

54. Wenham, *Genesis 16–50*, 72. We do not, however, need to assume Abimelech's righteousness in absolute sense. See Holmgren, "Looking Back on Abraham's Encounter with a Canaanite King," 375–76.

55. Alter, *Genesis*, 94. Alter says, "The repetition of the formula for introducing direct speech, with no intervening response from Abraham, is pointedly expressive. Abimelech vehemently castigates Abraham (with good reason), and Abraham stands

Abraham (20:11–13)

The direct speech with the *Wayyiqtol* form, including the change of the speaker in 11a, indicates a new beginning. In terms of its relation to the previous clauses, verse 11 is Abraham's attempt to answer Abimelech's question from verses 8–10. Since a common formula in sequence is the absence of the speaker and the presence of the addressee in pronoun form, the noun for the speaker and the absence of the addressee is unusual. This formula highlights a decisive intervention in which the appearance of the speaker may stress the importance of the speaker. Verse 11d is a good example of how the *WeQatal* functions as a sequence.[56] The particle רַק leads an asseverative clause, which is usually a non-verbal clause.[57] וְגַם in 12a is sometimes used independently to link two items. Abraham's speech is emphasized by the use of particles in 11a, 12a, and 12b.[58] Verse 13a is constructed as וַיְהִי+ temporal expression+ main clause, which functions as a complement- that is, it does not function on the mainline of the story.[59] Temporal clauses can be classified by their temporal relation to the main clause. Since 13a–b is used as a temporal clause, כַּאֲשֶׁר denotes a contemporary situation.[60]

Abraham responds to Abimelech's repeated accusatory questions.[61] Abraham intends to defend his action by arguing three things. First, Abraham has made an assumption about the people of Gerar, which is wrong (v. 11). Contrary to Abraham's assumption, verse 8 clearly refers to how Abimelech and his people show a strong fear of God when they hear what happened the previous night.

Second and more importantly, Abraham reveals the fact that Sarah is his half-sister, that is, she has the same father but a different mother (v. 12).

---

silent, not knowing what to say. And so Abimelech repeats his upbraiding, in shorter form."

56. Joüon and Muraoka, *A Grammar of Biblical Hebrew*, § 119.e.

57. Ibid., § 164.a; Merwe, "Old Testament Particles and the Interpretation of Old Testament Texts," 27–44. Merwe says, "The above-mentioned focus particles may therefore have been used to reveal the extent of a discourse concerning which speakers or authors assume their audience to share information with them or they may signal speakers' or authors' assessment of the relationship of two related propositions on the same topic."

58. Alter, *The Five Books of Moses*, 100. For Alter, 11a is a medial asseverative.

59. Longacre, *Joseph: A Story of Divine Providence*, 66–67.

60. *IBHS*, 643. In addition to this, if it is subordinate, it refers to a later situation mostly with עַד. For the following situation, most often אַחַר or אַחֲרֵי are used.

61. After 11a, the Samaritan Pentateuch adds כי יראתי ("because I feared"). It is to explain the motivation of Abraham so that the passage can be adapted to the other parallel passage. The MT, the LXX, and Targums keep the original.

In the patriarchal period, endogamy was not unusual. For example, Nahor married Milcah, who was the daughter of his brother, Haran. Isaac married his cousin Rebekah, and Jacob married his cousins Leah and Rachel.[62] Nevertheless, we might doubt if Abraham's defense is right or not and if he reveals the truth or not. In Gen 11:29, we are informed that Nahor's wife, Milcah, is the daughter of Haran, but in the same context, there is no further reference to Sarah's family history. Rather, Sarah was referred to Terah's daughter-in-Law in Gen 11:31.[63] Strictly speaking, then, we cannot confirm Sarah's real relationship with Abraham, so we also cannot confirm if Abraham reveals the full truth of their relationship. Even if Abraham is being faithful, he only revealed half of the truth when he introduced Sarah as his sister to the people of Gerar. Derek Kidner rightly points out that "using one half of the truth to conceal the other was so clearly a lie that on this occasion Abram attempted no defense."[64] Abraham tries to defend himself by using emphatic expressions in verses 11–12 (רַק and וְגַם־אָמְנָה), but we are not sure if Abimelech accepts Abraham's defense as a truth. In verse 16, Abimelech only gives compensations for the sake of Sarah without providing his own response to Abraham's speech.[65] Therefore, although it is difficult to prove Sarah's real relationship with Abraham, we can at least confirm that Abraham originally intended to lie.

Finally, Abraham introduces totally new information about his conversation with Sarah. Surprisingly Abraham may blame God for his deception. Verse 13 mentions, וַיְהִי כַּאֲשֶׁר הִתְעוּ אֹתִי אֱלֹהִים מִבֵּית אָבִי. In this phrase, we see the use of the Hiphil form of תָעָה, which means, "wander, err, or stagger." It is unclear why the plural form is used. There are two difficult issues here. First, the subject "God" usually takes a singular verb, but here takes a plural. Second, the Hiphil form can be translated as "cause to wander," which can mean that God leads Abraham astray. The Samaritan Pentateuch reads this as third person singular to resolve the first issue. On the other hand, Targum translations have tried to change the subject. Onkelos and Neofiti read "the nations" instead of God. On the same basis, Pseudo-Jonathan changes it to "idols." By doing this, these texts would

---

62. Mosaic Law strictly prohibits marriage with a half-sister. See, Lev 19:9, 11; 20:17; Deut 27:22; Ezek 22:11. But Abraham lived before the Mosaic prohibitions.

63. See Cassuto, *A Commentary on the Book of Genesis, Part 2*, 276; Turner, *Announcements of Plot in Genesis*, 65. Most scholars, however, simply acknowledge Abraham's face value. See, for example, Petersen, "A Thrice-Told Tale," 39–40.

64. Kidner, *Genesis*, 116; Bruckner, *Implied Law in the Abraham Narrative*, 181.

65. It is worth noting that Abimelech calls Abraham "brother" in v. 16. It is clear that although the relationship between Abraham and Sarah was already revealed Abimelech calls Abraham brother. In doing so, Abimelech appeals his uncomfortable mind.

avoid the concept that God makes Abraham to err. To simply change the subject, as the Targums do, is unacceptable, and changing the number of verb is not necessary, because a difficult reading is to be preferred. Mathews concludes, "Abimelech's polytheism may explain why the patriarch uses the plural verb 'wander' with God rather than the customary singular."[66] Furthermore, according to Mathews, if this is not a grammatical variation, it may manifest Abraham's "all-time religious low."[67] What Abraham says by means of the Hiphil form is that God caused him to wander from the house of the father. Just like Abimelech's question in Gen 20:9 reminds us of God's question in Gen 3:12, Abraham's defense reminds us of Adam's defense, in which he rebukes YHWH for giving Eve. Regarding the use of the name of God, however, when non-Israelites refer to God, or Israelites refer God to non-Israelites, it is usual to use אֱלֹהִים. Moreover, because it is not unusual for אֱלֹהִים to come with the plural verb form (Gen 35:7; 2 Sam 7:23), in my opinion it is not clear whether or not the plural use implies Abraham's spiritual digression.

Abimelech (20:14–16)

There is a sequence of the *Wayyiqtol* form in 14a. While the subject in Gen 20:11–13 is Abraham, now the subject changes to Abimelech. So, 14a is the main and independent clause and denotes a new beginning. Verse 15a introduces direct speech with the emphasis on the speaker, because the speaker is specified whereas the addressee is implied. Following 15b, the particle הִנֵּה is used two more times. הִנֵּה is followed by the clause, which denotes action or events in contemporary situations. In this case, הִנֵּה refers to a performative action, mainly with the *Qatal* form. Through this, the speaker gives worthy news to the addressee.[68] In particular, 16a is a common formula of the *We-X-Qatal* form, which denotes the beginning of a new topic so that the consistence of the mainline is broken. However, even though 16a functions syntactically as a thematic initial, the storyline is still continued throughout the story- that is, Abimelech is still speaking.[69]

---

66. Mathews, *Genesis 11:27—50:26*, 257; Wenham, *Genesis 16–50*, 73. For more detailed study on this verse, see Schmutzer, "Did the Gods Cause Abraham's Wandering?," 149–66.

67. Mathews, *Genesis 11:27—50:26*, 257–58.

68. Merwe, "A Cognitive Linguistic Perspective on הִנֵּה in the Pentateuch, Joshua, Judges, and Ruth," 101–40. See 131 especially.

69. Merwe, "Discourse Linguistics and Biblical Hebrew Grammar," 30–31.

Although we do not know whether Abraham's defense, which is in emphatic in its expression, was successful (vv. 11–13), Abimelech nevertheless restores Sarah with compensation. First, he brings livestock to Abraham and returns Sarah (v. 14). Second, he allows them to live in the land (v. 15). Third, he gives a thousand shekels of silver to Abraham in order to cover his guilt (v. 16).[70] Although Abimelech makes Abraham rich in the same way Pharaoh did in Story A (Gen 12:16), the purpose of those gifts is quite different. First, in Story A, the gifts are given for the marriage portion, but in Story B, they are given for Abimelech's vindication. Second, allowing Abraham to live in the land of Gerar is quite a different response from that found in Story A, where Abraham was immediately expelled from the land of Egypt.

Conclusion: Abraham's Prayer and Restoration

All three clauses from 17a to 17c have different subjects: Abraham, God, and they. These are all main clauses. As mentioned above in reference to 8a, this switch makes readers extend the thematic participant in the discourse. The syntactic function of 17c is to illustrate a consequence. Finally, verse18 contains the *Qatal* form, which denotes background information. The syntactic function of verse 18 is causal. Just as verses 1–2 function as an introduction, verses 17–18 form a conclusion to Story B.

By noting that the name Abraham is part of an *inclusio* in verses 17–18, the importance of Abraham's character becomes clear.[71] Abraham prays for Abimelech and his household as a prophet. As a result, God heals them so that they can give birth again. Through Abraham's prayer, women can bear children. Considering the flow of the narrative to Gen 21, this is very important because, like the women in Gerar, Sarah will bear a child—the promised seed, Isaac—in the very next verse in chapter 21. The last phrase, עַל־דְּבַר שָׂרָה אֵשֶׁת אַבְרָהָם, significantly defines the whole second wife/sister story and summarizes its main issue. Sarah is the wife of Abraham!

---

70. Waltke, *Genesis*, 287. According to Waltke, a thousand shekels is a large amount: a Babylonian laborer would have had to work 167 years to earn such a sum. Abraham bought the cave of Machpelah with four hundred shekels (Gen 23:15–16). Concerning 16d, the MT is grammatically obscure, so, BHS suggests to read ואת כֻּלּוֹ נכחת (et apud hos omnes iustificata es) or וְאַתְּ כֻּלּוֹ נכחת (et tu in omnibus his rebus iustificata es). That is, "and with everyone you will be justified" or "and in everything you will be justified." The MT probably placed waw with יכח (Niphal Participle form), which should be with כֹּל.

71. Mathews, *Genesis 11:27—50:26*, 259.

Type-Scene Analysis

In the previous section, we explored the textlinguistic features of Story B. We will now examine Story B from the type-scene perspective. As we have discussed, observing the similarities and variations between Story A and B is the most basic and important approach of a type-scene analysis. Since we investigated Story A in chapter four, in this chapter we will compare Story B to A, uncover how Story B develops its own theme and observe how Story B functions within the surrounding narrative and the entire book of Genesis.

Characterization

Characterization is an important device for conveying the intention of the author. Here we will focus on how the characters are described in Story B and how they develop from Story A.

Narrator

The narrator's point of view is crucial as we seek to determine narrative setting and understand the characters and the flow of the narrative. Not surprisingly, we see the existence of the narrator at the outset. Like Story A, Story B begins with the narrator, who introduces the basic setting of the narrative. In Gen 20:1, the narrator tells us of Abraham's journey to Gerar. On the other hand, the narrator intentionally unfolds the course of the plot more quickly in Story B than in Story A. Here the narrator includes in one verse (Gen 20:2) a storyline that was spread over 5 verses in Story A (Gen 12:11–15).[72]

While Story A includes a severe famine as a narrative setting, Story B has no mention of any crisis. The narrator wants us to recognize that Abraham has no need to depart from the promised land. For this reason, we must note that the issue of Story B is not the same as Story A. The narrator also reveals his intention to move the story forward more quickly. So, Story B describes Abraham's deception and Abimelech's taking of Sarah in a very brief way. Several elements are omitted in Story B. First, Story B does not inform us of the reason for Abraham's departure. Second, it does not explain the reason for his deception, which will be given when Abraham defends

---

72. The LXX adds, "ἐφοβήθη γὰρ εἰπεῖν ὅτι Γυνή μού ἐστιν, μήποτε ἀποκτείνωσιν αὐτὸν οἱ ἄνδρες τῆς πόλεως δι᾽ αὐτήν" ("for he was afraid to say, 'She is my wife,' lest the men of the city should kill him because of her"). Other secondary Aramaic versions follow the MT. Here, the LXX tried to assimilate to Gen 26:6.

himself. In Story A, the reason is given before Abraham's entering Egypt in direct speech form. Third, there is no recognition of Sarah's beauty. Fourth, there is no role for Abimelech's officers. At this point we might conclude that the author keeps Story A in mind and, as Van Seters suggests, excludes similar elements simply in order to avoid unnecessary repetition. In my opinion, the author has a different emphasis, and therefore does not want to include unimportant scenes. If the author only wanted to exclude parts of the story that appeared earlier, it would not be necessary to include new information in Abraham's speech to Abimelech (vv. 11–13). This implies that avoidance of repetition is not the author's only motivation.

The omniscient narrator gives us the most important information for understanding the whole story in Gen 20:4. Before the dialogue between God and Abimelech, the narrator confirms that Abimelech does not approach Sarah. This fact is so crucial in the narrative that Abimelech and God also confirm it in turn. This is where Story B significantly differs from Story A, which shows no concern for Sarah's purity.

Abraham

Abraham is one of three main characters, who have their own voices in Story B. The narrative itself begins with Abraham's journey and ends with Abraham's intercessional prayer. However, the narrator only refers to Abraham's journey and the following events. As we noted, Story A clearly establishes Abraham as the dominant character by introducing his intention for the journey, the reason for his deception, and even his dialogues with Sarah and Pharaoh. His dominant speech and action in Story A reveal his character well. Story B, however, is quite different: Abraham remains in silence until he defends himself before Abimelech in verse 11. This is the author's narrative strategy for the characterization of Abraham. In order to understand his character, therefore, it is worth noting that Abraham's first direct speech is his defense for what he has done.

Furthermore, from the context, we are to remember that Abraham has already been given God's promise that Sarah will give him a child, the promised seed, in the course of a year (Gen 18:10). We are not sure whether Sarah was pregnant at the time of Story B, but since Abraham already had God's promise of a son through Sarah he is characterized as much more unethical than in Story A. Abraham's deception is more understandable in Story A because there was a severe famine and the promise was not clearly understood. However, it is plausible that Abraham in Story B does not fully believe God's promise about Sarah. Peter D. Miscall rightly states:

The lack of regard for the wife is most serious in Genesis 20 because of its preceding context. Abraham, because of his experience in Egypt, must be well aware of the nearly inevitable result of his lie, and now this is not just his wife Sarah but the woman who has been twice designated by Yahweh as the future mother of Isaac, the next bearer of the promises (17:15–21, 18:10–15).[73]

We can conclude that Abraham' character has been bad throughout Stories A and B both ethically and spiritually.

Abraham's characterization appears more clearly in his direct speech in Gen 20:11–13. Even though Abraham wants to defend himself by raising the unknown fact of Sarah's identity as his half-sister, his attempt might not be successful. Just as his first defense—that he assumed Gerar has no fear of God—is clearly not true, his second defense—introducing Sarah as his half-sister—also has a negative effect. We need to note why the author postpones Abraham's direct speech until this point. Story B conveys direct speeches for the main flow of the story. Through Abraham's actions and the narrator's characterization, Abraham's unethical character is already apparent, but his final speech worsens his character. In order to enhance this, the author employs emphatic words such as רַק, וְגַם, and אַךְ, which reveal Abraham's desperate struggle to defend himself. It is therefore plausible to conclude that Abraham's speech of defense can also be understood negatively. Of course, based on verse 13, we can assume that Abraham's ruse should be expected as a regular practice whenever he goes to a foreign land. Our concern, however, is why the author includes this new information not in Story A, but in Story B. Furthermore, the context in which the information is located also must be observed. The author includes this in Abraham's direct speech in defense of his ruse. In doing this, the author reveals Abraham's ruse not for providing simple information, but for evaluating his ruse. From this context, even we cannot be sure whether Abraham is faithful or not. Based on this observation, Abraham's character in Story B emphasizes his ethical and spiritual weakness and his unfaithfulness to God's promise.

Lastly, verse 17 characterizes Abraham very differently. He seems like a different character from the one we see earlier in Story B when he prays for Abimelech and his household to be healed. This is the first time prayer appears in the Bible. Even though he has done wrong to Sarah, Abimelech, and the Promise itself, he now prays for healing and YHWH heals Abimelech and his household. Throughout the narrative, Abraham's characterization is

---

73. Miscall, "Literary Unity in Old Testament Narrative," 33; also see Turner, *Announcements of Plot in Genesis*, 84; Gossai, *Power and Marginality in the Abraham Narrative*, 82; Waltke, *Genesis*, 284. In this regard, it is not plausible to regard that Abraham's reputation in Story B as less damaging than in Story A. See Bruggemann, *Genesis*, 177

described negatively (vv. 1, 2, 7, 11, 13, and 17)—only when God mentions him is Abraham referred to in a positive way. In verse 7, God calls Abraham a prophet and verse 17 shows that Abraham has played as a prophet by praying for Abimelech and his household during an unethical situation. We therefore know that God's promise to make Abraham a blessing to the nations relies on God's faithfulness. In this regard, we are to extend this verse to Gen 21:1-2. As we noted, Gen 20 and 21 are closely linked to each other. When we read the text in order, after the women's fertility is restored in verses 17-18, we see that Sarah was pregnant and bore a son at the time God had promised (Gen 21:1-2). Abraham's prayer thus guides us to understand the fulfillment of YHWH's promise of prosperity.

Sarah

We see that Sarah is dominant in Story B because she is on stage at almost every moment. Sarah is referred to with various terms, such as wife, woman, sister, and third person feminine pronoun. In fact, Sarah is the most frequently mentioned character in Story B.[74] In Story A, Sarah's beauty is an important motif that leads the narrative, but in Story B we see no reference to her beauty, which raises the possibility of a different motivation behind Abimelech's taking of Sarah. In this regard, Abraham's deception would be much less motivated. As in Story A, Sarah is considered an object by others, but Story B is surprising in that she has an indirect voice. Sarah appears in Abimelech's speech in verse 5, where she talks about her status. In Story B, Sarah participates in Abraham's deception more actively.

The most important change that has taken place since Story A appears in the context of Story B. We can expect that Sarah will deliver her child within a year, so she might be pregnant around the incident of Story B. She also now knows that she is a part of the promises of YHWH. This fact requires us to read Story B differently from Story A.

Lastly, Sarah's developed role clearly appears when Abraham speaks to her in verse 13 and Abimelech speaks to her in verse 16. Here, for the first time, Sarah is referred to with the second person pronoun. This then occurs six more times. While Sarah was never a conversation partner in Story A, she clearly has a role as an interlocutor in Story B. In these ways, the author develops Sarah's characterization throughout Story A and B. However, it

---

74. Sarah is mentioned 16 times in nouns and 17 times in pronouns (Sarah: 2, 14, 16, 18; wife: 2, 7, 11, 12, 14, 18; woman: 3x2; sister: 2, 5, 12; daughter: 12; third person pronoun 2x2, 3, 4, 5x2, 6, 7, 12x2, 13; second person pronoun: 13x2, 16x4).

is necessary to note that Sarah's characterization, like Abraham's, becomes much more negative.

Abimelech

In Story B, the antagonist is Abimelech; in Story A, it is Pharaoh, the king of Egypt, who takes this role. From the point of view of the similar scene process, these two different foreign kings have a similar role. Even though there are slight differences in detail, they both take Sarah as their wife, suffer from God's judgment on account of Sarah, show a higher level of morality by rebuking Abraham, and return Sarah to Abraham, making him rich. However, Story B introduces Abimelech very differently from Pharaoh in Story A. First of all, he claims his innocence before God in verses 4–5. Second, God confirms this by repeating Abimelech's claim (v. 6). Abimelech received wrong information from both Abraham and Sarah, so he took Sarah with sincerity. God appears in his dream and warns him not to touch Sarah. God neither appears to nor speaks to Pharaoh; rather, God simply sends great plagues. Furthermore, Pharaoh might have a sexual relationship with Sarah, whereas Abimelech clearly does not approach her, as both God and Abimelech confirm. The author clearly intends at the outset to show that Abimelech's level of morality is higher than Pharaoh's.

We also see that, when God commands Abimelech to return Sarah, he returns her in the early morning of the very next day (v.8). This highlights Abimelech's quick obedience. When he summons Abraham and requests his defense, Abimelech continues to show his higher level of morality. He asks, "What have you done to us?" (v.9). Compare this to what the Pharaoh asks: "What have you done to me?" (Gen 12:18). We see here that Abimelech is concerned not only about himself but also about his people.[75] When it comes to the second and third questions, the difference is even clearer.[76]

We may conclude that Story B develops the character of the foreign king from Story A. This makes for a clear contrast between the main characters. Abraham and Sarah, who hold God's promise, regress through the stories, whereas the antagonists, Pharaoh and Abimelech, show higher levels of morality than Abraham and Sarah. From the course of the narratives, we cannot miss the clear contrast between God's promise holders and the foreign rulers. Above all, this contrast requests the readers to expect the appearance of the one who controls the entire narrative, God.

---

75. Wenham, *Genesis 16–50*, 72,
76. We do not need to repeat it here. See n54.

God

The Divine name, God, is used for the divine name in Story B, except in verse 18, where the personal and covenantal name YHWH appears. The contents of verse 18 are closely related to the theme of the seed, so verse 18 has to be read with Gen 21, where Sarah gives birth to Isaac, the promised seed. By and large, since the divine names Elohim and YHWH are interchangeable in the book of Genesis, there is no need to identify different sources here.

In terms of characterization, God in Story B is described quite differently from YHWH in Story A. YHWH in Story A only comes onto the scene in verse 17, and He appears in the narrator's explanation without any voice, even though His intervention is the most important turning point in Story A. On the other hand, in Story B God actively engages in the plotline of this narrative. The dialogue between God and Abimelech forms a major part of the first section. First, God appears in Abimelech's dream, speaks, warns him not to take Sarah, and gives instruction to Abimelech (vv. 3–7). More importantly, God clearly reveals His intention to protect Sarah and confirms that Sarah did not lie with Abimelech (v. 6). Compared to Story A, God's quick intervention makes a remarkable difference. In Story A, the author does not show concern for Sarah's status in the house of Pharaoh, while in Story B, the author strongly indicates that Sarah's purity is protected by God. God's active intervention is further enhanced by the reference to God's judgment on Abimelech and his household in the last statement. Through this background information in verse 18, we are surprised that God not only warns Abimelech not to touch Sarah, but also acts to protect her at the outset. We can see, therefore, that God is active in Story B: He speaks and acts.[77] This is considerably improved from Story A. The fact that God actively and directly intervenes in this narrative to protect Sarah, Abraham's seed, and God's promise is the most important feature, and it again confirms that God is the character who turns all situations toward His intention.

Nevertheless, we need to observe the narrative from Abraham's viewpoint. It is strange that, even though it is Abraham who has God's promise, God never shows himself to Abraham. It seems to me that Abraham has no access to any information about God. First, God never meets Abraham. Second, although Abimelech has met God, he does not mention this encounter, or God's command, to Abraham. Based on this, as we can assume that, according to God's instruction in his dream (v. 7), Abimelech might

---

77. Niditch, *A Prelude to Biblical Folklore*, 63. According to Niditch, theologically speaking, Genesis 20 emphasizes that God actively becomes "the spokesman for restoration," while in Genesis 12 God only appears as "plague sender."

ask Abraham to pray for him and his household. It is clear that, through prayer, Abraham puts himself into a special relationship with God. We may conclude, therefore, that God's intervention is envisioned particularly in the dream of the foreign ruler in Story B, while God still stays hidden from Abraham, the bearer of His promise.[78]

Minor Characters

The minor characters at play in Story B are the people of Gerar and those who are with Abraham. They all have unimportant roles: they only function to support the flow of the narrative. The Gerarites, first, appear implicitly in verse 2, which indicates that Abimelech sent for and took Sarah. We are not told how Abimelech knew of Sarah and her status. If we think of Story A, Abimelech might have received the information about Sarah from his officers, but Story B does not say anything about it. From a type-scene point of view, although the author considerably reduces the role of the Gerarites, the readers can assume their role from the information they get in Story A, in which the Egyptians introduce Sarah to Pharaoh and praise her.

The Gerarites come on the scene again the morning after Abimelech meets God in a dream. Unlike the Egyptians in Story A, they do not speak even in the narrator's voice. They are called "the officials" in Story A (Gen 12:15), while they are called "the servants" in Story B (Gen 20:8). In this case, we need to consider the surrounding context. The Sodom narrative precedes this one, so Story B should be read in relation to the Sodom narrative. When Abraham thinks of the Gerarites as having no fear of God, he might have come to this conclusion because of the incident with the Sodomites.[79] The Gerarites' response, however, indicates that Abraham's assumption was totally wrong. They are seized with a great fear of God, since a dream is considered a device of divine revelation.

Verse 16 introduces the people who are with Abraham, but they have no role except to function as observers. Finally, we can see Abimelech's wife and slave women, who are troubled with infertility on account of Sarah in verses 17–18. Through Abraham's prayer, they are healed and can have children again. We do not learn any other information about them; they are only secondary flat characters. Their function, however, is very important here: they can have children. These secondary characters, therefore, function as devices to let Abraham and Sarah know God's power to allow a birth

---

78. Humphreys, *The Character of God in the Book of Genesis*, 129.

79. Hamilton, *The Book of Genesis 18–50*, 67–68; Wenham, *Genesis 16–50*, 72; Mathews, *Genesis 11:27—50:26*, 256.

to whomever He wants. It is clear that YHWH allows Abraham to pray for bearing children and it is fulfilled. We then naturally have a question: Will he pray for his wife's fertility? Will Sarah also give a child to Abraham?[80] Through these minor characters, therefore, the narrator lets the reader prepare to see the fulfillment of God's promise of the seed (Gen 21).

Themes

In type-scene analysis an important step is to observe the repetition and variation of the stories. In particular, themes are crucial for the connection between the stories. I have discussed how various scholars view the theme of the wife/sister stories, but I have also argued that each story has its own primary theme, since the author puts each story into its own context. Three major themes of Genesis—that is, the promise of the seed, the land, and the blessings—also become common in the wife/sister stories. As we observed, Story A clearly has the promise of land as its primary theme.

As for Story B, however, we must observe its theme in relation to the text and its surrounding contexts. For example, after observing Story B's close relation to the Sodom narrative (Gen 18 and 19), Daniel H. Gordis argues that the primary theme of Story B must be a moral issue.[81] Likewise, David L. Petersen also insists that there are two important themes in Story B: the fear of Elohim and the dialectic of sin.[82] At a glance, these themes are important, but if we keep the entire book of Genesis in mind, they cannot be the primary themes of Story B. We need to apply the central themes of the whole book to the wife/sister stories.

Seed

As we have already observed the theme of the promised seed is the most important theme in the book of Genesis, particularly in the Abrahamic narrative. For this reason, we can see the theme of the seed in almost all of the scenes of the Abraham narrative. Story A, however, does not focus on this theme; instead, it centers on the theme of the land. In contrast, Story B gives less attention to the theme of the land, but is much more focused on the theme of the seed. In Story A the author hardly addresses Sarah's status at

---

80. See, Hamilton, *Genesis 18–50*, 71.
81. Gordis, "Lies, Wives and Sisters," 350–51.
82. Petersen, "A Thrice-Told Tale," 40–41.

the house of Pharaoh. Because of this, when we look at Story B, we cannot miss how much that author highlights Sarah's purity.

The most significant difference between Stories A and B is Story B's reference to the status of Sarah. The whole narrative begins with the indication of Sarah's status, the wife of Abraham (v. 2) and ends with the restoration of her status (v. 18). God actively protects Sarah from Abimelech by warning him not to approach her and by making his wife and the women in his house infertile as judgment.[83] Surprisingly, the author repeatedly mentions that Abimelech did not touch Sarah, not only through God and the narrator's voices (vv. 4, 6) but also through Abimelech's defense (v. 5). Indeed, the God of Story B is the God who makes people barren as well as fertile. This theme is maximized in the last verse of Story B, where God, who has made the Gerarite women barren, restores their fertility through Abraham's prayer. The readers, of course, can expect that God is going to restore Sarah from barrenness, as well.

This theme of the seed is clearer when we observe it in relation to the surrounding contexts. In Gen 18:10 and 14, we are told that God promises Sarah that she will deliver a child to Abraham in a year's time. Story B consists of subsequent events (20:1). It is best understood in light of God's annunciation. Without rapid intervention from God, the readers might be suspicious about the father of the child that Sarah will bear (Gen 21:1–2). This is why God's intervention is so quickly needed and why the text itself continues to confirm Sarah's purity in the house of Abimelech.

Verse 18 in particular clearly relates to the subsequent narrative, in which Sarah finally gives birth to the promised child, Isaac. After observing the close association between Gen 20 and 21, Sarna concludes, "a closer look reveals that their present position is intentional and purposeful. The relief of Sarah's infertility through the birth of a son is juxtaposed with the removal of the infirmity that afflicted Abimelech's household, thereby enabling the women to give birth (20:17f)."[84]

We need to be reminded of one more thing at this point. The previous Sodom narrative ends with the birth of Lot's descendants through his two daughters (Gen 19:30–38). The narrative flows in Gen 18 to 21 are all about the birth of descendants. At the end of the Sodom narrative we see Lot's seed; at the end of Story B, we also see the restoration of childbirth in Abimelech's house; and finally, at the beginning of the next narrative (Gen 21), God allows Abraham the promised seed.

---

83. See McKeown, *Genesis*, 110.
84. Sarna, *Genesis*, 145.

In terms of the primary theme of Story B, therefore, we can conclude that the author carefully deals with the theme of the seed throughout the narrative and its surrounding narratives.

Blessing

Because YHWH promises that Abraham will be blessed and will be a blessing to the nations, the encounter with the foreign rulers in the three wife/sister stories have the theme of blessing in common (Gen 12:3).[85] Story B contains considerable development of this theme compared to Story A. As mentioned above, the theme of blessing in Story A is not noticeable. The nations will receive blessings or curses from God in connection to their relationship with the patriarchs. In Story A, however, a curse is only seen because of Pharaoh's maltreatment of Abraham and Sarah. Abraham's ruse brings a curse to Pharaoh and his household. Therefore, he fails to bring a blessing to the nations.

Although the fact that Abraham shows lack of faith is the same in both narratives, Story B goes one step further. Verse 7 clearly indicates that Abraham is a prophet and his prayer will be the only way for Abimelech to live. Here, Story B highlights that Abraham could be a blessing or a curse to the nations. As a prophet, Abraham can mediate between God and the nations. Abraham already practiced this role in the Sodom narrative: through his intercession, Lot is saved from the destruction of Sodom. Likewise, Abimelech and his nation can be blessed through Abraham's intercession. In fact, the movement from infertility to fertility in verses 17–18 is an important sign of God's blessing. Therefore, while Abraham in Story A curses Pharaoh, his role in Story B is more developed by his prayer, which brings an actual blessing of restoration to the nation.

Finally, we need to observe how the theme of blessing appears in the two Abraham-Abimelech narratives (Gen 20:1–18 and 21:22–34). These two stories function as bookends for the story of the birth of Isaac (Gen 21:1–13) and the expulsion of Ishmael (Gen 21:14–21). In this second story, Abimelech sees that God is with Abraham in everything he does, so he requests a treaty with Abraham. Abimelech clearly acknowledges God's blessing upon Abraham. By establishing a covenant with Abraham, Abimelech just wants to make sure that the blessing and covenantal relationship will be passed on to his descendants. We may conclude, therefore, that the theme

---

85. Biddle, "The 'Endangered Ancestress' and Blessing for the Nations," 608; Mathews, *Genesis 11:27—50:26*, 122.

of blessing functions more importantly in Story B than in Story A, though it is not this story's primary theme.

Land

The theme of the land is the primary concern of Story A, which begins with departure from the land and ends with return to the land. In contrast, Story B does not concern the Promised Land itself. Although the exact location of Gerar is uncertain, it can be defined as the southern border of Canaan (Gen 10:19).[86] Abraham is still in the land of Canaan. Because of this, Gerar lacks thematic importance and only functions as a spatial background in verses 1–2. Furthermore, in Story A Pharaoh expels Abraham from Egypt resulting in Abraham's return to the land of Canaan. Surprisingly, however, in Story B, Abimelech shows generosity to Abraham and allows Abraham to stay in his territory (v. 15). It is worth noting how Abimelech refers to the land. He calls it "my land" in verse 15. So, by allowing Abraham to dwell in his land, in fact, Abimelech exercises his own rights over the land.[87] Although this land is included in the Promised Land, the narrative indicates that the land is still Abimelech's. From these observations, we can conclude that the land is not an important issue in Story B up to this point.

Plot

As a self-contained narrative, Story B has a plotline, including beginning, middle, and end. This plotline generates conflict and resolution. Compared with Story A, the plotline of Story B is more complicated.

---

86. Koch, *The Growth of the Biblical Tradition*, 128; Westermann, *Genesis 12–36*, 320; Hamilton, *The Book of Genesis 18–50*, 59; Matthews, "The Wells of Gerar," 118–26; Mathews, *Genesis 11:27—50:26*, 251; Oren, "Gerar," 989–91. In Gen 10:19, Gerar belongs to the territory of the land of Canaan, and, according to 1 Chr 4:39–41, the tribe of Simeon settled there and made it their own inheritance (as Oren suggests reading 1 Chr 4:39 following the LXX). Gerar is mentioned for the last time in 2 Chr 14:12–15. Asa, the king of Judah, chased Zerah and the Cushites from the Valley of Zephathat near Mareshah to Gerar. It seems that Gerar is a city on the way to Egypt. Among the candidates of the exact place for Gerar, at this point, Tell Haror (Tell Abu Hureirah) is a bit more relevant. Tell Haror is placed around 20 km from the west of Beer-Sheba and on the main road from Beer-Sheba to Gaza. Other possible sites have been suggested: Tell Jemmeh (six miles south of Gaza), Tell-Dshemme (14 km south of Gaza), Esh-Sheria (25 km southeast of Gaza), etc. See Koch, especially.

87. McKeown, "The Theme of Land in Genesis 1–11 and Its Significance for the Abraham Narrative, Part 2," 141.

Beginning

The narrative background is provided at the beginning of the story. We are given the spatial background, and the main character, Abraham, appears on the stage. Without explicit explanation, Abraham moves from Mamre to Negev and to Gerar. From this setting, the narrative prepares for the conflict. Abraham, who goes down to Gerar, might experience an unknown crisis like the one he met in Egypt. In Story A, narrative time slows down in order to describe the preparation of the major conflict (Gen 12:11–13), while Story B passes swiftly on in order to spend more time in the climax. We may consult Story A to more fully understand the situation in the beginning of Story B, although the narrator does not discuss it in detail.

Middle

The middle section of Story B is clearly different from that of Story A. Story A only describes God's intervention and judgment without explanation, while Story B contains two long dialogues between God and Abimelech and Abimelech and Abraham. In Story B, the narrative moves quickly to its climax without any development of crisis, and the climax itself is greatly expanded. On the same night Abimelech took Sarah to his house, God intervenes to protect Sarah from Abimelech (v. 3). Abimelech protests his innocence before God (vv. 4–5), and God confirms Abimelech's innocence (v. 6). This dialogue between God and Abimelech finally reaches a resolution through God's instruction (v. 7), that Abimelech should restore Sarah to Abraham and seek Abraham's prayer. The expression "early the next morning" in verse 8 makes it is clear that Abimelech will resolve the problem according to God's instruction.

Verse 8 functions as both the resolution of the story's first climax and the beginning of a new conflict. This conflict, however, is not at the same level as the first, because the original conflict generated in verse 2 is still not fully resolved. As we see in the diagram below, God's intervention in the first climax is the key to resolving all crises, while the second climax simply shows that Abraham is unqualified to be the key to resolve the crises. Abimelech summons and rebukes Abraham, which raises another crisis between Abimelech and Abraham. Abimelech accuses Abraham two times, and Abraham defends himself before Abimelech; this conversation serves as the story's second climax. Abimelech's resolution, then, is given in verses 14–16, which is much more expansive than Story A (Gen 12:20). When

Abimelech restores Sarah to Abraham and gives him gifts to cover his offense (v. 16), the original conflict is finally resolved.

End

The narrative now comes to the end. The conflict generated by God in verses 3 and 7 is finally resolved: Abimelech's wife and the women in his house can have children again through Abraham's intercessional prayer. As a result, all crises raised in the beginning of the story have been resolved.

The plotline of Story B can be depicted as follows:

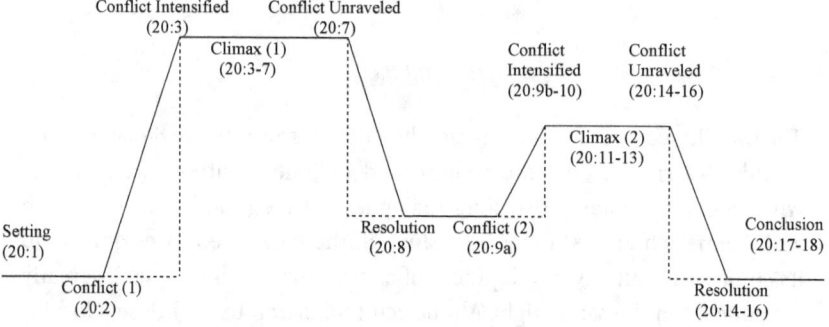

Figure 3: The Plotline of Story B.

Conclusion

In this chapter, we have explored the second wife/sister story in Genesis. First, by applying a textlinguistic perspective, we determined the extent of Story B, closely examined the surrounding narratives, and clarified the structure and the textual meaning of Story B. Second, from a type-scene point of view, we considered how Story B is closely related to Story A (Genesis 12:10—13:1) in terms of both similarities and variations. I have shown in this chapter that we must not overlook the considerable similarities between Stories A and B. On top of this, we have observed how these two narratives demonstrate developments in characters, themes, and plot.

First, God is always the main character, whose intervention is the turning point of the plotline. God is implied in the narrator's voice in Story A, as He preemptively speaks and acts in order to protect His promises and the bearers of His promises. We can conclude, therefore, that the characterization of God moves from elusive to explicit.

The human characters in the narratives also make progress, either positively or negatively. The characterizations of Abraham and Sarah change throughout the narratives. In Story A, they reveal their lack of faithfulness, but this is because of their misunderstanding of God's promise. In Story B, however, they clearly have God's promise- particularly the promise of the seed through Abraham and Sarah—but they have no fear of God, fearing Abimelech instead. As a result, Abraham deceives Abimelech and puts Sarah and God's promise in danger. Sarah's character is also more fully developed in Story B. She has no voice in Story A, but in Story B she is a little more active. Overall, she is a flat character throughout the narratives, but, in Story B she speaks to Abimelech and Abimelech speaks to her.

The character of the foreign rulers has been developed, as well. In comparison with Abraham and Sarah, both foreign rulers are shown to have a higher level of morality. When we compare Abimelech with Pharaoh, however, we can see that the moral characterization of Abimelech is more clearly developed. Abimelech protests his innocence before God, and God confirms it. Further, while Pharaoh expels Abraham and Sarah, Abimelech allows them to dwell wherever they want.

Second, we have examined the themes of each story in terms of God's promises to Abraham of seed, land, and blessing (Gen 12:1–3). From the study of these themes in each story, we have observed that each narrative has emphasized a specific theme, though all themes are discovered in each narrative. Story A highlights the theme of land, while Story B focuses on the theme of seed.

Third, in terms of plot, although the two narratives look very similar to one another, each plotline is quite different. Because it has complementary features, Story B should be understood in the light of Story A.

In conclusion, a close investigation on the second wife/sister story in relation to the first wife/sister story reveals that the author clearly keeps similarity and variations in mind and describes them from a type-scene point of view. The readers, therefore, should understand the two narratives together and synthesize them. This conclusion prepares us to look at the third and final wife/sister story in Gen 26:1–11. After exploring the third narrative in the next chapter, we will finally get the whole picture that the author portrays through the three wife/sister stories.

CHAPTER FOUR

The Third Wife/Sister Story
(Genesis 26:1–11)

IN THE PREVIOUS CHAPTERS, we explored Story A (Gen 12:10—13:1) and Story B (Gen 20:1–18). We now come to the last piece of the wife/sister motif. This chapter will examine the third wife/sister story (Story C), which appears in Gen 26:1–11. Story C is in part of the Isaac narrative, whereas Stories A and B are part of the Abraham narrative. Nevertheless, it is clear that Story C is closely related to Stories A and B, which use the same type-scene motif.

Among the three wife/sister motifs, only Story C concerns the story of Isaac and Rebekah. Although Isaac is considered as a patriarch, he only appears in seven chapters (21:1–7, 8–14; 22:1–19; 24:62–67; 25:19–28; 26:1–35; 29:1–46; and 35:27–29) and is mostly mentioned in relation to his father, Abraham, or his sons, Esau and Jacob. Genesis 26 is the only chapter of the Patriarchal narratives (Genesis 12–50) in which Isaac plays a central role. In relation to the whole Isaac narrative, then, it is reasonable to give special attention to Genesis 26. In this chapter, we will first examine the text in a textlinguistic method, carefully studying the literary style and structure, as well as its context. We will then specifically investigate Story C from a type-scene perspective.

Delimitation of the Discourse Unit

Delimiting Story C is far more difficult than delimiting Stories A and B. Scholars have offered a variety of views on the extent of Story C. These are listed in the following table.

THE THIRD WIFE/SISTER STORY

Table 7: Delimitation of Story C

	Delimitation	Scholars
A	26:1–11	McKeown, Matthews, Cotter, Hamilton, Wenham, Westermann, Thompson, Wagner[1]
B	26:6–11	Sailhamer, Towner, Fretheim, Sarna, Speiser, Driver[2]
C	26:7–11	Woychuk, Waltke, Gunkel, Brueggemann, von Rad, Maly, Skinner (363–65)[3]
D	26:1–13	Koch, Culley, Alexander, Weimar[4]
E	26:1–14	Schmitt[5]
F	26:1–16	Arnold, Kessler and Deurloo[6]
G	26:1–17	Currid, Ska, Niditch, Garrett, Coats[7]

As this table shows, there is no consensus on the extent of Story C. Most scholars have, however, come to agree on its beginning. The first word,

---

1. McKeown, *Genesis*, 129-30; Mathews, *Genesis 11:27—50:26*, 401-7; Cotter, *Genesis*, 193-94; Westermann, *Genesis 12-36*, 424-26; Hamilton, *The Book of Genesis 18-50*, 189-91; Wenham, *Genesis 16-50*, 184-88; Thompson, *The Origin Tradition of Ancient Israel*, 55; Van Seters, *Abraham in History and Tradition*, 167-83; Wagner, "Literary Analysis of Gen 12-36," 149.

2. Sailhamer, *Genesis*, 229-30; Sarna, *Genesis*, 184; Towner, *Genesis*, 142; Speiser, *Genesis*, 203; Fretheim, "The Book of Genesis," 527; Driver, *The Book of Genesis*, 249-51.

3. Woychuk, "The Rhetorical Functions of Genesis 26," 160; Waltke, *Genesis*, 368-69; Gunkel and Biddle, *Genesis*, 293-95; Brueggemann, *Genesis*, 127, 221; von Rad, *Genesis*, 270-71; Maly, "Genesis 12:10-20; 20:1-18; 26:7-11 and the Pentateuchal Question," 255; Skinner, A Critical and Exegetical Commentary on Genesis, 363-65. Regarding the extent, Brueggemann has been confused between 6-11 and 7-11. In his commentary he designates 7-11 for Story A, but 6-11 for Story C. Also, Waltke basically sees 2-16 as the extent, although he divides 7-11 for Story C.

4. Alexander, "The Wife/Sister Incidents of Genesis: Oral Variants?," 3-4; Weimar, *Untersuchungen zur Redaktionsgeschichte Des Pentateuch*, 16; Culley, *Studies in the Structure of Hebrew Narrative*, 33-41; Koch, *The Growth of the Biblical Tradition*, 111-32. Culley does not decide between 1-13 and 1-14.

5. Schmitt, "Zu Gen 26:1-14," 143-56.

6. Arnold, *Genesis*, 137-38; Kessler and Deurloo, *A Commentary on Genesis*, 147-48.

7. Ska, *Introduction to Reading the Pentateuch*, 56-57; Currid, *Genesis Chapters 25:19—50:26*, 24-30; Niditch, *A Prelude to Biblical Folklore*, 23-69; Garrett, *Rethinking Genesis*, 131-37; Coats, *Genesis*, 188-91. Ska's view is inconsistent between 1-11 and 1-17. On the other hand, Garrett considers vv. 2-6 to represent another source and eliminates these verses from Story C.

וַיְהִי, is a clear sign for a new beginning (cf. Gen 12:10). The narrator's voice follows: "besides the earlier famine of Abraham's time." This is, as Adele Berlin maintains, a common sign of "breaking frame."[8] Furthermore, the content of Story C itself is clearly different from the Esau and Jacob narrative that precedes it.

If we consider verse 6 or verse 7 as the beginning of Story C, we must explain that the divine promise in verses 2–5 has nothing to do with the wife/sister motif. Duane Garrett, for example, argues that the divine intervention in verses 2–5 comes from other sources; this is part of his attempt to rebuild three stories according to the same pattern: migration, deception, abduction, deliverance, confrontation, and conclusion.[9] In considering this position, we need to consider the following. First, as mentioned earlier, it is important to observe not only the similarity, but also variations. Second, based on the previous wife/sister stories (Gen 12 and 20), the divine intervention, which makes a turning point in the narrative (12:17; 20:3-7), is crucial to the wife/sister story. Van Seters, unlike many scholars, considers Gen 26 as a unified narrative and argues that the divine promise in verses 3–5 is primary in Isaac's narrative itself.[10] Third, verse 1 recalls Story A by mentioning a famine in the land, which is different from the earlier famine in Abraham's time. By adding this phrase, the author intends to connect Story C to Story A, while also establishing difference. The author then introduces Abimelech who has the same name as a similar character in Story B. In this regard, verse 1 plays a crucial role in connecting Story C to Stories A and B. We can conclude, therefore, that Story C begins with Gen 26:1.

Arguing that the story begins at verse 6 or verse 7 is not sustainable. Verse 6 clearly recalls and restates verse 1, so these two verses form an *inclusio*. Furthermore, verse 7 presupposes verse 6 by referring to "that place." Therefore, the reference in verse 6 to Isaac's stay in Gerar performs double duty here. For the first scene, it forms an *inclusio*, while for the second scene it provides a spatial background.

Scholars have made various attempts to identify the end of Story C. We must acknowledge two things at this point. First, there is no apparent ending point dividing the subunits in Gen 26, so scholars divide it in a number of

---

8. Berlin, *Poetics and Interpretation of Biblical Narrative*, 57–58. According to Berlin, the narrator uses two kinds of temporal frame in order to break narrative frame either by giving information from a later time or adding the story to some previous event.

9. Garrett, *Rethinking Genesis*, 132–33. By the same token, he eliminates vv. 14–16 from Story C.

10. Van Seters, *Prologue to History*, 267–70. Based on this understanding, he argues that Isaac's wealth in vv. 12–16 must be the fulfillment of YHWH's promise in vv. 3–5.

ways.[11] Second, Gen 26 has many close relationships to the Abraham narratives, as many scholars observe. This is true not only for the wife/sister story, but also for the other units in Gen 26. This means that, in terms of similarities, Gen 26 as a whole is widely connected to several narratives about Abraham's experiences. It is difficult, therefore, to determine the end of Story C by observing the similarities of certain story elements. Garrett and Coats, for example, emphasize the element of expulsion in the wife/sister stories, and from this perspective argue that Story C should end with verse 17, which describes Isaac's expulsion.[12] However, the deportation of the Patriarch is not a necessary part of the wife/sister stories—we must keep in mind that Story B does not contain this element, so the deportation theme is not required in Story C. Thematically speaking, the reason Abraham's deportation is included in Story A is that the major theme of Story A is the land. Stories B and C, therefore, need not include this element.

When it comes to the end of Story C, we need to observe that verse 11 provides a clear resolution for the wife/sister story, as the foreign ruler removes the tension in the narrative by proclaiming the safety of Isaac and Rebekah. Verses 12–16 contain a strife motif, which does not resemble the wife/sister narratives, but the strife of Abraham and Lot that immediately follows Story A. Gordon Wenham rightly declares, "Indeed, [Genesis 26] serves a most important function locking together the Abraham and Jacob cycles and highlighting the parallels between Abraham and his son. Its position and content invite the reader to reflect on the similarities and differences between the careers of Abraham and of Isaac."[13]

By observing similarities between Genesis 26 and the Abraham narratives, then, Story C can be seen as ending with verse 11.

Textlinguistic Analysis

Having reached a conclusion on the extent of Story C, we will now closely examine the story from a textlinguistic perspective.

---

11. So, for example, Gunkel divides it into five units: 1–6, 7–11, 12–17a, 17b–22, and 23–33, while Coats simply divides it into two units: 1–17 and 17–33. Gunkel, *Genesis*, 293; Coats, *Genesis*, 188–95.

12. Garrett, *Rethinking Genesis*, 133; Coats, *Genesis*, 190–91.

13. Wenham, *Genesis 16–50*, 187.

Story C within the Surrounding Narratives

Before beginning detailed discussion of the text, we must immediately recognize that there are significantly different views on the proper place of Gen 26. This lack of coherence has been a source of serious debate among scholars. Regarding the connection between Gen 26 and its contexts, Gerhard von Rad states, "These Isaac traditions were written down essentially in their ancient version, without being harmonized with the subsequent large composition of the patriarchal stories."[14] Likewise Westermann views Gen 26 as an "intentional composition"—that is, a later insertion that is not an original part of the Jacob *Toledot*: "Ch. 26 has been subsequently interpolated into an already existing sequence as a self-contained literary composition."[15]

Scholars have suggested the following problems. First, from the previous narrative, the readers know of the existence of Rebekah's two sons, Esau and Jacob, and even that they are grown (Gen 25:27–34). If Rebekah gave birth to two sons who are now fully grown, how can the people of Gerar not recognize her motherhood? We find no hint of the existence of two sons in Story C.[16] On the other hand, in the subsequent narrative, Isaac is in his old age and nearly blind. Isaac's situation in Gen 27 is an awkward fit with Gen 26.[17] With regard to wealth, although Abraham left everything he possessed to Isaac (Gen 25:5), Isaac does not seem particularly prosperous at the beginning of Story C. Then, in verses 12–16, we find a transparent indication of Isaac's wealth.[18]

These considerations prompt some scholars to suggest that Gen 26 should be placed before Gen 25. From a literary perspective, George G. Nicol emphasizes that Gen 26 is anachronical, functioning as a "flashback."[19]

---

14. von Rad, *Genesis*, 270.

15. Westermann, *Genesis 12–36*, 423.

16. Kuruvilla, *Genesis*, 305–6; Waltke, *Genesis*, 367; Fretheim, "The Book of Genesis," 526; Gunkel and Biddle, *Genesis*, 293. Gunkel places it before the time of Gen 25:22. Also, Kuruvilla argues that Story C should take place within the time of Rebekah's barrenness.

17. Vawter, *On Genesis*, 290. Vawter summarizes the place of Genesis 26 and critically concludes, "The whole is timeless in relation to what precedes and follows it: Isaac and his wife are a young couple, as in 24:67, unencumbered by the young adult sons of 25:27–34, and certainly decades removed from the advanced age they have attained by chapter 27."

18. Nicol, "The Chronology of Genesis: Genesis XXVI 1–33 as 'Flashback,'" 337.

19. Ibid., 330.

Gen. xxvi 1–33 as a "flashback," the retrospective narration of events supposed to have taken place before the birth of Esau and Jacob. Apart from this supposition, the promise of numerous progeny would not be threatened in any meaningful way. Since the narrative functions as "flashback," the reader already knows of Esau and Jacob so that the narrative is required only to resolve the circumstances that threatened the promise of progeny.[20]

In contrast, James A. Woychuk explains Nicol's observations in different ways. He argues, first of all, that the lack of reference to Esau and Jacob does not prove their absence.[21] John Ronning elaborates on this view, arguing that Isaac was probably very rich, and there is no reason to assume that only four family members came into Gerar. Isaac had many people working for him, as well as his own family, so he could have concealed his two sons in various ways.[22]

Second, the argument that Isaac does not prosper until 26:12–16 is also inferential. It is clear that Isaac is the successor of Abraham's great wealth (25:5, 11), and there is no conflict between the references to his wealth (25:5, 11 and 26:12–16). Just as God's promise of blessing appears twice (26:2–5 and 24), Isaac's prosperity can appear more than once.

Wenham goes one step further. He notes that there are eight explicit references to Abraham in Gen 26 (26:1, 3, 5, 15, 18x2, and 24x2). Besides these explicit expressions, a number of motifs in Gen 26 parallel the stories about Abraham.[23] He especially relates Gen 26 to both 12:10—14:20 and 20:1—21:31 as follows:[24]

---

20. Ibid., 343.

21. Woychuk, "The Rhetorical Functions of Genesis 26," 172; Vrolijk, *Jacob's Wealth*, 55–56.

22. Ronning, "The Naming of Isaac," 20.

23. Wenham, *Genesis 16–50*, 187. Regarding the place of Genesis 26, see chapter 3. Many scholars, including Fishbane, observe that Genesis 26 is closely connected to Genesis 34 in its functions within the Isaac *Toledot*. Fishbane, *Text and Texture*, 42, 47. Fishbane concludes, "Genesis 26 serves as an interlude between the opening oracle of strife and tension and its fulfillment. And Genesis 34 serves as an interlude bridging Jacob's reconciliation with Esau and the denouement at Beth-el." Also see Rendsburg, *The Redaction of Genesis*, 58–59: "they *(Genesis 26 and 34)* function in the same way within the Cycle, as important interludes craftly placed by our master compiler."

24. Wenham, *Genesis 16–50*, 187.

Table 8: Comparison between Genesis 26 and Genesis 12:10–14:20

26:1–11	Famine and the wife/sister	12:10–20
26:12–22	Wealth prompts quarrels between patriarch's herdsmen and others	13:2–10
26:23	Separation	13:11–12
26:24	Divine promise of descendants	13:14–17
26:25	Altar built, patriarch encamps	13:18
26:26–31	Good relations established with foreigners	chap. 14
26:29	Patriarch blessed by foreign king	14:19–20

Likewise there are certain connections between Genesis 26 and 20:1—21:31

Table 9: Comparison between Genesis 26 and Genesis 20:1—21:31

26:1–11	The wife/sister	20:1–18
26:15–21	Disputes about wells	21:25
26:26	Abimelek and Phicol	21:22
26:28	"The Lord has been with you"	21:22
26:28	Let there be an oath	21:23
26:30–31	Treaty made	21:24–31
26:32–33	Well of Beersheba named	21:31

Wenham concludes, "Indeed, [Genesis 26] serves a most important function locking together the Abraham and Jacob Cycles and highlighting the parallels between Abraham and his son. Its position and content invite the reader to reflect on the similarities and differences between the careers of Abraham and of Isaac."[25] Based on these observations, it is plausible that Gen 26 is properly placed in the Isaac *Toledot* as well as in relation to the Abraham narratives. Therefore, we can confidently say that Gen 26 is hardly misplaced in its present context, since the text itself calls readers to read it within the context. It is clear that this story about Isaac is intended to refer back to Abraham's story, while also making connections to the Jacob narratives.

25. Ibid.

Structure

We have now explored the place of Story C within its context and concluded that Story C is well placed in its current context. Now we must narrow our focus from the context to the structure of Story C. As we observed, the three wife/sister stories have clear similarities, though each story is distinct. In comparison to Stories A and B, however, Story C does not seem to have the same apparent structure.

Alexander observes the structural similarities among the wife/sister stories. He identifies the following structural elements: reason for locale (vv. 1–6a), the deception (vv. 6b–7), discovery of ruse (v. 8), interview with foreigner (vv. 9–10), and final outcome (vv. 11–13).[26] On the other hand, Cotter divides Story C into five sections: exposition (1a), development (1b–6), turning point (7), resolution (8), and conclusion (9).[27] Finally, Weimar dissects Story C into three units. Since he maintains the extent of Story C as vv 1–13, if we only focus only on verses 1–11, he identifies two units:[28]

Exposition (26,1aαb)

I. Szene (26.2aα.3a.6: Jahwe-Isaak

    1. Erscheinungsrede Jahwes (26,2aα.3a)

    2. Ausführungsnotiz (Isaak) (26,6)

II. Szene (26,7–9, 11)

    1. Bericht-Rede-Bericht (26, 7–8)

    2. Wechselrede Abimelek-Isaak +Edikt Abimeleks (26,9 +11)

III. Szene (26, 12–13): Isaak

    1. Bericht (Segen Jahwes) (26, 12)

    2. Konstatierende Notiz (26, 13)

As mentioned above, Gen 26:1 is clearly the beginning of Story C. Furthermore, verses 1b and 6 form an *inclusio*.[29] Verse 1 states that Isaac is moving toward Gerar and verse 6 states that he stays in Gerar. It is plausible, therefore, to view verses 1–6 as the first unit. The divine intervention is placed in the center of this unit.

---

26. Alexander, *Abraham in the Negev*, 42.
27. Cotter, *Genesis*, 193.
28. Weimar, *Untersuchungen zur Redaktionsgeschichte Des Pentateuch*, 93.
29. Gunkel, *Genesis*, 294. Wenham, *Genesis 16–50*, 184.

The divine promise in verses 2–5 can also be divided into two subunits. Verse 2 contains a simple command to stay in the land that God designates, while verses 3–5 contain divine promises. In particular, verses 3–5 share the same structure as YHWH's promise in Gen 12:2–3.

Verses 7–11 can be identified as the second unit of Story C. These verses clearly parallel Stories A and B. This unit also contains two subunits. In verses 7–10, the narrative crisis is growing, while verse 11 provides a resolution.

Based on these observations, we can outline the structure of Story C as follows:

I. Scene One (vv. 1–6)

   A Isaac in Gerar (v. 1)

     B God's Promise (vv. 2–5)

        a God's Command (vv. 2–3a)

        b God's Promises (vv. 3b–5)

   A' Isaac in Gerar (v. 6)

II. Scene Two (vv. 7–11)

   A Deception (vv. 6b–7)

   B Crisis (v. 8)

     a Abimelech's Witness (v. 8)

     b Abimelech and Isaac (vv. 9–10)

   C Resolution

Textual Analysis

Based on the structural analysis, this section will present more specific study on each unit. Of course, from a type-scene perspective, Story C should be considered in relation to Story A and B.

Scene One (26:1–6)

Scene one narrates the arrival of a famine, Isaac's move to Gerar, God's intervention with promises, and Isaac's stay in Gerar in response to God's command. The basic role of this scene is to provide the background for scene two. Based on our understanding of God's promises we can properly evaluate Isaac and Rebekah in scene two. In addition, Gerar provides the spatial background for scene two. As mentioned above, we can confirm that verses 1–6 form a unit by observing the *inclusio* between verse 1 and 6. The divine intervention in verses 2–5 thus forms the center of scene one.

Isaac in Gerar (26:1)

The first phrase, וַיְהִי רָעָב בָּאָרֶץ, is identical to the beginning of Story A. The use of this same expression indicates the beginning of a new unit and it reveals its connection to Story A. Following this introductory phrase, the narrator clarifies that this famine is different from the one that took place in Abraham's time. This comment is often viewed, as the work of a later redactor who wanted to connect Story C to the Abraham narratives. However, if we look at the story from a type-scene perspective, this phrase is revealed as a well-designed device that helps readers relate Story C to Story A, while maintaining both similarity and variation. The narrator's voice in 1b is not a later insertion, but a literary device that recalls the previous story.

As a result of the famine, Isaac goes to Abimelech, the king of the Philistines, in Gerar. By referring to Abimelech, Story C also recalls Story B. Although the same name, Abimelech, is used in both Story B and C, it is not necessary to view these characters as the same person. It is worth noting that Abimelech is called "king of Gerar" in Story B and "king of Philistines" in Gerar in Story C. On the other hand, some scholars argue that the characters named Abimelech in Story B and C represent the same person.[30] It appears that these scholars are trying to explain these two stories as variants of the same tradition.[31] Kenneth A. Mathews, however, argues that (1) the term "Abimelech" may be understood as a throne title, and (2) Gerar is a small city-state, while the Philistines are a larger ethnic group. He concludes that "the broader title 'king of the Philistines' in verse 1 is not a literary variant but a rhetorical device that contributes to the chapter's emphasis on divine blessing for the nations."[32]

---

30. Clines, "The Ancestor in Danger: But Not the Same Danger," 79–80. BHS includes a dagesh in מ in the name Abimelech. Because the place of this dagesh is unusual, many manuscripts remove it. According to E. A. Knauf, dagesh is added to distinguish Abimelech in Story C from the previous one in Story B. Knauf, "Dagesh Agrammaticum im Codex Leningradensis," 23–35. Re-cited from Wenham, *Genesis 16–50*, 183.

31. Mathews, *Genesis 11:27—50:26*, 402–3.

32. Ibid., 403.

The reference to the Philistines is problematic. The term "Philistines" as an ethnicity first appeared during the reign of Ramesses III, who opposed the Sea people in the twelfth century. The name is mentioned several times in the patriarchal narratives (Gen 21:32, 34; 26:1; Exod 23:17, 31). Consequently many scholars, including Van Seters, view this as an evidence of anachronism.[33] Kitchen raises some important questions concerning the possibility of different non-Canaanite people from the Aegean, who settled in the five cities of the coastal plain. According to him, the Philistines in Gerar may not be the same as the people in the five cities.[34] There is thus no need to view the appearance of the Philistines as anachronism.

Divine Intervention (26:2–5)

In comparison with the previous wife/sister stories, Story C presents an impressive level of divine intervention. From the eyes of Abraham, YHWH is elusive in Story A and implicit in Story B, but in Story C God's intervention is direct and preemptive. The narration of this divine intervention can be divided into two subunits: God's command (vv. 2–3a) and God's promises (vv. 3b–5). God's intervention begins with the expression, וַיֵּרָא אֵלָיו יְהוָה, which indicates a theophany. Particularly, וַיֵּרָא is the Niphal form of ראה, which is commonly used for God's self-revelation.[35] As Sarna notes, this expression appears only in Genesis. It occurs six times in the book of Genesis with each occurrence referring to divine self-revelation to one of the three Patriarchs: Abraham (12:7; 17:1; 18:1), Isaac (26:2, 24), and Jacob (35:9).[36] It is clear, therefore, that this expression is used in relation to Isaac in order to connect him to his father Abraham. This becomes clearer if we note divine commands in verses 2–3a.

God's commands contain three imperatives:

אַל־תֵּרֵד מִצְרָיְמָה

שְׁכֹן בָּאָרֶץ

אֲשֶׁר אֹמַר אֵלֶיךָ:

גּוּר בָּאָרֶץ הַזֹּאת

---

33. Van Seters, *Abraham in History and Tradition*, 52–54.

34. Kitchen, *On the Reliability of the Old Testament*, 340–41. For a general review of research history on Palestine, see Ortiz, "Rewriting Philistine History," 191–204. Wenham agrees with Kitchen's argument by noting "archaeological evidence of Aegean contact with the Levant as early as the third millennium B.C." Wenham, *Genesis 16–50*, 189.

35. *HALOT*, 1160; Sarna, *Genesis*, 91–92.

36. Ibid.,

Just like the first introductory expression that recalls God's promise to Abraham, YHWH's commands appear to be associated with God's commands to Abraham. First, YHWH's threefold commands are closely connected to God's threefold commands to Abraham in Gen 12:1–3 and 22:2. Second, each command recalls the previous ones. The first command, אַל־תֵּרֵד מִצְרָיְמָה, is related to Story A, where Abraham goes down to Egypt in order to flee from a severe famine. God's commanding Isaac not to go down to Egypt reminds us of Abraham's case.[37] The second command, שְׁכֹן בָּאָרֶץ אֲשֶׁר אֹמַר אֵלֶיךָ:, echoes Abraham in Gen 12:2 and 22:2 more clearly.

Table 10: Comparison of God's Promise

Gen 26:2	Gen 12:2	Gen 22:2
שְׁכֹן בָּאָרֶץ אֲשֶׁר אֹמַר אֵלֶיךָ:	לֶךְ־לְךָ ... אֶל־הָאָרֶץ אֲשֶׁר אַרְאֶךָּ	לֶךְ־לְךָ אֶל־אֶרֶץ הַמֹּרִיָּה אֲשֶׁר אֹמַר אֵלֶיךָ

According to Wenham, "These allusions make it clear that even if Isaac is not to walk in his father's footsteps geographically, he must follow him spiritually."[38] As observed above, if we identify Gerar as the border of the land of Canaan, the use of שְׁכֹן, which usually indicates permanent residence, is not problematic.[39] The third command, גּוּר בָּאָרֶץ הַזֹּאת, contains a common verb that appears in all three wife/sister stories. This word implies that Isaac temporarily sojourns in Gerar as an alien. This third command is also intended to highlight Isaac's connection to Abraham.

YHWH's three promises (vv. 3–5) immediately follow His three repetitive commands (vv. 3–5): His presence with Isaac (protection: v. 3), blessing (v. 3), and great descendants (v. 4). Not surprisingly, these promises also closely correspond to the promises given to Abraham (Gen 12:1–3). Throughout the promises, the author intentionally uses the "I will" form six times. In terms of keywords, the term "land" occurs five times (vv. 2–4), the term "bless" occurs two times, and the term "seed" occurs four times. The repetition of these keywords clearly emphasizes their relationship with the promises given to Abraham. Another important

---

37. Nevertheless, we should be cautious to conclude that, based on this command, Abraham's going down to Egypt in Story A can be condemned. At the least, Story A has no explicit command not to go down to Egypt. YHWH's command is particularly given to Isaac, and Story C does not simply intend to give an answer of the event in Story A.

38. Wenham, *Genesis 16–50*, 189; Mathews, *Genesis 11:27—50:26*, 403; and Kuruvilla, *Genesis*, 308. In fact, Gen 26:2 is closer to Gen 22:2.

39. *HALOT*, 1497.

keyword is "Abraham," which occurs eight times in Gen 26 (vv. 1, 3, 5, 15, 18, and 24). It is worth noting that the name Abraham occurs only fifteen times from Gen 27 to 50.[40] Its appearance eight times in Gen 26 is thus very impressive. Needless to say, this establishes a strong and explicit connection between Abraham and Isaac.

In order to make this connection even clearer, the author adds the reason for YHWH's blessing to Isaac. Verse 3 indicates that the promise is an oath given by YHWH. The oath in verse 3 also reflects the case of Abraham in Gen 22:16, where the divine oath only appears once. In order to highlight the object of the oath, לְךָ וּלְזַרְעֲךָ comes first in verse 3. Here, the promise of land is given to two separate recipients: Isaac (v. 3) and his descendants (v. 4). The expressions of בָּאָרֶץ in verse 2 and בָּאָרֶץ הַזֹּאת in verse 3 are in singular, while the expression אֶת־כָּל־הָאֲרָצֹת הָאֵל, which is repeats in verses 3 and 4, is in plural.[41] We need to recognize the change of number: "land" is singular in 3a, but it changes to "all these lands" in 3cα and 3f. Why does the text render "land" in plural form if it refers to the land of Canaan? This question led the LXX to modify the text from plural to singular (πᾶσαν τὴν γῆν ταύτην). However, if we recognize that the singular expression "the land" aptly indicates the land of Canaan, we can interpret "the lands" as a reference to the expansion of the land.[42] If so, "all these lands" would apparently refer to Isaac's wealth and strife, as portrayed in verses 12-33. As Mathews notes, this expression serves in its context to foreshadow the strife with the land of Gerar similar to the case of Lot in Gen 13.[43] We should, however, be careful concluding that Gerar does not initially belong to the Promised Land. Isaac stays in the land of Gerar and we are already told that "this land" indicates Gerar.[44]

The divine promises also emphasize that Isaac's descendants will be a great nation and a blessing for the nations. The blessing given to Isaac is motivated not only by God's oath, but also by Abraham's obedience to

---

40. Wenham, *Genesis 16–50*, 187. In this regard, most scholars acknowledge that the central theme of Genesis 26 is the passing of YHWH's blessing from Abraham to Isaac as a new Abraham. See Fokkelman, *Narrative Art in Genesis*, 113; Waltke, *Genesis*, 367.

41. The Samaritan Pentateuch has more usual form, האלה, of הָאֵל (cf. Gen 19:8, 25)

42. Westermann, *Genesis 12–36*, 424; Coats, *Genesis*, 189; Wenham, *Genesis 16–50*, 189–90; Mathews, *Genesis 11:27—50:26*, 404. Also, Sarna (*Genesis*, 183) suggests that "all these lands" can be understood in terms of idealized boundaries of the Promised Land.

43. Mathews, *Genesis 11:27—50:26*, 404.

44. Contra, Vawter, *On Genesis*, 291.

God's commands, decrees, and laws (v. 5).[45] This recalls Gen 22:18, where Abraham obeys God's voice.

From a type-scene perspective, we need to pay attention to God's remarkable intervention in Story C. In Story A YHWH's involvement is only implied in the narrator's words, and in Story B, God explicitly appears in a dream to Abimelech, but not to Abraham. In Story C, however, YHWH reveals Himself to Isaac clearly, directly, and preemptively. In terms of God's intervention, therefore, there is thematic development from elusiveness to fullness over the course of the three stories.

Isaac in Gerar (26:6)

The place name Gerar reappears in verse 6, which contains only three words and functions as a bridge to connect verse 1 with verse 6. As a conclusion, this short statement emphasizes Isaac's simple obedience. Although we cannot confirm the duration of his residence in Gerar, we know that it is quite long (v. 8).

In sum, we can see that scene one focuses on establishing a close connection between Isaac and Abraham. And, by connecting verse 1 to 6, scene one as a whole provides background for the next scene.

Scene Two (26:7–11)

Although scene one contains only a divine monologue, scene two incorporates the dialogue of several characters. This scene clearly parallels the other wife/sister stories. While Isaac immediately obeys God and stays in Gerar, this raises a crisis just like those experienced by his father Abraham.

Deception (26:7)

The scene begins with the Gerarites' inquiry about Isaac's wife. This is the first conversation to appear in Story C. This deception unit is shorter than its equivalent Story A or B. The author thus presupposes some knowledge of how Stories A and B progress.

The change of the subject indicates a new beginning of a unit. Verse 7 contains three elements: question, lie, and reason for the deception. The Gerarites simply ask about Rebekah, the wife of Isaac. The word אִשָּׁה can be

---

45. The LXX and the Samaritan Penatateuch add "your father." This seems to emphasize their relationship, but modification is unnecessary.

translated as both "a wife" and "a woman," and can be understood in either sense in the context of the men of Gerar's inquiry. This is just a question- no more, no less. However, just like his father, Isaac passes off Rebekah as his sister. There are two כִּי clauses that explain why Isaac would lie: his fear, and Rebekah's beauty. Although there is no evidence that the Gerarites posed a threat, Isaac identifies Rebekah not as his wife, but as his sister. If we seriously consider the divine promise of blessing and protection, Isaac's deception appears more problematic. Unlike Stories A and B, Story C contains no dialogue between the spouses regarding the deception. Because God delivers the promises at the outset, Isaac's lie shows that he does not fully trust in God. As a result of his unfaithfulness, he cannot remain under the promise of God. Isaac's lie is worse than Abraham's because YHWH did not show Himself to Abraham but did appear to Isaac.

Recalling the plotline of Stories A and B, we expect that something might happen to Rebekah. In Story C, however, nothing happens to Rebekah or Isaac. The men of Gerar are not evil, as Isaac expected. They neither report back to the king, Abimelech, nor praise Rebekah's beauty. There is literally no threat: the danger exists only in Isaac's unfaithful mind.

Crisis (26:8–10)

This section can be divided into two units: Abimelech's witness (v. 8) and dialogue between Abimelech and Isaac (vv. 9–10).

Abimelech's Witness (v. 8): The word וַיְהִי marks the beginning of another new unit by indicating the passing of time. A long time has passed since Isaac's deception, and it is clear that Isaac's fear is unrealistic.[46] By chance, one day Abimelech witnesses Isaac fondling Rebekah through the window (יִצְחָק מְצַחֵק).

The exact meaning of מְצַחֵק is unclear, and the word has been translated in various ways. RSV translates it as "fondling"; NASB, NIV, NLT, and NET have "caressing"; ASV, JPS, and KJV prefer "sporting"; but NEB and ESV translate the word as "laughing." The issue is whether this term suggests sexual implications. Although some scholars observe the Piel form of צחק and argue that the Piel form has a sexual connotation, the term is still

---

46. There is no clear subject in 8a. Gramatically speaking, both Isaac and Abimelech are possible. If the subject is Isaac, it seems that 8a is considered as a continuation of v. 7. However, if we regard Abimelech as the subject, highlighting that v. 8 is a new beginning, then 8a functions as a subordinate of 8b, where Abimelech is the subject. For detailed discussion see Dickman, *Segen für Isaak*, 256–57.

ambiguous, since it is used in various ways throughout the Old Testament.⁴⁷ The word generally means "laugh" (Gen 17:17; 18:12, 15) in the Qal form. In the Piel form, it can be understood to mean "joke" in Gen 19:14, "make fun" in Gen 21:9, or "amuse or play" in Exod 32:6. We must be careful to note that the term can be used to express either sexual or non-sexual meaning.⁴⁸ It is clear, however, that its meaning here can be confirmed from the context and its place in the text. From the context of Story C, when Abimelech saw Isaac's fondling, he immediately recognizes that Rebekah is Isaac's wife rather than his sister. It is natural, therefore, to infer that Isaac's action is uniquely appropriate to the relation of husband and wife. Alter comments, "The meaning of the verb here is clearly sexual, implying either fondling or actual sexual 'play.'"⁴⁹ From its context, therefore, we can assume that the meaning of the verb in verse 8 is "fondling, caressing, or foreplaying." Furthermore, there is unmistakable wordplay in the phrase יִצְחָק מְצַחֵק especially since we already have some information for the wordplay using the name Isaac (Gen 17:17; 18:12–13; 21:9).⁵⁰

The discovery of the deception in Story C occurs in a most natural way. Unlike Stories A and B, in which Sarah is taken by the foreign rulers, Story C involves neither crisis nor captivity. Isaac's lie is very smoothly revealed as Abimelech looks down from the window by chance.⁵¹ There is no need for YHWH's special intervention. In this regard, Story C clearly differs from the previous wife/sister stories.

Abimelech and Isaac (vv. 9–10): The second conversation in scene two begins with the two major characters: Abimelech and Isaac. When Abimelech finds out the truth about Isaac and Rebekah, he is surprised. In order to denote Abimelech's feelings, verse 8 begins with an exclamation, הִנֵּה. His feeling is exaggerated even more in verse 9 through the use of a double exclamation: אַךְ הִנֵּה. Furthermore, in the very next clause (9d),

---

47. Sasson, "The Worship of the Golden Calf," 154–57.

48. Hamilton, *The Book of Genesis 18–50*, 195–96 and 468. According to Hamilton, we need more textual evidence to confirm a sexual connotation.

49. Alter, *Genesis*, 133; Wenham also notes that this situation clearly implies a euphemism indicating intimacy between spouses. Wenham, *Genesis 16–50*, 190.

50. Mathews, *Genesis 11:27—50:26*, 406; Janzen, *Abraham and All the Families of the Earth*, 101. In order to make it clear, Mathews comments, "Isaak was Issaking."

51. Zlotowitz and Scherman, *Bereishis=Genesis*, 1087. Some scholars note that the action of looking down from a window has negative implication. Traditionally, looking down denotes an evil or immoral purpose (Judg 5:28; 2 Sam 6:16; 2 Kgs 9:30). I doubt this is the case. Sarna notes that there is a definite article on the word window, which indicates a specific window of the royal palace. Sarna, *Genesis*, 184.

another sign of exclamation appears: אַךְ. This interrogative is also used as an expression of astonishment.⁵²

Isaac's short defense is centered between Abimelech's two accusations. Abimelech's question contains a verbatim repetition of Isaac's lie in verse 7 (אֲחֹתִי הִוא). Readers have no idea whether Abimelech was there when Isaac lied or heard of his words from the men of Gerar. In this regard, Story C is distinct from Story A, in which the officers of Pharaoh praise Sarah's beauty to Pharaoh. Isaac's defense is similar to what we see in Story B, but his explanation is shorter than Abraham's defense in Gen 20:11–13. Isaac also quotes his earlier statement in verse 7.

Table 11: Isaac's Defense

Verse 7	Verse 9
Because he was afraid to say, "She is my wife." He thought, "The men of this place might kill me on account of Rebekah, because she is beautiful	Because I thought I might lose my life on account of her

As we see in this table, the quotation is shortened considerably and is certainly modified. First, Isaac does not say anything about "the men of this place." In this way, Isaac wisely conceals his aggressive assumption about the people of Gerar. Second, Isaac only mentions fearing "on her account," and omits mention of "her beauty." This is also intended to reduce offensiveness by increasing ambiguity.⁵³ According to Savran, "When Isaac is called to task for his deception of Abimelech in Gen. 26:9, he tactfully rephrases his actual thoughts, which showed his mistrust of the locals (26:7), into a less offensive quotation that describes his fears in an indefinite, even passive way (26:9)."⁵⁴

Abimelech continues to raise questions and accuse Isaac. First, he demands to know the reasons behind Isaac's lie; second, he offers his own evaluation of what Isaac has done. Abimelech's question is developed one step beyond what we see in Stories A and B. Story A indicates that Pharaoh commits an actual sin and is punished with great plagues as a result. In

---

52. *GKC*, §148ab; *IBHS*, §18.4de.

53. Savran, *Telling and Retelling*, 24–35; Yoo, "A Rhetorical Reading of the Rebekah Narratives," 207–08. Savran comments there are four basic patterns of biblical quotations: X quotes Y to Z, X quotes X to Y, X quotes Y to Y, and small amount of repetition. According to Savran's analysis, Abimelech's quotation is XYY, while Isaac's quotation is XXY. Also see Hamilton, *The Book of Genesis 18–50*, 196.

54. Savran, *Telling and Retelling*, 34.

Story B, God prevents Abimelech from committing an actual sin when he takes Sarah into his house. In Story C, however, there is no actual incident, nor even an implied crisis. Nevertheless, Abimelech responds to Isaac much as the previous foreign rulers do. Although the punishment from YHWH is only potential, Abimelech stops himself from sinning and orders his people not to commit sin to avoid any potential guilt: "One of the men might well have slept with your wife, and you would have brought guilt upon us" (v. 10). The word אָשָׁם, which is not frequently used in the Old Testament, normally means "guilt." Hamilton, however, thinks that translating the word as guilt is too weak; he suggests "retribution."[55] In particular, this term is used for the guilt offering in a cultic system, with reference to unwitting sin and it is connected to the guilt that damage or loss has been incurred. Since this word is used in a cultic context, it is clear that Abimelech assumes that touching someone's wife is a serious sin.[56]

Resolution (26:11)

Verse 11 functions as the end of Story C. By ordering the people of Gerar not to touch Isaac and Rebekah, Abimelech resolves the crisis and tension. Isaac's security is thus established by royal decree. Furthermore, Abimelech's command is very strong (מוֹת יוּמָת). יוּמָת is the Hophal form of מות. It is probable that the Hophal form assumes that the death penalty will be in human's hands.[57] The term נגע reappears here after previously appearing in Gen 12:17 and 20: 6. It is clear that in Stories A and B נגע carries a sexual meaning in relation to Sarah. In Story C, however, this word can be understood in two ways, since it applies to both Isaac and Rebekah. Hamilton describes the meaning of this word as "a double entendre."[58] In reference to Isaac, to touch means to injure or to hit him, while in reference to Rebekah, implies sexual abuse.

The fact that there is no subsequent action in verse 11 is surprising. In Story A, Pharaoh expels Abraham to the land of Canaan, while in Story B, Abraham is allowed to stay wherever he wants. Story C, however, offers no

---

55. Hamilton, *The Book of Genesis 18–50*, 197.

56. Milgrom, *Cult and Conscience*, 3–12. Milgrom calls this term "consequential *asham*"; Snaith, "The Sin-Offering and the Guilt-Offering," 73–80; Biddle, "The 'Endangered Ancestress' and Blessing for the Nations," 605–06; Yoo, "A Rhetorical Reading of the Rebekah Narratives," 209–10; Hamilton, *The Book of Genesis 18–50*, 197–98.

57. Ibid., 198. Hamilton notes that the Hophal form preceded by the infinitive absolute refers to execution by human hands, while the Qal form refers to death directed by the work of God. See n37 above.

58. Ibid., 197.

additional comment. We are also left with no idea how Isaac responds. Abimelech does not present gifts as compensation, which indicates that Isaac's wealth in Story C has nothing to do with Abimelech.

The fact that there is no reference to Isaac's wealth in verse 11 that directly connects it to the following narrative. Although Abimelech does not make Isaac rich, God blesses Isaac and makes him very rich. Verse 11 thus concludes Story C and at the same time it provides a background for the following narrative, which highlights Isaac's wealth as a result of YHWH's blessing.

Type-Scene Approach

In the previous section, we examined Story C from a textlinguistic perspective. Based on this analysis, we will now examine Story C from a type-scene perspective in this section. Throughout the entire process, it is important to look at Story C in relation to Stories A and B. We will examine how the author develops the wife/sister stories in terms of characterization, themes, and plot, through the use of similarities and variations. By doing so, we will gain a better understanding of Story C and how three stories work together within the surrounding narratives and the entire book of Genesis.

Characterization

Story C features new major characters compared to Stories A and B. Isaac and Rebekah replace Abraham and Sarah as protagonists, and the antagonist is Abimelech, which connects only to Story B.

Narrator

We should begin with the existence of the narrator in the story. In a narrative, the narrator provides everything we see, hear, and feel.[59] Story C starts with the narrator's voice giving the background information of the story. The narrator introduces a famine and describes Isaac going to Abimelech king of the Philistines in Gerar. The narrator then adds important information to this general introductory statement. By adding the phrase "besides the earlier famine of Abraham's time," the narrator indicates that he wants to distinguish the famine in the story from the famine in Story A. At the

---

59. Bar-Efrat, *Narrative Art in the Bible*, 13; Berlin, *Poetics and Interpretation of Biblical Narrative*, 44.

same time, however, the narrator wants to connect this story to the story of Abraham in Story A. The narrator also informs us that Isaac's destination is the territory of Abimelech, king of the Philistines in Gerar. The names Abimelech and Gerar are closely connected to Abimelech the king of Gerar who appears in Story B. The narrator thus shows that he wants readers to consider Story C in relation to Stories A and B.

Of course, in addition to the similarities among the three stories, there are variations that we should not miss. Like Story A, but not Story B, Story C mentions a famine in the land. On the other hand, the geographical information in Story C is clearly different from Story A, and the author's concerns also differentiate the two stories. In contrast, Story B does not mention famine, but does share a similar spatial background with Story C. In terms of setting, then, Stories A and C share a similar situation, while Stories B and C share similar spatial information.

In verse 7, Isaac's deception is briefly introduced through the narrator's voice. The narrator also tells us about the people of Gerar's question about Rebekah. The omniscient narrator then reveals the reason for Isaac's deception, which exists only in Isaac's mind: "because he was afraid to say, 'She is my wife.' He thought, 'the men of this place might kill me on account of Rebekah, because she is beautiful'" (v. 7). In light of the promise of YHWH given to Isaac right before he gets to Gerar (vv. 2–5), Isaac's fear shows his unfaithfulness to the promise of YHWH. The expression כִּי אָרְכוּ־לוֹ שָׁם הַיָּמִים in verse 8 indicates the duration of time. By indicating the length of time, the narrator highlights that Isaac and Rebekah spent a long time deceiving the people of Gerar. The narrator's report finally reveals Isaac's incorrect expectations concerning the threats on account of Rebekah's beauty.

Isaac

Isaac is the most passive character in the patriarchal narratives (Genesis 12–50). In contrast to his father Abraham and son Jacob, he is the only patriarch who remains in the land of Canaan throughout his entire life. Even in the process of his marriage, he does not take any meaningful action. God appears to Rebekah at a very significant moment in order to reveal His plan for Esau and Jacob (Gen 25:19–26) before He appears to Isaac.

Story C shows us that YHWH first appears to Isaac and commands him not to go down to Egypt, then, gives Isaac the promises given to his father, Abraham. We should pay attention to the fact that Isaac remains silent, especially in verses 1–6. Although YHWH gives the promises to him, there is no response from Isaac, other than obedience. It seems as if the author wanted to highlight Isaac's obedient and silent characteristics at the beginning of the story.

After YHWH gives his promises, Isaac begins to speak. Isaac's speech only reveals his deceptive and unfaithful character. When the people of Gerar ask about Rebekah, he deceives them by telling them that Rebekah is his sister, repeating the incidents involving his father Abraham. It is obvious that although Isaac's ruse follows his father's, there is no actual threat to Isaac and Rebekah. Isaac's unfaithful action is thus more pronounced than Abraham's in the previous wife/sister stories (Gen 12 and 20). He does not fully trust in YHWH, who promises protection and blessings. Instead, he only cares about his own life. Verse 8 gives us a clue that Isaac stays in Gerar for a long time without facing any threat. It is ridiculous that his ruse is revealed by chance. Perhaps Isaac and Rebekah linger in times of peace for so long that they forget about their ruse, which may have given Abimelech the opportunity to see Isaac caressing Rebekah through the window. Again, although Abimelech raises two questions to Isaac, the narrator intentionally does not report how Isaac responds to them. As with his father, Isaac's silence may imply that he is guilty.

Rebekah

Rebekah's characterization in this passage is striking in light of the surrounding context. Rebekah has been very active. In chapter 24, Rebekah actively decides to leave her hometown, her kin, and her father's house to marry Isaac, whom she has never seen. This act is very similar to Abraham's departure in Gen 12:1–4. In chapter 25, God appears to Rebekah in a dream and reveals His future plan. This also contributes to the strong contrast between Rebekah's activity and Isaac's passivity. Following Gen 26, Rebekah plays a leadership role in making Isaac bless Jacob instead of Esau. Only in Gen 26, is Rebekah totally silent, though she plays a crucial role in the plot of Story C. In relation to the surrounding narratives, Rebekah's total silence in this story accentuates Isaac's flawed character as he manipulates the situation.[60]

In verse 1, the narrator introduces important characters in the story, but intentionally avoids mentioning Rebekah. She is mentioned in the context of deception in verse 7, in which she is presented as Isaac's sister, not his wife.[61] We can therefore conclude that even though she plays a very important role in Story C, she only appears as a flat character.

60. Choi, "Significance of Narrative Interruptions in the Patriarchal History," 71.
61. Yoo, "A Rhetorical Reading of the Rebekah Narratives," 193. However, I am not

Abimelech

Unlike Isaac, the foreign ruler Abimelech is portrayed as a moral character. Isaac deceives him and Abimelech shows a higher level of morality than Isaac, higher even than the rulers in the previous wife/sister stories. Although Rebekah was identified as Isaac's sister, he does not take her to his harem, and when the ruse is revealed, he protects Isaac and Rebekah and his people by warning the people of Gerar not to touch Rebekah. Although YHWH intervened in the story prior to this point, His intervention has nothing to do with the discovery of the ruse. This is quite different from the previous stories in which YHWH intervenes to protect Sarah from the foreign rulers who took her. It is interesting to note at a glance that the one who protects Isaac and Rebekah here is not YHWH, but Abimelech. In the last scene, Abimelech's moral acts vividly display that he places a higher value on morality than the patriarch Isaac, who cannot defend himself against Abimelech's accusation.

YHWH

YHWH takes the initiative to intervene directly in this story. In Stories A and B, the patriarchs do not themselves interact with YHWH; we only hear about YHWH's indirect intervention through the narrator's voice and his speech to Abimelech, respectively. In this story, however, YHWH appears directly to the patriarch for the first time and gives Isaac promises that are similar to those given to Abraham (Gen 12:1–3, 7). By narrating the gift of these promises, which are very closely connected to Abraham, the author stresses that YHWH's faithfulness continues from generation to generation.[62]

It is more striking, however, that we do not see YHWH's intervention in verses 7–11. In light of the previous wife/sister stories, we naturally expect YHWH to intervene at this stage to directly protect His people and judge those who sin. While the whole story progresses in Gerar, though, we do not see any trace of YHWH's action, whether implicitly or explicitly. Isaac's ruse is discovered by chance. No threats are implied in the scene. Abimelech protects Isaac and Rebekah by warning his people not to touch Rebekah. There is no place for the intervention of YHWH in verses 7–11. A probable conclusion is that YHWH's intervention is unnecessary because

---

convinced of Yoo's argument concerning the significance of Rebekah. Yoo argues that the whole story should be read from the perspective of Rebekah. Of course, she still plays a very important role in this narrative plot, although Isaac is the main character in this story. This might be a reason for Rebekah's silence in the story.

62. Choi, "Significance of Narrative Interruptions," 72.

there is no threat and there is no need for protection from evil foreigners. In this regard, YHWH's absence highlights Isaac's unfaithful character.[63]

Minor Characters

Minor characters also play a role in the plot of Story C. In most cases, minor characters are secondary in relation to major characters, serving as background to the main storyline and assisting the main characters.[64] In this story, the people of Gerar and Abraham can be viewed as the minor characters. The people of Gerar simply appear, described in the narrator's voice in verse 7. Their question concerning Rebekah's status is described indirectly. While their role in the story is secondary, they do play an important part in the development of the plot. Isaac assumes they are evil, but this is not the case. They reappear in verse 11 as the recipients of Abimelech's command.

Abraham

In fact, Abraham does not actually appear on stage, but—as mentioned above—his character plays very important role in relation to Isaac.[65] In Story C, Abraham is only described in the context of YHWH's promises. YHWH refers to Abraham as a model for Isaac, who should follow his father's footsteps. Just as Abraham obeyed YHWH and kept YHWH's commandments, Isaac is required to obey YHWH's commandments. In terms of the character of YHWH, His references to Abraham are important in helping to clarify the character of His promise. Here, Abraham serves as evidence of YHWH's faithfulness. As YHWH was faithful to Abraham, He will be faithful to Isaac.

Theme

In this section, we continue our examination of the major themes of the book of Genesis. As Gen 12:1–3 declare, these themes are seed, land, and blessings. We will first investigate these three themes in Story C, and then look at them within the surrounding narratives. As we have seen, Story

---

63. Humphreys, *The Character of God in the Book of Genesis*, 160–61.
64. Bar-Efrat, *Narrative Art in the Bible*, 86–88.
65. On types of characters including the off-stage character, see Choi, "Luke's Thematic Characterization," 39–47. Choi categorizes two different off-stage characters; setting character and potential character.

A centers on the promise of land, while Story B focuses primarily on the promise of seed. It is apparent that Story C also has a central theme that contributes to the message of the wife/sister stories as a whole. In order to demonstrate this, I will apply the three major themes to Story C.

Before we examine each theme, we must refer to YHWH's promises to Isaac in Gen 26:2–5. When Isaac goes down to Gerar, YHWH shows Himself to Isaac for the first time and makes promises that are almost the same as those he made to Abraham. Not surprisingly, the promises overflow with the major themes of the book of Genesis- that is, seed, land, and blessings. For example, the term זרע occurs four times in verses 3–4 and the term ארץ occurs five times in verses 2–4. With regard to blessing for both Isaac and his descendants and the nations, the term ברך directly appears twice in verses 3–4 and is implied by the use of different terms such as אֶהְיֶה עִמְּךָ (v. 3) and הִרְבֵּיתִי (v. 4).

The author uses YHWH's theophany in verses 2–5 to establish a thematic connection between Abraham and Isaac. In this regard, the promises given to Isaac immediately remind us of the Abrahamic covenant presented in Gen 12:1–3. Thematically speaking, the theophany does not focus on a particular theme; rather, it emphasizes that Isaac has what Abraham had. Isaac is now the bearer of the Abrahamic covenant, and YHWH will show His faithfulness to Isaac despite Isaac's flaws, just as He did to Abraham.

Seed

Although the seed is one of the major themes of the entire book of Genesis, we have to be cautious about concluding that the promise of seed is one of the themes of the three wife/sister stories. According to Jon Choi

> More importantly, Isaac jeopardizes God's promise of descendants (v. 4) by placing his wife in danger. The danger is that one of the foreigners will take her, impregnate her, and prevent Isaac from continuing the family line through Rebekah. Just as Abraham jeopardizes the promise of God by lying about his wife, Isaac's deception also endangers the promise of God concerning the seed of the patriarch.[66]

As we have observed, however, there are two questionable things about Choi's argument. First, unlike Story A and B, in Story C the crisis appears only in Isaac's mind. Although Isaac is afraid of the men of Gerar, they do not do anything to Isaac and Rebekah. Second, we must consider the

---

66. Choi, "Significance of Narrative Interruptions," 70.

existence of Isaac's two sons. In Gen 25:21–34, Esau and Jacob are already fully grown. Although Story C apparently does not say anything about them, reading it within its context helps us to conclude that the crisis is only potential for Rebekah and is not about the seed.[67] Instead, the previous narrative clearly tells us who will be the seed of Isaac through the story of the strife between Esau and Jacob. Esau sells his birthright because he despises it. Based on the conclusion of the previous narrative (Gen 25:34), we can easily confirm the identity of the promised seed before we reach Story C. The fact that Esau and Jacob are the major players who could serve as Isaac's seed does not play a role in Story C. This indicates that the theme of seed is not the primary concern of Story C.

Land

At first glance, the theme of land is remarkably observed. In fact, the term ארץ occurs six times in verses 1–4. At first, it seems that land is an issue because verse 1 indicates that there is a famine in the land. This clearly reminds us of Story A, in which the theme of land is primary issue. Here, however, the author specifically notes that we should not to think of the famines in Story A and C as the same.

We might assume that Isaac would go down to Egypt to avoid the famine, but in verse 2, YHWH commands Isaac not to go to Egypt, but to live in the land where Isaac stays. The land is more particularly indicated in verse 3 by adding a demonstrative pronoun. When Isaac stays in Gerar, YHWH prohibits him from going down to Egypt and commands him to stay in "this land"—that is, Gerar. Here, although there is a crisis of land, the crisis is only implied. Furthermore, Isaac is still in Gerar, and YHWH allows him to stay in Gerar. As mentioned above, since Gerar is considered as a place within the Promised Land, Isaac does not actually depart from the land. The crisis of land is only the result of a famine; it is not tied to the patriarch's departure as it was in Story A. The implied crisis of the loss of the land is thus resolved at the outset through the intervention of YHWH. Although the promise of land is a significant feature of YHWH's promise in verses 2–5, the theme of land does not affect the plotline of Story C after this point.

---

67. Clines, "The Ancestor in Danger: But Not the Same Danger," 79. He maintains that the dangers in the three stories are not the same.

Blessings

If we compare the theme of blessing to other major themes mentioned above, the theme of blessing is not explicitly described in Story C. The term ברך occurs only twice in the context of YHWH's promises in verses 3–4, though the blessing theme is implicitly in the expressions "I will be with you" and "I will make your descendants as numerous as the stars."

Most strikingly, unlike Abraham in Stories A and B, Isaac does not receive any benefits after the discovery of his ruse. In Story A, Pharaoh gives a marriage portion to Abraham (Gen 12:16) and in Story B, Abimelech gives compensation for his eyes to Abraham. The previous narratives thus share the concept of wealth given by foreign rulers. Story C, on the other hand, does not share this idea. Only after the incident is passed does the theme of blessing prevail in the narratives. In particular, verses 12–16 show that Isaac becomes rich and his wealth continues to grow, to the point that Abimelech finally recognizes that Isaac has become too powerful.[68] It is worth noting that this blessing is given to Isaac directly by YHWH. This is clearly different from the situation in Stories A and B, in which foreign rulers serve as devices of blessing the wife/sister stories to some extent function to make Abraham rich. This indicates that Story C is more highlighted in terms of YHWH's blessing. As Brueggemann argues, "The entire chapter is preoccupied with the theme of blessing."[69]

We should also observe that the theme of blessing is developed throughout the three wife/sister stories. With regard to blessing of the nations, Story A only describes the possibility of curse when the Patriarch does not follow YHWH's promise. Story B adds the possibility of blessing, for though Abimelech falls into the covenantal curse, he is healed and restored by Abraham's intercessional prayer. In Story C, Isaac also plays a role as a mediator who may bring blessings or curses to the nations. If we consider the entire chapter, Abimelech not only acts in good conscience, but also acknowledges that YHWH is with Isaac (v. 28) and that Isaac is a bearer of YHWH's blessing (v. 29). Finally, Abimelech wants to establish a covenant with Isaac. Clearly, then, we can see the development of the blessing theme through the three wife/sister stories.[70]

---

68. Ibid., 82. According to Clines, unlike its predecessors, Story C does not have clear point of closure. For this reason, the readers need to consider Story C in relation to the subsequent narratives.

69. Brueggeman, *Genesis*, 221; Waltke, *Genesis*, 367. Waltke identifies the key words of Genesis 26 as "blessing" and "Abraham his father." In light of this observation, the theme can be summarized as "Isaac inherits his father's divine blessing."

70. Biddle, "The 'Endangered Ancestress' and Blessing for the Nations," 608–10.

The theme of blessing is also closely connected to the surrounding narratives. It is worth noting two features within Gen 25. First, Gen 25:11 declares that God blessed Isaac after Abraham died. Second, the main theme of Gen 25:19–34 is the struggle for the birthright. The birthright is closely connected to the blessing theme. In terms of vocabulary, these two words are clearly related to each other through wordplay (בְּכֹרָה and בְּרָכָה).[71] Wenham observes, "it may also be significant that בכרה 'rights of firstborn' is an anagram of ברכה 'blessing,' the subject of chaps. 26–27 and a key theme in Genesis."[72] Esau and Jacob struggle for the birthright from the very beginning of their lives—that is, in their mother's womb. The second battlefield emerges when they grow up. While Esau returns home from hunting, Jacob cooks some stew. Because Esau is so tired and hungry, he sells his birthright to Jacob for the red stew. Jacob, who had wanted to get the birthright from his mother's womb, thus finally wins it.

The connection between Gen 26 and the subsequent narratives is also apparent. In these chapters, the theme of blessing is more directly observed in relation to the strife for the birthright. With the help of Rebekah, Jacob takes the firstborn's birthright (בְּכֹרָה) by obtaining Isaac's blessing (בְּרָכָה), which is supposed to be given to Esau.[73] Chapters 25, 26, and 27 all generally contain the theme of blessing, which passes down through three patriarchal generations: Abraham, Isaac, and Jacob.[74]

Based on all these observations, we can conclude that, although Story C contains elements of all three major themes, the theme of blessing is its primary concern. Together, then, the three wife/sister stories establish the three major themes of the book of Genesis: Land, Seed, and Blessing, respectively.

Plot

As a last consideration, the plot of Story C should be added to our type-scene analysis. Because Story C is a self-contained narrative unit, it is natural that the plotline can be observed. Just like Stories A and B, Story C generates conflict and resolution. It includes following plotlines: introductory exposition (vv. 1–6), conflict and climax (vv. 7–10), and resolution (v. 11).

---

71. Fokkelman, *Narrative Art in Genesis*, 115.
72. Wenham, *Genesis 16–50*, 178.
73. Fokkelman, *Narrative Art in Genesis*, 98.
74. Ibid., 115; Choi, "Significance of Narrative Interruptions," 39.

Beginning

The setting of Story C is presented in Gen 26:1–6. A famine generates a crisis for Isaac who, like his father, decides to depart from the Promised Land. Although this is a crisis similar to the famine in Story A, Story C clearly guides the reader to avoid identifying the two famines too closely. The first crisis is not important to the plotline of Story C because YHWH quickly intervenes and dissolves the crisis generated.

Unlike Stories A and B, Story C is notable for the inclusion divine intervention and promises to Isaac as a significant feature of its setting. As mentioned above, the divine promises play a significant role in distinguishing Story C from Stories A and B. We have also observed that there is a development in divine intervention from one story to the next. Story A only implies that such intervention is occurring using the narrator's voice (Gen 12:17), while in Story B, God appears in a dream to a foreign ruler, but not to the Patriarch. Story C, however, dramatically portrays YHWH's appearance directly to Isaac. Not surprisingly, YHWH reiterates the promises of land, seed, and blessing of the nations. In addition, the timing of this divine intervention is noteworthy. In Story C, YHWH intervenes preemptively, such that Rebekah is never in crisis. Through this characterization, the author emphasizes YHWH's obvious protection of His own promises and the Patriarchs.

The reason for the divine promise, we should note, has nothing to do with Isaac, but follows Abraham's obedience. This raises the question of whether Isaac would follow YHWH's words as his father did. We recognize that Isaac obeys YHWH's command to stay in Gerar (v. 6)—however, this is not the end of the story.

Middle

Staying in Gerar is an expression of Isaac's faith, but it also generates tension and another crisis. In the beginning of the middle part of the plot, the men of "that place" ask Isaac about his wife. We do not know exactly what they ask about Rebekah, and we do not know how they think of Rebekah. They just ask him about his wife and then the situation is distorted in Isaac's mind. It is not the men of Gerar who escalate the tension of the situation, it is Isaac. In fear, he passes Rebekah off as his sister, yet—contrary to Isaac's expectations—it is clear that no crisis actually develops following this ruse. Story C's crisis reaches a climax in verse 8, when, by chance, Abimelech sees Isaac caressing Rebekah, Abimelech summons Isaac without delay and accuses him with questions. In this climactic scene, there is clear contrast between Abimelech and Isaac in terms of their relative morality. Ironically, the foreigner—one who must be blessed by the Patriarch—accuses the bearer of YHWH's blessing. The foreigner cares for his people and takes steps to guard them against any potential sin, whereas Isaac seems to neglect taking care of his wife for the sake of his own life. Who is actually in crisis at this point? Most importantly, YHWH's promise is in crisis. As a result, the foreigners in Gerar are also in danger.

End

Unlike Stories A and B, this narrative does not have a clear conclusion. The resolution therefore naturally functions as a conclusion. In the previous stories, the resolution results from YHWH's intervention. In Story C, however, YHWH has no explicit role in the resolution, as Abimelech strongly commands his people not to touch both Isaac and Rebekah. Through Abimelech's command, the tension and the crisis are dissolved. Also, unlike Stories A and B, Story C makes no reference to the wealth theme, which must wait for subsequent stories.

The plotline of Story C can be captured as follows

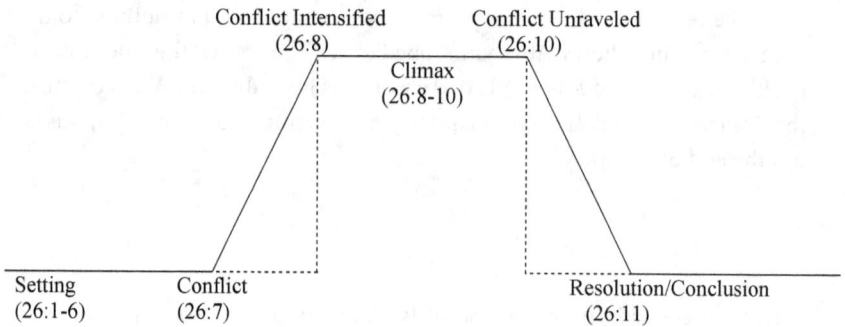

Figure 4: The Plotline of Story C.

Conclusion

In this chapter, we examined the third wife/sister story (Gen 26:1–11). From a textlinguistic perspective, we first decided on the extent of Story C, then explored the surrounding narratives, the structure of Story C, and the textual meaning of its literary units. Then, from a type-scene perspective, we studied Story C in relation to Stories A and B focusing on similarities and variations in characterization, themes, and plot. Through this process, we have confirmed that there are clear developments in characters, themes, and plot, through the three wife/sister stories.

First, in terms of characterization, the character of YHWH has been developed from elusiveness to fullness. Story A indicates YHWH's intervention only indirectly, through the narrator's voice, while in Story B God clearly appears in the dream of the foreign ruler but does not appear to the Patriarch. In Story C, however, YHWH, for the first time, reveals Himself to the Patriarch and preemptively removes a possible crisis.

Two major human characters, the Patriarchs and the foreign rulers, are also developed throughout the stories. Although Isaac experiences both fuller intervention from YHWH and far less threatening circumstances than Abraham, he does not trust in YHWH and therefore actively passes his wife off as his sister. If we observe God's intervention here in comparison with the previous stories, Isaac is the only person who meets YHWH directly. Therefore, his responsibility for his guilt is more apparent than that of his father in the previous stories. Abimelech, on the other hand, adheres to a higher standard of morality than either Isaac or the previous foreign rulers. Not only does he not take Rebekah, he also protects himself, his people, and Isaac and Rebekah from potential sin.

Second, Story C contains YHWH's promises to Isaac, which are the same as the promises given to Abraham (Gen 12:1–3). Story C also highlights three major themes: Seed, Land, and Blessings. However, as I have argued, each of the three wife/sister stories emphasizes a specific theme. Story A is clearly related to the theme of land, Story B focuses on the theme of seed, and Story C stresses the theme of blessing the nations. All blessings in Genesis 26 come from YHWH. This finally leads the foreigners to acknowledge that YHWH is with Isaac and to make a covenant with Isaac, the bearer of YHWH's blessings.

Finally, the plot of Story C should be understood in light of Stories A and B, as the author continues to provide signs pointing back to Stories A and B. The plotline of Story C is quite simple in comparison to that of Story B.

In sum, this study of the third wife/sister story in relation to the first and second wife/sister stories allows us to conclude that the author continuously reveals similarities and variations among the three stories. It follows that, in order to obtain a fuller understanding of Story C, we should keep the previous stories in mind and synthesize all three stories. In doing so, we can finally reach a proper understanding of the whole picture of the three stories, which will in turn give us a more concrete understanding of each individual story.

CHAPTER FIVE

Conclusion

I WANT TO SUMMARIZE here the findings of my investigation and clarify the significance of the three wife/sister stories within the book of Genesis as a whole. In this book, I applied textlinguistic and literary type-scene analysis to the three wife/sister stories. Through these two approaches, we can confidently conclude that the three wife/sister stories play an important role in the patriarchal narrative and that they are not products of different authors or sources but should be recognized as well-organized stories reflecting a single author's literary and theological intention. Throughout the three wife/sister stories, the author highlights the major themes of the patriarchal narrative (Gen 12–36), and even those of the entire book of Genesis. Furthermore, the three stories are not simple repetitions of the same story but use repetition as a technique to clarify themes and develop characterization, themes, and plot.

Summary

The three wife/sister stories have inspired a variety of discussions throughout the history of research on Genesis. Traditional studies of the stories have employed source critical, form critical, socio-historical, and literary approaches. Source critics have looked for evidence of various sources, such as J, E, JE, and R. Form critics, on the other hand, have discussed the oral stage that preceded the current written stories. As a consequence, the wife/sister stories have been widely acknowledged as apparent evidence of different sources contributed by different authors. Therefore, Introduction traces the history of scholarly discussions from source criticism to literary criticism.

Although source critics basically agree that different sources have been used in the wife/sister stories, they have not reached any agreement on the details. Even among source critics, Baden argues that the wife/sister stories do not represent different sources. Scholars taking a form critical approach have observed remarkable similarities in the form and structure of the wife/

sister stories. Based on these similarities, form critics argue that the wife/sister stories are variants of a single story or ur-story.

Other scholars take a social-historical approach to the wife/sister stories, pointing to many parallels between the biblical accounts and Near Eastern texts. E. A. Speiser, for example, maintains that the wife/sister stories can be understood in light of Hurrian customs at Nuzi. Although Speiser's argument has inspired lengthy discussions, recent studies broadly acknowledge that his argument has been excessively exaggerated from a small number of sources. James K. Hoffmeier's argument regarding the wife/sister stories as representing diplomatic marriage is more probable, but this argument raises questions in relation to the patriarch's deception. If these are stories about diplomatic marriage, why did the patriarchs deceive the foreign rulers?

Finally, from a synchronic perspective, some scholars have attempted to observe the connections between the wife/sister stories. Robert Alter proposes the wife/sister stories as a type-scene. Following Alter, we need to explore the relationship and the thematic development of the stories. In doing so, a type-scene model gives us a good method to observe the relationship between the stories by studying their similarities and variations.

Also, methodological considerations apply to the wife/sister stories. Linguistic analysis addresses various linguistic levels, including syntactics, semantics, and pragmatics. This study also uses innerbiblical interpretation and functional sentence perspective approaches to determine the relationship among the three wife/sister stories, observe textual coherence, and examine thematic development. A type-scene approach is also an important method for this study. However, I attempted to add a new approach to the traditional of type-scene method by exploring recurrent fixed motifs. On top of the traditional approach, this new approach examines similarities and variations through similar sets of characteristics. I therefore proposed three dimensions—characterization, theme, and plot—as a developed type-scene method. This approach will help us observe the three wife/sister stories as a whole within the larger context of the book of Genesis.

Before undertaking the study of each wife/sister story, I investigated the place of the wife/sister stories within their own context and within the book of Genesis. In order to understand the macrostructure of the book of Genesis, we must first focus on the *Toledot* formula. So, Chapter 1 begins with the narrative structure of the *Toledot* of Terah and Isaac, in which the three wife/sister stories are located. In the beginning of this dissertation, I questioned why the first two stories are located in the *Toledot* of Terah, while the third story is in the *Toledot* of Isaac. If we consider each *Toledot* formula as a self-contained unit, we must explain how the three stories function together despite being located in different *Toledot* sections. In this section, I proposed viewing all three stories as belonging to the *Toledot* of Shem. This view allows us to see the three stories within one larger context. As I mentioned, the *Toledot* of Shem is an independent *Toledot* that continues to the *Toledot* of Esau (Gen 11:10–37:1). This larger context highlights the fact that YHWH gives promises to the patriarchs and keeps His promises in spite of the patriarchs' weakness. Based on this observation, I explored YHWH's three major promises—seed, land, and blessings on the nations. Our study of the three wife/sister stories gives a special attention to these themes.

Chapters 2 to 4 explore the three wife/sister stories in the book of Genesis. Each of these chapters begins by analyzing the story's delimitation, placing it in its context, and observing its narrative structure from a textlinguistic point of view. Based on these preliminary observations, a type-scene analysis on each story has been presented. Again, while type-scene study has focused primarily on recurrent scenes, I developed this analysis in the areas of characterization, theme, and plot.

Chapter 2, which examines Story A (Gen 12:10—13:1), is particularly important, because Story A provides a starting point and the following stories should be understood in relation to it. In terms of the larger context, I explored how Story A is well located in the current place. By investigating the relationship between Story A and its close context, I clarified that Story A is particularly focused on the theme of land. I also observed that, although the main character is YHWH, who changes the paradigm of Story A, the author only implies YHWH's intervention through the narrator's explanation.

Chapter 3 explores Story B (Gen 20:1–18). Although many scholars have questioned the placement of Story B, I proposed that Story B is well placed in its current position. In fact, its context reveals Story B's main concern. Based on this observation, I concluded that although Story B is closely connected to Story A as a type-scene, it is clear that Story B has a very different concern from that of Story A—that is, it is focused on the theme of seed. In terms of characterization, God appears in the dream of the foreign ruler and warns Abimelech not to take Sarah. By including this information, Story B shows that the main concern is to protect Abraham's seed. We should note, however that God's intervention remains unknown to Abraham in this story, because God only speaks to Abimelech.

Chapter 4 describes the third wife/sister story (Gen 26:1–11). As in the previous chapters, I examined the textlinguistic and type-scene features of the third wife/sister story, which led me to suggest that the main concern of Story C is the theme of blessing. The relationship between Story C and the surrounding context confirms that blessing is the major theme of Story C. At the same time, it is important to note that in this story

YHWH finally meets Isaac and directly gives him the promises, as He did to Abraham in Gen 12:1–3 and 22:16–18. We can see, therefore, that the three stories demonstrate clear development in terms of the explicitness of YHWH's intervention.

By examining the three wife/sister stories all together, I argued that our main concerns in studying these narratives should be uncovering how the author utilizes characters, major themes, and plot and how the author clarifies his purpose for each story in relation to its surrounding narrative. Furthermore, I suggested that we must keep in mind the developments that appear through the sequence of three stories. The characterization of God clearly moves from elusiveness to fullness, while the characterization of Abraham/Isaac and Sarah/Rebekah reveals a downward trend in terms of their morality and faith. Based on these observations, we can confidently conclude that the three wife/sister stories are not formidable evidence for the existence of sources, but in fact work together beautifully for the purpose of the author. Taken together, these stories play a significant role in enhancing readers' knowledge of YHWH, who keeps His promises in spite of the patriarchs' weakness and unfaithfulness.

Significance of Three Stories

I raised some questions in the beginning of this work. Why does Genesis include three wife/sister stories in which the patriarch's faith seems to fail? How do these three stories function within the whole narrative of Genesis? What are the literary intentions behind the three stories?

To put it simply, for an author to include three such similar stories, those stories must play important roles and convey important messages in a narrative plot. As Robert Alter emphasizes, type-scenes only occur at crucial points in the lives of biblical heroes, such as conception, birth, betrothal, and deathbed. Further, the type-scene does not occur for every major hero.[1] Based on these observations, the triple appearance of the wife/sister story indicates its importance in the book of Genesis. All three stories show a certain crisis in the life of the patriarchs. Whose crisis is it? The patriarchs bring crisis upon themselves by deceiving foreign rulers for their own sake. In the patriarchs' minds, they are in danger, and as a result they put Sarah and Rebekah in danger. Sarah is taken into the harem of Pharaoh in Story A, and is also in danger in Story B, though here God protects her from any harm, including sexual contact. In Story C, the crisis exists only in the minds of Isaac and Rebekah—they actually bring potential crisis

---

1. Alter, *The Art of Biblical Narrative*, 51.

with them. Each of the three wife/sister stories has a distinct emphasis. On the surface, the three stories look very similar and convey similar crises, but a more careful look reveals that each story represents a different crisis. Story A clearly focuses on the crisis of land, Story B on the crisis of seed, and Story C on the crisis of blessing.

This conclusion becomes clearer with close examination of the surrounding narratives. The surrounding narratives basically describe good characteristics of the patriarchs. For example, Gen 12:1–9, which is followed by Story A, highlights YHWH's promises and how beautifully Abraham obeys YHWH's command. After he receives YHWH's promises, Story A indicates that Abraham leaves the Promised Land. The long stories in Gen 17 to 21 take place in a single year. In Gen 17, God gives Abraham the promise of seed again, and this time God clearly mentions that Sarah will be a part of this promise. In Gen 18, God promises again that Abraham and Sarah will have a son in one year. Surprisingly, in Story B, right after God's promise, Abraham moves to Gerar for no clear reason and puts Sarah in danger by passing her off as his sister. In Story C, although they receive the promises of YHWH, Isaac and Rebekah fear a potential crisis, which precipitates an actual crisis. Therefore, we see that the three wife/sister stories take place immediately following God's great promises. The three stories are about anti-promises and the crisis of promises, not about the patriarch or the wife. As John Goldingay argues, "12:10—13:4 relate a further threat to the promise. YHWH intends to make Abram a great nation, to make him a blessing to the nations, and to give the land of Canaan to his descendants. But as a result of an entirely human response to a real crisis, each element in this promise receives a kind of anti-fulfilment."[2]

Based on these observations, we can conclude that the crisis in each of the three wife/sister stories is primarily a crisis of promises. The three stories thus emphasize that God will protect His promises to the patriarchs, in spite of their weaknesses. As we see throughout the three wife/sister stories, the patriarchs' weakness and unfaithfulness repeatedly place the promises in jeopardy, but God faithfully keeps His promises to the patriarchs. This is why the patriarchs' characterization becomes progressively more negative, while YHWH's intervention becomes increasingly explicit.

Contributions to scholarly discussions

I attempt, in this book, to extend scholarly discussions of type-scene analysis by applying a different perspective. Scholars who apply the type-scene

---

2. Goldingay, "The Patriarchs in Scripture and History," 3.

approach to biblical texts tend to use it from a form critical perspective. On the other hand, following Robert Alter, other scholars attempt to identify recurrent fixed motifs in the texts. This book, however, focuses much more on literary aspects such as characterization, theme, and plot. This approach has been utilized in the type-scene studies on the New Testament texts,[3] so it is hoped that applying this approach to the wife/sister stories will be a good starting point for better understandings of Old Testament narratives. Second, although most scholars refer to the wife/sister stories as a type-scene, only a few have discussed these stories at a high level. The present work, then, may be one of the most extended studies on the wife/sister stories. Third, previous scholarship has tended to read the three stories to discover evidence of different sources, while this study attempts to provide a holistic reading of the three stories. By reading the three stories together, we come to the conclusion that the three stories are intentional products of a single author. A textlinguistic and type-scene reading allows us to look at the thematic development of the three stories and recognize how well these stories work together to highlight God's faithfulness to His promises.

3. McMahan, "Meals as Type-Scenes in the Gospel of Luke."

Bibliography

Abela, Anthony. "The Redactional Structuring within the Abraham Narrative in Genesis." In *Veterum Exempla: Essays in Honour of Mgr. Prof. Emeritus Joseph Lupi*, edited by Vincent Borg, 35-82. Malta: University of Malta, 1991.

———. *The Themes of the Abraham Narrative: Thematic Coherence within the Abraham Literary Unit of Genesis 11, 27-25, 18*. Malta: Studia, 1989.

Albright, William Foxwell. "Abram the Hebrew: A New Archaeological Interpretation." *Bulletin of the American Schools of Oriental Research* 163 (1961) 36-54.

———. "Historical Framework of Palestinian Archaeology between 2100 and 1600 BC (EB IV, MB I, MB IIA-B)." *Bulletin of the American Schools of Oriental Research*, 209 (1973) 12-18.

Alexander, T. Desmond. *Abraham in the Negev: A Source-Critical Investigation of Genesis 20:1—22:19*. Carlisle, Cumbria: Paternoster, 1997.

———. "Are the Wife/Sister Incidents of Genesis Literary Compositional Variants?" *Vetus Testamentum* 42, no. 2 (1992) 145-53.

———. "From Adam to Judah: The Significance of the Family Tree in Genesis." *Evangelical Quarterly* 61 (1989) 5-19.

———. *From Paradise to the Promised Land: An Introduction to the Pentateuch*. 2nd ed. Grand Rapids: Baker, 2002.

———. "Further Observations on the Term 'Seed' in Genesis." *Tyndale Bulletin* 48, no. 2 (1997) 363-67.

———. "Genealogies, Seed and the Compositional Unity of Genesis." *Tyndale Bulletin* 44, no. 2 (1993) 255-70.

———. "A Literary Analysis of the Abraham Narrative in Genesis." PhD diss., University of Belfast, 1982.

———. "The Wife/Sister Incidents of Genesis: Oral Variants?" *Irish Biblical Studies* 11 (1989) 2-22.

Alexander, T. Desmond, and David W. Baker, eds. *Dictionary of the Old Testament: Pentateuch*. IVP Bible Dictionary Series. Downers Grove, IL: InterVarsity, 2003.

Alter, Robert. *The Art of Biblical Narrative*. New York: Basic, 1981.

———. *The Five Books of Moses: A Translation with Commentary*. New York: Norton, 2004.

———. *Genesis: Translation and Commentary*. New York: Norton, 1997.

———. "How Convention Helps Us Read: The Case of the Bible's Annunciation Type-Scene." *Prooftexts* 3 (1983) 115-30.

Andersen, Francis I. *The Hebrew Verbless Clause in the Pentateuch*. Journal of Biblical Literature Monograph Series 14. Nashville: Abingdon, 1970.

———. *The Sentence in Biblical Hebrew*. The Hague: Mouton, 1980.

Arend, Walter. *Die Typischen Szenen bei Homer*. Berlin: Weidmann, 1933.

Aristotle. *Poetics: Translated with Introduction and Notes*. Translated by Joe Sachs. Newburyport: Focus, 2006.

Arnold, Bill T. *Genesis*. New Cambridge Bible Commentary. New York: Cambridge University Press, 2009.

Averbeck, Richard E. "Factors in Reading the Patriarchal Narratives: Literary, Historical, and Theological Dimensions." In *Giving the Sense: Understanding and Using Old Testament Historical Books*, edited by David M. Howard Jr. and Michael A. Grisanti, 115–37. Grand Rapids: Kregel, 2003.

Avigad, Nahman, and Yigael Yadin. *A Genesis Apocryphon: A Scroll from the Wilderness of Judaea*. Jerusalem: Magnes, 1956.

Baden, Joel S. *The Composition of the Pentateuch: Renewing the Documentary Hypothesis*. New Haven: Yale University Press, 2012.

———. *J, E, and the Redaction of the Pentateuch*. Forschungen Zum Alten Testament 68. Tübingen: Mohr/Siebeck, 2009.

Baker, David W. "Diversity and Unity in the Literary Structure of Genesis." In *Essays on the Patriarchal Narratives*, edited by A. R. Millard and D. J. Wiseman, 197–215. Winona Lake, IN: Eisenbrauns, 1980.

Bar-Efrat, Shimon. *Narrative Art in the Bible*. Bible and Literature Series 17. Decatur: Almond, 1989.

Barr, James. *Semantics of Biblical Language*. London: Oxford University Press, 1961.

Beaugrande, Robert Alain de, and Wolfgang Ulrich Dressler. *Introduction to Text Linguistics*. New York: Longman, 1981.

Berlin, Adele. *Poetics and Interpretation of Biblical Narrative*. Winona Lake, IN: Eisenbrauns, 1994.

Biddle, Mark E. "The 'Endangered Ancestress' and Blessing for the Nations." *Journal of Biblical Literature* 109 (1990) 599–611.

Boda, Mark J. *A Severe Mercy: Sin and Its Remedy in the Old Testament*. Winona Lake, IN: Eisenbrauns, 2009.

Bodine, Walter R. "Introduction." In *Discourse Analysis of Biblical Literature: What It Is and What It Offers*, edited by Walter R. Bodine, 1–18. Atlanta: Scholars, 1995.

Botterweck, G., Johannes, Helmer Ringgren, and Heinz-Josef Fabry, eds. *Theological Dictionary of the Old Testament*. 15 vols. Grand Rapids: Eerdmans, 1974–2006.

Britt, Brian. "Prophetic Concealment in a Biblical Type Scene." *Catholic Biblical Quarterly* 64 (2002) 37–58.

Brodie, Thomas L. *Genesis as Dialogue: A Literary, Historical, and Theological Commentary*. Oxford: Oxford University Press, 2001.

Bruckner, James K. *Implied Law in the Abraham Narrative: A Literary and Theological Analysis*, edited by David J. A. Clines and Philip R. Davies. JSOTSup 335. London: Sheffield, 2001.

Brueggemann, Walter. *Genesis*. Interpretation: A Bible Commentary for Teaching and Preaching 1. Atlanta: Knox, 1982.

———. *The Land: Place as Gift, Promise, and Challenge in Biblical Faith*. 2nd ed. Overtures to Biblical Theology. Minneapolis: Fortress, 2002.

Bullard, Jeremy. "Genesis 18:1–15 through the Lens of a Covenant Meal Type-Scene." MA thesis, Trinity Evangelical Divinity School, 2010.

Calvin, John. *Genesis*. Edited by Alister McGrath and J. I. Packer. Crossway Classic Commentaries 25. Wheaton, IL: Crossway, 2001.

Carden, Michael. "Endangered Ancestress Revisited: Sarah's Miraculous Motherhood and the Restoration of Eden." *Bible and Critical Theory* 1, no. 3 (2005) 1–14.

Carson, D. A. *Exegetical Fallacies*. 2nd ed. Grand Rapids: Baker, 1996.

Casanowicz, Immanuel M. "Paronomasia in the Old Testament." *Journal of Biblical Literature* 12, no. 2 (1893) 105–67.

Cassuto, Umberto. *A Commentary on the Book of Genesis: From Adam to Noah*. Translated by Israel Abrahams. Jerusalem: Magnes, 1964.

———. *A Commentary on the Book of Genesis: From Noah to Abraham*. Jerusalem: Magnes, 1964.

———. *The Documentary Hypothesis and the Composition of the Pentateuch; Eight Lectures*. Jerusalem: Magnes, Hebrew University, 1961.

Choi, Byung Pill. "Luke's Thematic Characterization: The Infancy Narrative (Luke 1–2) and Beyond." PhD diss., McMaster Divinity College, 2014.

Choi, Jon. "Significance of Narrative Interruptions in the Patriarchal History." PhD diss., Southwestern Baptist Theological Seminary, 2005.

Clines, David J. A. "The Ancestor in Danger: But Not the Same Danger." In *What Does Eve Do to Help? And Other Readerly Questions to the Old Testament*, 67–84. JSOTSup 94. Sheffield, UK: JSOT, 1990.

———. *The Theme of the Pentateuch*. JSOTSup 10. Sheffield, UK: University of Sheffield, 1978.

Coats, George W. *Genesis, with an Introduction to Narrative*. Forms of the Old Testament Literature 1. Grand Rapids: Eerdmans, 1983.

Cotter, David W. *Genesis*. Berit Olam: Studies in Hebrew Narrative and Poetry. Collegeville, MN: Glazier, 2003.

Cotterell, Peter. "Semantics, Interpretation, and Theology." In *A Guide to Old Testament Theology and Exegesis*, edited by Willem A. VanGemeren, 131–57. Grand Rapids: Zondervan, 1997.

Cotterell, Peter, and Max Turner. *Linguistics & Biblical Interpretation*. Downers Grove, IL: InterVarsity, 1989.

Cross, Frank Moore. *Canaanite Myth and Hebrew Epic: Essays in the History of the Religion of Israel*. Cambridge, MA: Harvard University Press, 1973.

Culley, Robert C. *Studies in the Structure of Hebrew Narrative*. Semeia Supplements. Philadelphia: Fortress, 1976.

Culpepper, R. Alan. *Anatomy of the Fourth Gospel: A Study in Literary Design*. Philadelphia: Fortress, 1983.

Daneš, František. "Functional Sentence Perspective and the Organization of the Text." In *Papers on Functional Sentence Perpective*, edited by František Daneš, 106–28. Prague: Academia Publishing House of the Czechoslovak Academy, 1974.

Davis, John J. "The Camel in Biblical Narratives." In *Tribute to Gleason Archer*, edited by Walter C. Kaiser Jr. and Ronald F. Youngblood, 141–52. Chicago: Moody, 1986.

Dawson, David Allan. *Text-Linguistics and Biblical Hebrew*. JSOTSup 177. Sheffield, UK: Sheffield, 1994.

DeRoche, Michael Paul. "The Dynamics of Promise: Narrative Logic in the Abraham Story." PhD diss., McMaster University, 1986.

Dieckmann, Detlef. *Segen für Isaak: Eine Rezeptionsästhetische Auslegung von Gen 26 unt Kotexten*. Beihefte zur Zeitschrift für die Alttestamentliche Wissenschaft 329. Berlin: de Gruyter, 2003.

Dorsey, David A. *The Literary Structure of the Old Testament: A Commentary on Genesis-Malachi*. Grand Rapids: Baker, 1999.

Driver, S. R. *An Introduction to the Literature of the Old Testament*. New York: Meridian, 1960.

Eco, Umberto. *Interpretation and Overinterpretation*. Cambridge: Cambridge University Press, 1992.

———. *The Limits of Interpretation*. Bloomington: Indiana University Press, 1990.

———. *The Role of the Reader: Explorations in the Semiotics of Texts*. Bloomington: Indiana University Press, 1979.

Edelman, Diana V. "An Appraisal of Robert Alter's Approach." *Biblical Research* 31 (1986) 19–25.

Edwards, Mark W. "Homer and Oral Tradition: The Type-Scene." *Oral Tradition* 7, no. 2 (1992) 284–330.

Eichler, Barry L. "Nuzi and the Bible: A Retrospective." In *DUMU-E2-DUB-BA-A: Studies in Honor of Åke W. Sjöberg*, 107–19. Philadelphia: Samuel Noah Kramer Fund, 1989.

Fishbane, Michael A. *Biblical Interpretation in Ancient Israel*. Oxford: Clarendon, 1984.

———. "Composition and Structure in the Jacob Cycle (Gen 25:19—35:22)." *Journal of Jewish Studies* 26 (1975) 15–38.

———. *Text and Texture: Close Readings of Selected Biblical Texts*. New York: Schocken, 1979.

Fitzmyer, Joseph A. *The Genesis Apocryphon of Qumran Cave I: A Commentary*. Biblica et Orientalia 18. Rome: Pontifical Biblical Institute, 1966.

Fleming, D. M. "The Divine Council as Type-Scene in the Hebrew Bible." PhD diss., Southern Baptist Theological Seminary, 1989.

Fokkelman, J. P. "Genesis." In *The Literary Guide to the Bible*, edited by Robert Alter and Frank Kermode, 36–55. Cambridge, MA: Belknap, 1987.

———. *Narrative Art in Genesis: Specimens of Stylistic and Structural Analysis*. Amsterdam: Van Gorcum, 1975.

Foley, John Miles. *The Theory of Oral Composition: History and Methodology*. Folkloristics. Bloomington: Indiana University Press, 1988.

———. *Traditional Oral Epic: The Odyssey, Beowulf, and the Serbo-Croatian Return Song*. Berkeley: University of California Press, 1990.

Forster, E. M. *Aspects of the Novel*. San Diego: A Harvest, 1927.

Freedman, David A., ed. *The Anchor Bible Dictionary*. 5 vols. New York: Doubleday, 1992.

———. "A New Approach to the Nuzi Sistership Contract." *The Journal of the Ancient Near Eastern Society of Columbia University* 2 (1970) 77–85.

Freedman, David Noel, Allen C. Myers, and Astrid B. Beck, eds. *Eerdmans Dictionary of the Bible*. Grand Rapids: Eerdmans, 2000.

Fretheim, Terence E. "The Book of Genesis." In *The New Interpreter's Bible: 1 Genesis to Leviticus*, edited by Walter Brueggemann et al., 319–674. Nashville: Abingdon, 1994.

Friedman, Richard E. *The Bible with Sources Revealed: A New View into the Five Books of Moses*. New York: HarperCollins, 2005.

Fuchs, Esther. "Structure, Ideology and Politics in the Biblical Betrothal Type-Scene." In *Feminist Companion to Genesis*, 273–81. Sheffield, UK: JSOT, 1993.
Gadamer, Hans-Georg. *Truth and Method*. London: Bloomsbury, 2013.
Gammie, John G. "Theological Interpretation by Way of Literary and Tradition Analysis: Genesis 25–36." In *Encounter with the Text: Form and History in the Hebrew Bible*, edited by Martin J. Buss, 117–34. Society of Biblical Literature Semeia Supplements 8. Philadelphia: Fortress, 1979.
Garrett, Duane A. *Rethinking Genesis: The Sources and Authorship of the First Book of the Pentateuch*. Grand Rapids: Baker, 1991.
Genette, Gérard. *Narrative Discourse: An Essay in Method*. Ithaca, NY: Cornell University Press, 1980.
Gesenius, Wilhelm, E. Kautzsch, and A. E. Cowley. *Gesenius' Hebrew Grammar*. 2nd ed. Oxford: Clarendon, 2010.
Gibson, John C. L. *Genesis 12–50*. Daily Study Bible Series. Edinburgh: Saint Andrew, 1982.
Glück, J. J. "Paronomasia in Biblical Literature." *Semitics* 1 (1970) 50–78.
Goldingay, John. "The Patriarchs in Scripture and History." In *Essays on the Patriarchal Narratives*, edited by A. R. Millard and D. J. Wiseman, 1–34. Winona Lake, IN: Eisenbrauns, 1980.
Gordis, Daniel H. "Lies, Wives and Sisters: The Wife-Sister Motif Revisited." *Judaism* 34, no. 3 (1985) 344–59.
Gordon, Cyrus H. "Biblical Customs and the Nuzi Tablets." *Biblical Archaeologist* 3, no. 1 (1940) 1–12.
Gossai, Hemchand. *Power and Marginality in the Abraham Narrative*. 2nd ed. Princeton Theological Monograph. Eugene, OR: Wipf and Stock, 2010.
Green, Christopher Charles. "A Type-Scene Approach to Jacob's Encounter at the Jabbok." MA thesis, Trinity Evangelical Divinity School, 2001.
Greengus, Samuel. "The Patriarchs' Wives as Sisters: Is the Anchor Bible Wrong?" *Biblical Archaeology Review* 1, no. 3 (1975) 22–26.
———. "Sisterhood Adoption at Nuzi and the 'Wife-Sister' in Genesis." *Hebrew Union College Annual* 46 (1975) 5–31.
Greidanus, Sidney. *Preaching Christ from Genesis: Foundations for Expository Sermons*. Grand Rapids: Eerdmans, 2007.
Groom, Susan Anne. *Linguistic Analysis of Biblical Hebrew*. Carlisle: Paternoster, 2003.
Gropp, Douglas M. "Toward a Discourse Grammar of Biblical Hebrew Narrative: The Abraham Story." MA Thesis, Westminster Theological Seminary, 1979.
Guillaume, A. "Paronomasia in the Old Testament." *Journal of Semitic Studies* 9 (1964) 282–96.
Gunkel, Hermann. *The Folktale in the Old Testament*. Sheffield, UK: Almond, 1987.
Gunkel, Hermann, and Mark E. Biddle. *Genesis*. Mercer Library of Biblical Studies. Macon, GA: Mercer University Press, 1997.
Gunn, David M., and Danna Nolan Fewell. *Narrative in the Hebrew Bible*. Oxford: Oxford University Press, 1993.
Halliday, Michael A. K. "Text as Semantic Choice in Social Contexts." In *Grammars and Descriptions: Studies in Text Theory and Text Analysis*, edited by Teun Adrianus van Dijk and János S. Petőfi, 176–225. Research in Text Theory 1. Berlin: de Gruyter, 1977.

Halliday, Michael A. K., and Ruqaiya Hasan. *Cohesion in English*. English Language Series. Essex: Longman, 1976.

Halliday, Michael A. K., and Christian Matthiessen. *An Introduction to Functional Grammar*. 4th ed. London: Routledge, 2014.

Hamilton, Victor P. *The Book of Genesis 1–17*. NICOT 1. Grand Rapids: Eerdmans, 1990.

———. *The Book of Genesis 18–50*. NICOT 2. Grand Rapids: Eerdmans, 1995.

Harrison, Roland K. *Introduction to the Old Testament*. Peabody, MA: Prince, 1999.

Hartley, John E. *Genesis*. New International Biblical Commentary 1. Peabody, MA: Hendrickson, 2000.

Harvey, David. *The Condition of Postmodernity: An Enquiry into the Origins of Cultural Change*. Oxford: Blackwell, 1990.

Harvey, W. J. *Character and the Novel*. New York: Cornell University Press, 1968.

Heide, Martin. "The Domestication of the Camel: Biological, Archaeological and Inscriptional Evidence from Mesopotamia, Egypt, Israel and Arabia, and Literary Evidence from the Hebrew Bible." *Ugarit-Forschungen* 42 (2010) 331–84.

Heimerdinger, Jean-Marc. *Topic, Focus and Foreground in Ancient Hebrew Narratives*. JSOTSup 295. Sheffield, UK: Sheffield, 1999.

Helyer, Larry R. "The Separation of Abram and Lot: Its Significance in the Patriarchal Narratives." *Journal for the Study of the Old Testament* 26 (1983) 77–88.

Hirsch, E. D., Jr. *Validity in Interpretation*. New Haven: Yale University Press, 1967.

Hoffmeier, James K. "The Wives' Tales of Genesis 12, 20 and 26 and the Covenants at Beer-Sheba." *Tyndale Bulletin* 43 (1992) 81–99.

Holmgren, Fredrick Carlson. "Looking Back on Abraham's Encounter with a Canaanite King: A Reversal of Expectations (Genesis 20:1–18)." *Currents in Theology and Mission* 37, no. 5 (2010) 366–77.

Hoop, R. de. "The Use of the Past to Address the Present: The Wife-Sister-Incidents (Gen 12,10–20; 20,1–18; 26,1–16)." In *Studies in the Book of Genesis*, 359–69. Leuven: Leuven University Press, 2001.

Horowitz, Wayne. "'Sweeter Than Camel's Milk': The Camel in Sumerian, The Bactrian Camel in Genesis?" *Bible Lands e-Review* (2014) 1–9. https://biblelandsreview.files.wordpress.com/2014/05/horowitz-bler-2014-s3.pdf.

Humphreys, W. Lee. *The Character of God in the Book of Genesis: A Narrative Appraisal*. Louisville: Westminster John Knox, 2001.

Jacobs, Mignon R. *Gender, Power, and Persuasion: The Genesis Narratives and Contemporary Portraits*. Grand Rapids: Baker, 2007.

Janzen, J. Gerald. *Abraham and All the Families of the Earth: A Commentary on the Book of Genesis 12–50*. Grand Rapids: Eerdmans, 1993.

Jeanrond, Werner G. *Text and Interpretation as Categories of Theological Thinking*. New York: Crossroad, 1988.

Joüon, Paul, and T. Muraoka. *A Grammar of Biblical Hebrew*. 2nd ed. Roma: Biblical Institute, 2006.

Kaminski, Carol M. *From Noah to Israel: Realization of the Primaeval Blessing After the Flood*. JSOTSup 413. London: T. & T. Clark, 2004.

Keck, Leander E. "Will the Historical-Critical Method Survive? Some Observations." In *Orientation by Disorientation: Studies in Literary Criticism and Biblical Literary Criticism*, edited by Richard A. Spencer, 115–27. Pittsburgh Theological Monograph Series 35. Pittsburgh: Pickwick, 1980.

Kee, Min Suk. "The Heavenly Council and Its Type-Scene." *Journal for the Study of the Old Testament* 31, no. 3 (2007) 259–73.
Kennedy, Elisabeth Robertson. *Seeking a Homeland*. Leiden: Brill, 2011.
Kessler, Martin, and Karel Deurloo. *A Commentary on Genesis: The Book of Beginnings*. New York: Paulist, 2004.
Kidner, Derek. *Genesis: An Introduction and Commentary*. TOTC 1. Downers Grove, IL: InterVarsity, 1967.
Kim, Koowon. *Incubation as a Type-Scene in the Aqhatu, Kirta, and Hannah Stories: A Form-Critical and Narratological Study of KTU 1.14 I–1.15 III, 1.17 I–II, and 1 Samuel 1:1—2:11*. Supplements to Vetus Testamentum 145. Boston: Brill, 2011.
Kitchen, Kenneth A. *On the Reliability of the Old Testament*. Grand Rapids: Eerdmans, 2003.
Koch, Klaus. "Die Toledot-Formeln als Strukturprinzip des Buches Genesis: Festschrift für Horst Seebass zum 65. Geburtstag." In *Recht und Ethos im Alten Testament*, edited by Stefan Beyerle, Günter Mayer, and Hans Strauß, 183–90. Neukirchen-Vluyn: Neukirchener, 1999.
———. *The Growth of the Biblical Tradition: the Form-Critical Method*. New York: Scribner, 1969.
Kruschwitz, Jonathan. "The Type-Scene Connection between Genesis 38 and the Joseph Story." *Journal for the Study of the Old Testament* 36, no. 4 (2012) 383–410.
Kuruvilla, Abraham. *Genesis: A Theological Commentary for Preachers*. Eugene, OR: Resourse, 2014.
Levinson, Stephen C. *Pragmatics*. Cambridge: Cambridge University Press, 1983.
Lindner, Monika. "Integrationsformen Der Intertextualität." In *Intertextualität: Formen, Funktionen, Anglistische Fallstudien*, edited by Ulrich Broich and Manfred Pfister, 116–35. Tübingen: Niemeyer, 1985.
Lipton, Diana. *Revisions of the Night: Politics and Promises in the Patriarchal Dreams of Genesis*. Sheffield, UK: Sheffield Academic, 2009.
Longacre, Robert E. "Discourse Perspective on the Hebrew Verb: Affirmation and Restatement." In *Linguistics and Biblical Hebrew*, edited by Walter R. Bodine, 177–89. Winona Lake, IN: Eisenbrauns, 1992.
———. *The Grammar of Discourse*. 2nd ed. New York: Plenum, 1996.
———. *Joseph: A Story of Divine Providence*. Winona Lake, IN: Eisenbrauns, 1989.
———. "Weqatal Forms in Biblical Hebrew Prose: A Discourse-Modular Approach." In *Biblical Hebrew and Discourse Linguistics*, edited by Robert D. Bergen, 50–98. Winona Lake, IN: Eisenbrauns, 1994.
Longman III, Tremper. *Literary Approaches to Biblical Interpretation*. Vol. 3. Foundations of Contemporary Interpretation. Grand Rapids: Academie, 1987.
Louw, J. P. *Semantics of New Testament Greek*. Philadelphia: Fortress, 1982.
Lowery, Kirk E. "The Theoretical Foundations of Hebrew Discourse Grammar." In *Discourse Analysis of Biblical Literature: What It Is and What It Offers*, edited by Walter R. Bodine, 103–30. Atlanta: Scholars, 1995.
Lyons, John. *Language and Linguistics: An Introduction*. Cambridge: Cambridge University Press, 1981.
Malamat, Abraham. "King Lists of the Old Babylonian Period and Biblical Genealogies." In *"I Studied Inscriptions Form before the Flood": Ancient Near Eastern, Literary, and Linguistic Approaches to Genesis 1–11*, edited by Richard S. Hess and David

Toshio Tsumura, 183–99. Sources for Biblical and Theological Study 4. Winona Lake, IN: Eisenbrauns, 1994.

Maly, Eugene H. "Genesis 12:10–20; 20:1–18; 26:7–11 and the Pentateuchal Question." *The Catholic Biblical Quarterly* 18, no. 3 (1956) 255–62.

Manor, Dale W. "Kadesh." In *Eerdmans Dictionary of the Bible*, edited by David N. Freedman, Allen C. Myers, and Astrid B. Beck, 359–60. Grand Rapids: Eerdmans, 2000.

Mathews, Kenneth A. *Genesis 1—11:26*. NAC 1a. Nashville: Broadman and Holman, 1996.

———. *Genesis 11:27—50:26*. NAC 1b. Nashville: Broadman and Holman, 2005.

Matthews, Victor H. "Pastoralists and Patriarchs." *Biblical Archaeologist* 44, no. 4 (1981) 215–18.

———. "The Wells of Gerar." *Biblical Archaeologist* 49, no. 2 (1986) 118–26.

McKeown, James. "Blessings and Curses." Edited by T. Desmond Alexander and David W. Baker. *Dictionary of the Old Testament: Pentateuch*. Downers Grove, IL: InterVarsity, 2003.

———. *Genesis*. Grand Rapids: Eerdmans, 2008.

———. "The Theme of Land in Genesis 1–11 and Its Significance for the Abraham Narrative, Part 1." *Irish Biblical Studies* 19, no. 2 (1997) 51–64.

———. "The Theme of Land in Genesis 1–11 and Its Significance for the Abraham Narrative, Part 2." *Irish Biblical Studies* 19, no. 3 (1997) 133–44.

McMahan, Craig Thomas. "Meals as Type-Scenes in the Gospel of Luke." PhD diss., Southern Baptist Theological Seminary, 1987.

Merrill, Eugene H. "Ebla and Biblical Historical Inerrancy." *Bibliotheca Sacra* 140, no. 560 (1983) 302–21.

Milgrom, Jacob. *Cult and Conscience: The ASHAM and the Priestly Doctrine of Repentance*. Leiden: Brill, 1976.

Miscall, Peter D. "Literary Unity in Old Testament Narrative." *Semeia* 15 (1979) 27–44.

Morris, James F. "'Dream Scenes' in Homer, A Study in Variation." *Transactions of the American Philological Association* 113 (1983) 39–54.

Mullo Weir, C. J. "The Alleged Hurrian Wife-Sister Motif in Genesis." In *Glasgow University Oriental Society*, 14–25. Glasgow: Glasgow University Oriental Society, 1970.

Nagler, Michael N. *Spontaneity and Tradition: A Study in the Oral Art of Homer*. Berkeley: University of California Press, 1974.

———. "Toward a Generative View of the Oral Formula." *Transactions and Proceedings of the American Philological Association* 98 (1967) 269–311.

Nahkola, Aulikki. *Double Narratives in the Old Testament: The Foundations of Method in Biblical Criticism*. Beihefte zur Zeitschrift für die Alttestamentliche Wissenschaft 290. Berlin: de Gruyter, 2001.

Niccacci, Alviero. "Analysis of Biblical Narrative." In *Biblical Hebrew and Discourse Linguistics*, edited by Robert D. Bergen, 175–98. Winona Lake, IN: Eisenbrauns, 1994.

———. "On the Hebrew Verbal System." In *Biblical Hebrew and Discourse Linguistics*, edited by Robert D. Bergen, 117–37. Winona Lake, IN: Eisenbrauns, 1994.

Nicol, George G. "The Chronology of Genesis: Genesis XXVI 1–33 as 'Flashback.'" *Vetus Testamentum* 46, no. 3 (1996) 331–38.

———. "The Narrative Structure and Interpretation of Genesis XXVI 1–33." *Vetus Testamentum* 46, no. 3 (1996) 339–60.

———. "Story-Patterning in Genesis." In *Text as Pretext: Essays in Hournour of Robert Davidson*, edited by Robert P. Carroll, 215–33. JSOTSup 138. Sheffield, UK: JSOT, 1992.

Niditch, Susan. *A Prelude to Biblical Folklore: Underdogs and Tricksters*. Urbana: University of Illinois Press, 2000.

Noth, Martin. *A History of Pentateuchal Traditions*. Translated by Bernhard W. Anderson. Chico, CA: Scholars, 1981.

Novick, Tzvi. "'Almost, at Times, the Fool': Abimelekh and Genesis 20." *Prooftexts* 24 (2004) 277–90.

Olrik, Axel. "Epic Laws of Folk Narrative." In *The Study of Folklore*. Englewood Cliffs, NJ: Prentice-Hall, 1965.

Oppenheim, A. Leo. "The Interpretation of Dreams in the Ancient Near East: With a Translation of an Assyrian Dream Book." *Transactions of the American Philological Association* 46 (1956) 179–373.

Oren, Eliezer D. "Gerar." In *Anchor Bible Dictionary*, edited by David N. Freedman, et al., 989–91. New York: Doubleday, 1992.

Ortiz, Steven M. "Rewriting Philistine History: Recent Trends in Philistine Archaeology and Biblical Studies." In *Critical Issues in Early Israelite History*, 191–204. Winona Lake, IN: Eisenbrauns, 2008.

Osborne, Grant R. *The Hermeneutical Spiral: A Comprehensive Introduction to Biblical Interpretation*. Downers Grove, IL: InterVarsity, 1991.

Palmer, F. R. *Semantics*. 2nd ed. Cambridge: Cambridge University Press, 1981.

Pappas, Harry S. "Deception as Patriarchal Self-Defense in a Foreign Land: A Form Critical Study of the Wife-Sister Stories in Genesis." *Greek Orthodox Theological Review* 29, no. 1 (1984) 35–50.

Patterson, Todd. "The Righteousness and Survival of the Seed: The Role of Plot in the Exegesis and Theology of Genesis." PhD diss., Trinity Evangelical Divinity School, 2012.

Payne, David F. "Old Testament Textual Criticism: Its Principles and Practice." *Tyndale Bulletin* 25 (1974) 99–112.

Payne, Geoffrey. "Functional Sentence Perspective: Theme in Biblical Hebrew." *Scandinavian Journal of the Old Testament* 1 (1991) 62–82.

Peleg, Yitzhak. "Was the Ancestress of Israel in Danger?" *Zeitschrift für die Alttestamentliche Wissenschaft* 118 (2006) 197–208.

Petersen, David L. "A Thrice-Told Tale: Genre, Theme, and Motif." *Biblical Research* 18 (1973) 30–43.

Pettinato, Giovanni. "Ebla and the Bible." *Biblical Archaeologist* 43, no. 4 (1980) 203–16.

Polzin, Robert. "'The Ancestress of Israel in Danger' in Danger." *Semeia* 3 (1975) 81–98.

Porter, Stanley E. "Discourse Analysis and the New Testament Studies: An Introductory Survey." In *Discourse Analysis and Other Topics in Biblical Greek*, edited by Stanley E. Porter and D. A. Carson, 14–35. Sheffield, UK: Sheffield, 1995.

Pratt, Richard L. "Pictures, Windows, and Mirrors in Old Testament Exegesis." *Westminster Theological Journal* 45 (1983) 156–67.

Radday, Yehuda T. "Chiasmus in Hebrew Biblical Narrative." In *Chiasmus in Antiquity: Structures, Analyses, Exegesis*, edited by John W. Welch, 50–117. Provo, UT: Maxwell Institute, 1998.

Reed, Jeffrey T. "Discourse Analysis as New Testament Hermeneutic: A Retrospective and Prospective Appraisal." *Journal of the Evangelical Theological Society* 39, no. 2 (1996) 223–40.

Reinhartz, Adele. *"Why Ask My Name?" Anonymity and Identity in Biblical Narrative.* Oxford: Oxford University Press, 1998.

Reis, Pamela Tamarkin. "Take My Wife, Please: On the Utility of the Wife/Sister Motif." *Judaism* 41, no. 4 (1992) 306–15.

Rendsburg, Gary A. *The Redaction of Genesis.* Winona Lake, IN: Eisenbrauns, 1986.

Revell, E. J. *The Designation of the Individual: Expressive Usage in Biblical Narrative.* Kampen: Kok Pharos, 1996.

Rickett, Dan. "Rethinking the Place and Purpose of Genesis 13." *Journal for the Study of the Old Testament* 36, no. 1 (2011) 31–53.

Ricoeur, Paul. *Interpretation Theory: Discourse and the Surplus of Meaning.* Fort Worth: Texas Christian University Press, 1976.

Rieser, Hannes. "On the Development of Text Grammar." In *Current Trends in Textlinguistics*, edited by Wolfgang U Dressler, 6–20. Berlin: de Gruyter, 1978.

Robinson, Robert B. "Literary Functions of the Genealogies of Genesis." *Catholic Biblical Quarterly* 48 (1986) 595–608.

Ronning, John L. "The Naming of Isaac: The Role of the Wife/Sister Episodes in the Redaction of Genesis." *Westminster Theological Journal* 53, no. 1 (1991) 1–27.

Roop, Eugene F. *Genesis.* Believers Church Bible Commentary. Scottdale: Herald, 1987.

Rosenberg, Joel. *King and Kin: Political Allegory in the Hebrew Bible.* Bloomington: Indiana University Press, 1986.

Russell, Bertrand. *A History of Western Philosophy.* 2nd ed. Routledge Classics. London: Routledge, 2004.

Sailhamer, John H. *Genesis*, edited by Tremper Longman III and David E. Garland. Rev. ed. Expositor's Bible Commentary 1. Grand Rapids: Zondervan, 2008.

———. "Genesis 1:1—2:4a." *Trinity Journal* 5 (1984) 73–82.

———. *Introduction to Old Testament Theology: An Canonical Approach.* Grand Rapids: Zondervan, 1995.

———. *The Pentateuch as Narrative: A Biblical-Theological Commentary.* Grand Rapids: Zondervan, 1992.

Salanga, Victor R. *Three Stories of the Endangered Wife: Gen 12,10–20; 20,1–18; 26,1–11: A Narrative and Stylistic Analysis.* Rome: Pontificia Universitas Gregoriana, 1993.

Sarna, Nahum M. "The Anticipatory Use of Information as a Literary Feature of the Genesis Narratives." In *The Creation of Sacred Literature: Composition and Redaction of the Biblical Text*, edited by Richard E. Friedman, 76–82. Near Eastern Studies. Berkeley: University of California Press, 1981.

———. *Genesis.* The JPS Torah Commentary. Philadelphia: Jewish Publication Society, 1989.

———. *Understanding Genesis: The Heritage of Biblical Israel.* New York: Schocken, 1972.

Sasson, J. M. "The Worship of the Golden Calf." In *Orient and Occident: Essays Presented to Cyrus H. Gordon on the Occasion of His Sixty-Fifth Birthday*, edited by Cyrus H. Gordon and H. A. Hoffner Jr., 154–57. Alter Orient und Altes Testament 22. Kevelaer: Neukirchener, 1973.

Saussure, Ferdinand de. *Course in General Linguistics.* Edited by Charles Bally, Albert Sechehaye, and Albert Riedlinger. LaSalle: Open Court, 1986.

Savran, George W. "Theophany as Type Scene." *Prooftexts* 23, no. 2 (2003) 119–49.

———. *Telling and Retelling: Quotation in Biblical Narrative*. Edited by Herbert Marks and Robert Polzin. Indian Studies in Biblical Literature. Bloomington: Indiana University Press, 1988.

Scharbert, Josef. "Der Sinn der Toledot-Formel in der Priesterschrift." In *Wort, Gebot, Glaube: Beiträge zur Theologie des Alten Testaments: Walther Eichrodt zum 80. Geburtstag*, edited by Walther Eichrodt, Hans Joachim Stoebe, and O. Cullmann. 45–56. Abhandlungen zur Theologie des Alten und Neuen Testaments 59. Zürich: Zwingli, 1970.

Schmitt, Götz. "Zu Gen 26:1–14." *Zeitschrift für die Alttestamentliche Wissenschaft* 85, no. 2 (1973) 143–56.

Schmutzer, Andrew J. "Did the Gods Cause Abraham's Wandering? An Examination of התעו אתי אלהים in Genesis 20.13." *Journal for the Study of the Old Testament* 35, no. 2 (2010) 149–66.

Schniedewind, W. M. "Innerbiblical Exegesis." In *Dictionary of the Old Testament: Historical Books*, edited by Bill T. Arnold and Hugh G. M. Williamson, 502–9. IVP Old Testament Dictionary Series 2. Downers Grove, IL: InterVarsity, 2005.

Scinto, Leonard F. M. "Functional Connectivity and the Communicative Structure of Text." In *Micro and Macro Connexity of Text*, edited by János S. Petöfi and Emel Sözer, 73–115. Papiere zur Textlinguistik Band 45. Hamburg: Buske, 1983.

Seebass. "לָקַח." In *Theological Dictionary of the Old Testament*, vol. 8, edited by G. Johannes Botterweck, Helmer Ringgren, and Heinez-Josef Fabry, 16–21. Grand Rapids: Eerdmans, 1997.

Ska, Jean L. "Essai sur la Nature et la Signification du Cycle d'Abraham (Gn 11,27–25,11)." In *Studies in the Book of Genesis: Literature, Redaction and History*, edited by André Wénin, 153–77. Peeters: Leuven University Press, 2001.

———. *Introduction to Reading the Pentateuch*. Winona Lake, IN: Eisenbrauns, 2006.

Skinner, John. *A Critical and Exegetical Commentary on Genesis*. 2nd ed. Edinburgh: T. & T. Clark, 1930.

Snaith, Norman H. "The Sin-Offering and the Guilt-Offering." *Vetus Testamentum* 15, no. 1 (1965) 73–80.

Speiser, E. A. *Genesis: A New Translation with Introduction and Commentary*. ABC 1. Garden City, NY: Doubleday, 1964.

———. *Oriental and Biblical Studies*; Philadelphia: University of Pennsylvania Press, 1967.

———. "The Wife-Sister Motif in the Patriarchal Narratives." In *Oriental and Biblical Studies: Collected Writings of E. A. Speiser*, edited by J. J. Finkelstein and Moshe Greenberg, 62–82. Phildadelphia: University of Pennsylvania Press, 1967.

Steinberg, Naomi. "The Genealogical Framework of the Family Stories in Genesis." *Semeia*, no. 46 (1989) 41–50.

Sternberg, Meir. *The Poetics of Biblical Narrative: Ideological Literature and the Drama of Reading*. Bloomington: Indiana University Press, 1987.

Stubbs, Michael. *Discourse Analysis: The Sociolinguistic Analysis of Natural Language*. Language in Society 4. Chicago: University of Chicago Press, 1983.

Sutherland, Dixon. "The Organization of the Abraham Promise Narratives." *Zeitschrift für die Alttestamentliche Wissenschaft* 95, no. 3 (1983) 337–43.

Sweeney, Marvin A. "Form Criticism: The Question of the Endangered Matriarchs in Genesis." In *Method Matters: Essays on the Interpretation of the Hebrew Bible in*

Honor of David L. Petersen, edited by J. M. LeMon and K. H. Richards, 17–38. SBL Resources for Biblical Study 56. Atlanta: SBL, 2009.

Sykes, David K. "Patterns in Genesis." PhD diss., Yeshiva University, 1985.

Tannehill, Robert C. "The Composition of Acts 3–5: Narrative Development and Echo Effect." *Society of Biblical Literature Seminar Papers* 23 (1984) 217–40.

———. *The Narrative Unity of Luke-Acts: A Literary Interpretation*. Vol. 2. Foundations and Facets. Philadelphia: Fortress, 1986.

Thimmes, Pamela Lee. *Studies in the Biblical Sea-Storm Type-Scene: Convention and Invention*. San Francisco: Mellen Research University Press, 1992.

Thiselton, Anthony C. *Hermeneutics: An Introduction*. Grand Rapids: Eerdmans, 2009.

———. "On Models and Methods: A Conversation with Robert Morgan." In *Bible in Three Dimensions: Essays in Celebration of Forty Years of Biblical Studies in the University of Sheffield*, edited by David J. A. Clines, Stephen E. Fowl, and Stanley E. Porter, 337–56. JSOTSup 87. Sheffield, UK: JSOT, 1990.

Thomas, Matthew A. *These Are the Generations: Identity, Covenant, and the Toledot Formula*. New York: T. & T. Clark, 2011.

Thompson, Thomas L. *Historicity of the Patriarchal Narratives: The Quest for the Historical Abraham*. Harrisburg, PA: Trinity, 2002.

———. *The Origin Tradition of Ancient Israel*. JSOTSup 55. Sheffield, UK: JSOT, 1987.

Tolmie, Francois. *Narratology and Biblical Narratives: A Practical Guide*. Eugene, OR: Wipf and Stock, 2012.

Towner, W. Sibley. *Genesis*. Westminster Bible Companion. Louisville: Westminster John Knox, 2001.

Tucker, Gene M. *Form Criticism of the Old Testament*. Philadelphia: Fortress, 1971.

Turner, Laurence A. *Announcements of Plot in Genesis*. JSOTSup 96. Sheffield, UK: JSOT, 1990.

———. *Genesis*. Sheffield, UK: Sheffield Academic, 2000.

———. "Genesis, Book of." In *Dictionary of the Old Testament: Penatateuch*, edited by T. Desmond Alexander and David W. Baker, 350–59. Downers Grove, IL: InterVarsity, 2003.

Van der Merwe, C. H. J. "A Cognitive Linguistic Perspective on הִנֵּה in the Pentateuch, Joshua, Judges, and Ruth." *Hebrew Studies* 48 (2007) 101–40.

———. "Old Testament Particles and the Interpretation of Old Testament Texts." *Journal for the Study of the Old Testament* 60 (1993) 27–44.

Van der Merwe, Christo H. J. "Discourse Linguistics and Biblical Hebrew Grammar." In *Biblical Hebrew and Discourse Linguistics*, edited by Robert D. Bergen, 13–49. Winona Lake, IN: Eisenbrauns, 1994.

Van der Merwe, Christo H. J., Jan H. Kroeze, and Jackie A. Naudé. *A Biblical Hebrew Reference Grammar*. Sheffield, UK: Sheffield Academic, 1998.

Van Dijk, Teun A. "Episodes as Units of Discourse Analysis." In *Analyzing Discourse: Text and Talk*, edited by D. Tannen, 177–95. Washington, DC: Georgetown University Press, 1982.

Van Dijk, Teun Adrianus. *Text and Context: Explorations in the Semantics and Pragmatics of Discourse*. London: Longman, 1977.

VanGemeren, Willem A. "Preface." In *A Guide to Old Testament Theology and Exegesis*, 7–9. Grand Rapids: Zondervan, 1999.

Vanhoozer, Kevin J. *Is There a Meaning in This Text?* Grand Rapids: Zondervan, 1998.

———. "Language, Literature, Hermeneutics and Biblical Theology: What's Theological About a Theological Dictionary?" In *A Guide to Old Testament Theology and Exegesis*, edited by Willem A. VanGemeren, 11–47. Grand Rapids: Zondervan, 1997.

———. "The Reader in New Testament Interpretation." In *Hearing the New Testament: Strategies for Interpretation*, edited by Joel B. Green, 301–28. Grand Rapids: Eerdmans, 1995.

Van Seters, John. *Abraham in History and Tradition*. New Haven: Yale University Press, 1975.

———. *Prologue to History: The Yahwist as Historian in Genesis*. Louisville: Westminster John Knox, 1992.

Vawter, Bruce. *On Genesis: A New Reading*. Garden City, NY: Doubleday, 1977.

Von Rad, Gerhard. *Genesis: A Commentary*. 2nd ed. Old Testament Library. Philadelphia: Westminster, 1972.

Vrolijk, Paul D. *Jacob's Wealth: An Examination into the Nature and Role of Material Possessions in the Jacob-Cycle (Gen 25:19—35:29)*. Supplements to Vetus Testamentum 146. Leiden: Brill, 2011.

Wacholder, Ben Zion. "How Long Did Abram Stay in Egypt?" *Hebrew Union College Annual* 35 (1964) 43–56.

Wagner, Norman Ernest. "Literary Analysis of Gen 12–36." ThD diss., University of Toronto, 1965.

Wallace, Howard. "On Account of Sarai: Gen 12:10—13:1." *Australian Biblical Review* 44 (1996) 32–41.

Walsh, Jerome T. *Style And Structure In Biblical Hebrew Narrative*. Collegeville, MN: Glazier, 2001.

Waltke, Bruce K. *Genesis*. Grand Rapids: Zondervan, 2001.

Waltke, Bruce K., and Michael P. O'Connor. *An Introduction to Biblical Hebrew Syntax*. Winona Lake, IN: Eisenbrauns, 1990.

Walton, John H. *Genesis*. NIV Application Commentary. Grand Rapids: Zondervan, 2001.

Weimar, Peter. "Die Toledot-Formel in der Priesterschriftlichen Geschichtsdarstellung." *Biblische Zeitschrift* 18 (1974) 65–93.

———. *Untersuchungen zur Redaktionsgeschichte des Pentateuch*. Berlin: de Gruyter, 1977.

Wenham, Gordon J. *Genesis 1–15*. WBC 1a. Waco, TX: Word, 1987.

———. *Genesis 16–50*. WBC 1b. Dallas: Word, 1994.

Westermann, Claus. *Genesis 1–11*. A Continental Commentary. Minneapolis: Fortress, 1994.

———. *Genesis 12–36: A Commentary*. Minneapolis: Augsburg, 1995.

Wheaton, Byron. "Focus and Structure in the Abraham Narratives." *Trinity Journal* 27 (2006) 143–62.

Whybray, R. N. *The Making of the Pentateuch: A Methodological Study*. JSOTSup 53. Sheffield, UK: JSOT, 1994.

Wiklander, Bertil. *Prophecy as Literature: A Text-Linguistic and Rhetorical Approach to Isaiah 2–4*. Coniectanea Biblica. Old Testament Series 22. Lund: Gleerup, 1984.

Williams, James G. "The Beautiful and the Barren: Conventions in Biblical Type-Scenes." *Journal for the Study of the Old Testament* 17 (1980) 107–19.

Williamson, Paul R. *Abraham, Israel and the Nations: The Patriarchal Promise and Its Covenantal Development in Genesis*. JSOTSup 315. Sheffield, UK: Sheffield, 2000.

Williams, Paul R. "Abraham." Edited by T. Desmond Alexander and David W. Baker. *Dictionary of the Old Testament: Pentateuch*. Downers Grove, IL: InterVarsity, 2003.

Williams, Ronald J., and John C. Beckman. *Williams Hebrew Syntax*. 3rd ed. Toronto: University of Toronto Press, 2007.

Wilson, Robert R. *Genealogy and History in the Biblical World*. New Haven and London: Yale University Press, 1977.

Winnett, Frederick Victor. "Re-Examining the Foundations." *Journal of Biblical Literature* 84, no. 1 (1965) 1–19.

Wiseman, D. J. "Abraham Reassessed." In *Essays on the Patriarchal Narratives*, edited by A. R. Millard and D. J. Wiseman, 141–60. Winona Lake, IN: Eisenbrauns, 1980.

Wood, D. R. W., and I. Howard Marshall, eds. *New Bible Dictionary*. Leicester and Downers Grove, IL: InterVarsity, 1996.

Woudstra, Marten H. "The Toledot of the Book of Genesis and Their Redemptive-Historical Significance." *Calvin Theological Journal* 5 (1970) 184–89.

Woychuk, James Arthur. "The Rhetorical Functions of Genesis 26 in the Argument of Genesis." PhD diss., Dallas Theological Seminary, 2003.

Yoo, Yeon Hee. "A Rhetorical Reading of the Rebekah Narratives in the Book of Genesis." PhD diss., Union Theological Seminary, 2001.

Yudkowsky, Rachel. "Chaos or Chiasm? The Structure of Abraham's Life." *Jewish Bible Quarterly* 35, no. 2 (2007) 109–14.

Yule, George. *Pragmatics*. Oxford Introductions to Language Study. Oxford: Oxford University Press, 1996.

Zakovitch, Yair. "Juxtaposition in the Abraham Cycle." In *Pomegranates and Golden Bells*, 509–24. Winona Lake, IN: Eisenbrauns, 1995.

Zeelander, Susan. *Closure in Biblical Narrative*, edited by Paul Anderson and Yvonne Sherwood. Biblical Interpretation Series 111. Leiden: Brill, 2012.

Zlotowitz, Meir, and Nosson Scherman. *Bereishis=Genesis: A New Tranlation with a Commentary Anthologized from Talmudic, Midrashic and Rabbinic Sources*. 2nd ed. Vol. 1. ArtScroll Tanach. Brooklyn: Mesorah, 1986.

www.ingramcontent.com/pod-product-compliance
Lightning Source LLC
Chambersburg PA
CBHW070314240426
43663CB00038BA/2254